THE MEASURE OF PROGRESS

The Measure of Progress

COUNTING WHAT REALLY MATTERS

DIANE COYLE

PRINCETON UNIVERSITY PRESS

PRINCETON & OXFORD

Published by Princeton University Press
41 William Street, Princeton, New Jersey 08540
99 Banbury Road, Oxford OX2 6JX

press.princeton.edu

All Rights Reserved

Library of Congress Cataloging-in-Publication Data

Names: Coyle, Diane, author.
Title: The measure of progress : counting what really matters / Diane
    Coyle.
Description: Princeton : Princeton University Press, [2025] | Includes
    bibliographical references and index.
Identifiers: LCCN 2024036081 (print) | LCCN 2024036082 (ebook) | ISBN
    9780691179025 (hardback) | ISBN 9780691271286 (ebook)
Subjects: LCSH: Econometrics. | Economic development. | Electronic
    commerce. | Information technology—Economic aspects. | BISAC: BUSINESS
    & ECONOMICS / Statistics | POLITICAL SCIENCE / Public Policy / Economic
    Policy
Classification: LCC HB139 .C69 2025 (print) | LCC HB139 (ebook) | DDC
    330.9—dc23/eng/20240823
LC record available at https://lccn.loc.gov/2024036081
LC ebook record available at https://lccn.loc.gov/2024036082

British Library Cataloging-in-Publication Data is available

Editorial: Hannah Paul, Josh Drake
Production Editorial: Elizabeth Byrd
Jacket: Karl Spurzem
Production: Erin Suydam
Publicity: James Schneider (US), Kate Farquhar-Thomson (UK)
Copyeditor: Christina Roth

Jacket Credit: Pixel-Shot / Shutterstock

This book has been composed in Arno

Printed in the United States of America

10 9 8 7 6 5 4 3 2 1

CONTENTS

LIST OF FIGURES AND TABLES

Images

Figures

Tables

THE MEASURE OF PROGRESS

Introduction

TREATMENTS FOR neurological diseases such as Parkinson's have not much progressed since the 1960s. The standard medication, levodopa, has been in use for over half a century; it was introduced in Western medicine in 1967. The active compound was in fact in use in ancient Indian ayurvedic medicine as the powdered seeds of *Mucuna pruriens*, a type of legume that grows in Africa and parts of Asia (Ovallath and Suthana 2017). The most significant recent weapon added to the treatment arsenal for Parkinson's has been deep brain stimulation (DBS), which involves implanting electrodes in the brain through holes drilled in the skull, controlled via a wire linking them to a pacemaker-type device implanted under the skin of the chest. DBS is often effective, but certainly invasive. Recently, though, my husband Rory (who has Parkinson's and writes about health technology) was invited to watch a potential new treatment using ultrasound (Cellan-Jones 2024). Ultrasound is familiar from its everyday use for everything from prenatal scans to investigating soft tissue injuries from sport or falls. In this innovative application to tackle the tremors that characterise diseases such as Parkinson's, an MRI scanner is used to direct focused ultrasound beams that burn away the brain cells causing debilitating symptoms. For the patients Rory observed being treated at the Queen's Square Imaging Centre in London, the beneficial results of the ultrasound therapy were immediate and striking.

What does this have to do with measuring economic progress? It is one of many astonishing examples of technological progress that hold great promise for health, or for the convenience and enjoyment of life. Innovations in biomedicine, personalised cell and gene therapies, mRNA-based vaccines, and medications such as the new generation of weight loss drugs all leap to mind. But there are also innovations in digital, such as generative artificial intelligence (AI)—an astonishingly powerful technology even if you think it's overhyped—and in materials and low-carbon energy. How do these all get reflected in the gross domestic product (GDP) growth figures that dominate media comment and political debate? After all, the ultrasound example is not new technology but a clever reuse of an existing one. If the therapy becomes widespread, it will surely be a good thing but will reduce the use of other treatments; sales of levodopa might fall. How is what is clearly a potential improvement in many people's lives captured in the way we measure progress? And what about who gets the treatment: will access be widespread, and fair?

Other new ideas improve outcomes but might even reduce the economic footprint of an activity. Another health example is the possibility of substituting Avastin for Lucentis in treating age-related macular degeneration (Nakamura 2020). Lucentis is the approved treatment in the United States, requiring a monthly injection. Avastin, a cancer medicine, turns out to be at least as effective, and cheaper (about $55 compared with over $2,000 per dose in the United States). The manufacturers have long fought to prevent doctors from prescribing it instead of Lucentis, as it would reduce their revenues (D. Cohen 2018); the United Kingdom's National Health Service (NHS) won the right to do so only in 2018 after a court battle (Sagonowski 2018). Consumers would pay less, directly or indirectly, but the measurement of health output in GDP makes it likely a switch in the drug used would reduce the measured size of the economy (Sheiner and Reinsdorf 2024). Are we measuring productivity in a way that captures such shifts from material to ideas? Almost certainly not.

There are other areas where an innovation would bring tremendous benefits in the shape of a lighter footprint on the planet. The use of ideas to innovate is constantly shrinking the need for stuff (Coyle 1997). For example, for decades the aim in making silicon chips has been to make them more powerful at computation, and very successful it has been (Coyle and Hampton 2023). But now the priority may be to make them more energy efficient. "Better" now means "more efficient" rather than just "more powerful computationally" (Conway 2024). How could this change of definition be captured in measuring output of the chip industry? How does an energy-saving chip compare with a conventional chip in the economic statistics when carbon emissions are not priced?

All these modern marvels suggest the possibility of a dawning new era of human progress. But innovation often has transformational effects that are hard to crystallise in economic statistics. How on earth could you measure the impact of a treatment that can immediately reverse disabling symptoms and restore a patient's ability to lead an independent life?

At the same time, many aspects of modern life are all too obviously pointing to things getting worse. In some countries—notably the United States—improvements in life expectancy have halted or reversed. This is not just due to COVID but also to the increase in "deaths of despair" (Case and Deaton 2020). Inequality of incomes, wealth, and also health and leisure remain as high as they have ever been in modern times. A burst of inflation has left many households unable to afford heating, or has left them homeless or using food banks, in supposedly prosperous countries. Young people—and their parents—no longer expect steady improvements over time in living standards, with housing becoming less and less affordable and too many people having to hold down more than one job. We might question, too, the benefits of some innovations, whether social media that eats people's attention and spreads misinformation or harmful behaviours, or novel financial instruments that turn out to impoverish customers or increase risk rather than mitigate it. Although free online search and maps are useful, using many everyday services has turned into a nightmare of complicated tariffs, unhelpful chatbots, and higher prices, often deceptively designed into online interfaces using "dark patterns." The experience of having to spend time in the labyrinth of online chat or voicemail menus trying to sort out a problem that doesn't seem to fit the automated script, or of puzzling over a comparison website trying to figure out which of hundreds of different policies or contracts will be best, is all too familiar. This "time tax" is one of the new costs of doing business as a human being in today's advanced economies, to the extent that, in August 2024, the Biden Administration launched a "Time Is Money" regulatory crackdown on corporations involving measures such as making it easier for people to cancel subscriptions or get automatic refunds, instead of getting caught in customer service "doom loops." Corporations seem to have forgotten that their purpose is to serve customers rather than raise their share prices (Mayer 2023), so that pharmaceutical companies profit from illness, financial services companies profit when customers lose out, insurance companies only want the customers unlikely to need to claim, and food companies make more when they sell people the most processed and unhealthy products.

In short, it seems nigh on impossible to evaluate what is going on in the economy—is it getting better or worse, and for whom? This is hampering policymakers' ability to tackle slow growth in productivity and living standards. Meaningful economic statistics are needed for governments to devise policies, manage their societies effectively, and deliver for their voters; after all, the word *statistics* derives from *state*. Inevitably, though, the statistical lens through which we all try to understand the economy will become blurred at a time when the economy is changing significantly and rapidly—as it is now with the two technological revolutions of AI and digital and of energy transition from carbon-based to net zero. These two—information and energy—are the fundamental "general purpose technologies" that decisively shape the structure of the economy in each era.

This is a new era, and a new statistical framework will be needed. The current System of National Accounts (SNA), including the all-important figure for GDP, dates from the 1940s when physical capital was the binding constraint on growth in the postwar era, natural resources seemed free, and the pressing economic policy challenge was seen as effective demand management so the Great Depression could never recur. Now, nature is the binding constraint. Extreme weather will destroy much physical and human capital, biodiversity loss will reduce agricultural productivity, and new zoonotic diseases seem likely to emerge as humans press harder upon natural habitats. And the main economic policy challenge is now on the supply side, restarting the economy's productivity engine to drive improving living standards, at a time when there are headwinds such as climate shocks, conflict, and ageing societies.

Just as important a reason for rethinking the approach to economic measurement lies in the signs of a substantial shift in the public philosophy that started to emerge from the aftermath of multiple economic shocks: the 2008 financial crisis, the 2020 pandemic, the cost-of-living crisis since 2022, the reemergence of geopolitical tension and conflict. Protests against what is often described as the "neoliberal" era of globalisation and financialisation predate 2008. But the past decade or two have seen doubts about the assumptions underpinning economic policies—that individual interests will add up to societal well-being, and that individual choice in markets will bring about the best outcomes—spread far beyond groups of activists or fringe politicians. Although many finance and economics ministries remain bastions of 1980s-vintage free market economics, a large number of voters could not be making it clearer that the resulting economic system is not working for them. Economic discontent is one important contributor to the rage expressed in volatile and extremist politics today.

There is no obvious fully formed new public philosophy replacing the one that has predominated globally since the Reagan and Thatcher governments, but a fragmented picture is starting to take shape. The ongoing digital transformation of work and leisure will be part of this, enabling creativity and satisfying new uses of individuals' time on the one hand and dangerous concentrations of money and power on the other hand. An ostensibly free market approach has created the most powerful corporations the world has seen, raising questions about individual and collective freedom, and indeed about the power of the state. The environmental crises also play into an emerging sense of collective interest being at odds with market outcomes. There is a feedback loop between events (like the crises from 2008 on), politics, and economic ideas; political priorities shape what is measured, and the measures in turn define ideas about the economy and thus political choices (Coyle 2020). Articulating a new political economy, if it is indeed starting to emerge, will require a different framework of economic statistics. The underlying structure of the economy and society is changing with the dual transition in general purpose technologies, zero carbon energy, and the ongoing digital and information revolution.

These big questions—are things getting better? For whom? What does "better" mean?—motivate this book. It reflects over a decade's worth of research on questions of economic statistics and measurement, particularly on the digital economy. Some of this is rather detailed and technical (although technical sections are confined to boxes in the text). But there are also some questions of philosophy and politics involved. The fundamental issue is the definition of value. Economic measurement is deeply value laden, and (in contrast to many fellow economists) I believe it is important to engage with other disciplines and literatures; equally, the consideration of deep questions of value or power needs to be rooted in technical knowledge, whether of economic theory or computer science. The book makes a virtue of drawing on a wide range of research not limited to economics.

Unfortunately, the revision to the SNA to be adopted by the United Nations, SNA25, makes only incremental changes to the measurement framework, rather than the significant conceptual shift that is needed. Although welcome, the changes will not provide policymakers the information they need about the environmental sustainability of economic activity, or the importance of investment in human capital for living standards and progress. Much of the additional information governments and businesses need about the digital economy or unpaid household work will be contained in supplementary thematic tables that many countries might never get around to creating. Most of the chapters of this book set out the shortcomings in standard economic measurement, explaining why the current metrics miss important considerations. Each chapter focuses on specific areas, particularly regarding digital aspects of the economy where the absence of relevant statistics is striking.

The final two chapters broaden out to sketch an alternative approach to economic measurement, the generational conceptual shift we need.

This approach has two elements. One is the introduction of an asset-based framework, in effect a broadly defined balance sheet for the economy, with the associated flows of services for the assets, valued at shadow prices reflecting societal values rather than market exchange values. This new element has two key advantages over the current SNA. First, it embeds sustainability considerations because the appropriately measured value of assets and the services they provide today depends on their future condition. Second, by defining the assets society needs to have a functioning economy to more broadly include not only physical capital and infrastructure but also human and social or organisational capital, natural capital, and intangible capital, it illuminates how these assets operate as a portfolio. Different assets may complement each other—like human capital and many intangibles—or substitute for each other—like concrete flood defences and wetlands. Just as investors make good decisions by taking the correlations into account, so can policymakers improve their economic decision-making.

The downside of this capitals approach compared with today's measurement framework is that it is not an accounting framework: there is nothing the components need to add up to. It is worth underlining that the SNA itself is an accounting framework only when expressed in current price or nominal terms; the real terms measures often used by economists and commentators do not add up and indeed at an aggregate level are conceptually incoherent.

However, the second new element I set out in the book is an accounting framework based on time use. Everybody has twenty-four hours a day and must spend them all every day. The "user" side of this account involves a choice along several margins, allocating time to paid work, unpaid work in the household, consumption, and leisure. The "producer" side of the account also involves several margins, over the standard factors of production (including land, materials, and energy as well as capital and labour), location, and time: What production techniques and combinations of machines, other capitals, nature and energy, ideas, and humans are used to deliver what products or services? Productivity gains may correspond to time saving in production or higher quality in products and services provided—for in addition to the standard, intuitive metric of labour productivity, we should look at the productivity of the other inputs too, including output per unit of carbon and other resources, and per unit of time.

This is not to argue for throwing away all the current statistics; for instance, a measure of nominal GDP growth and short-term inflation measures will continue to be important for macroeconomic policymakers who need tools for managing demand over the business cycle. Rather, the measures I advocate—of an economy's asset base and of the use of time for either efficiency (in production) or well-being (in consumption and leisure)—speak directly to the motivating question: Is there economic progress? That depends on whether people can lead the lives they want, and what resources they can access to help them do so. Many of the resources any of us needs or wants are collective: clean air, an energy grid, public transport or road networks, broadband, a school system. Such a framework speaks to the need to shift how the economy is understood—in policy and in academic economics—decisively away from seeing society as the sum of individual decisions, or GDP as the sum of individual incomes and spending decisions. Introducing time use and time saving as a criterion similarly shifts the focus for thinking about economic analysis and policy away from markets as the organising mechanism, and instead toward transaction costs and how institutions are organised.

This shift in focus, from individual and simple choices in markets to collective and complex choices in organisations or institutions, also represents a personal intellectual journey that began more than forty years ago, when I was an economics graduate student at the height of the discipline's insistence on rational, individual choice. The story begins at Harvard in 1982.

1

"Political Arithmetick"

HERE ARE TWO OF MY FELLOW PhD students (Jonathan Leape and Don Hanna) at the Harvard Economics Department summer picnic in 1982.

Behind us stand two faculty members chatting, looking mildly uncomfortable with their arms folded; the one on the right is Professor Zvi Griliches, one of our econometrics lecturers. An immigrant to the United States, Zvi had trained as an agricultural economist and written his 1957 PhD dissertation on the diffusion of hybrid corn seed in the American Midwest. This was one of several studies around that time demonstrating empirically the now well-known S-shaped logistic curve for the spread of innovations—slow at first, then rapid, then slow again as their use approaches saturation. His contribution was to provide an economic explanation for the S-pattern based on the costs of adopting the technology, its average profitability (relative to the older seed technology), and the market potential (measured by population density). The new type of seed corn was more costly but produced higher yields per acre; worth the investment if the farmer was confident of producing and selling enough to cover the upfront expense. A simple economic model fit the data well for the spread of hybrid corn across US states. Zvi's subsequent research explored in depth the economics of innovation and measurement. I had no idea forty years ago as we played softball and ate hamburgers at the picnic that his work, along with that of Professor Dale Jorgenson, another of my Harvard econometrics lecturers, would be so foundational for my own future research. Not only was

IMAGE 1.1. Harvard Economics Department summer picnic, 1982.
© Diane Coyle.

I more interested then in macroeconomics, but I was also terrified by
the plunge into advanced econometrics with such brilliant professors
after my non-technical Oxford Philosophy, Politics, and Economics
(PPE) degree. (Indeed, terror was the prevailing emotion of my first
year in the United States, down to the smallest things. The impact
of walking into a local supermarket and being frozen in front of the

vast array of toothpaste brands, unable to choose, is still vivid in my memory.)

Why are the economics of innovation and issues of economic measurement both interesting? It's because the central question in economics is the question of progress. What causes it, enabling people to be healthier, live longer, and have more convenient and comfortable lives? Economic growth has always been a process of continuing innovation, and dramatically so since the Industrial Revolution. But how, why, and when do economies innovate and grow, and how can we evaluate whether the path the economy takes is indeed making people better off? This question can be deconstructed into a number of other questions, some factual but also including value judgments about which people count and who are the "we" doing the evaluation. It also raises questions about how to define and measure economic growth and the evaluation of economic welfare. In an earlier book (Coyle 2014) I recounted how the answers to these questions have changed in the past. How they need to change for the future is my concern in this book.

The story begins with a 1994 paper in the *American Economic Review*, "Productivity, R&D, and the Data Constraint," a write-up of Zvi's presidential address to the American Economic Association. It begins, "Forty years ago, economists discovered the 'residual.'"

The *residual*—famously described as "the measure of our ignorance" by Moses Abramovitz (1956)—is the measured economic growth beyond that which can be accounted for by the growth in inputs used. The concept was made systematic in the KLEMS (capital, labour, energy, materials, and services) growth accounting framework (Solow 1957, Jorgenson and Griliches 1967, Jorgenson 2012), as these are the measured inputs used to produce output. The residual came to be regarded as an indicator of technological progress (although it includes in addition measurement error, omitted variables, and the effects of shocks or structural changes). It is generally described as *total factor productivity* (TFP): what we get out of the economy for what we put in. This interpretation raises the further question of how to explain why this residual itself grows at different rates over time. Is it because of variations in the success of research efforts and the diffusion of innovations? What are the

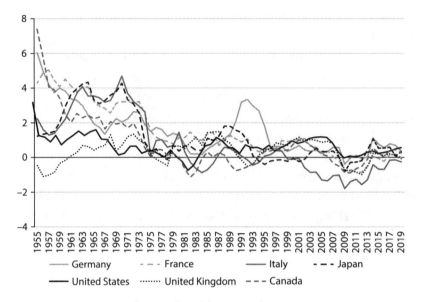

FIGURE 1.1. Growth rate of total factor productivity, G7 economies, 1955–2019. *Source:* Penn World Tables. *Note:* 5-year moving average.

roles of scientific discovery and technical advances on the one hand, and economic factors driving usage of new technologies on the other hand? What might explain changes in the rate of this metric of technological progress?

There is no definitive or consensus answer among economists, and the question has become a live one again as the growth rate of the residual (or TFP) has slowed substantially since its previous acceleration in the late 1990s—which was itself less impressive than postwar progress in the 1950s and 1960s (see Figure 1.1). But, as Zvi asked in his 1994 paper, how is it that we don't know what determines this rate of progress when it has been the subject of so much research by so many scholars? "What is it about our data and data acquisition structure, and possibly also our intellectual framework, that prevents us from making more progress on this topic?" he wrote. We still don't know.

This is the question motivating this book. At one level, the puzzle is why TFP growth has slowed or stagnated in so many of the richest economies since the mid-2000s. It is an important puzzle because TFP growth is necessary (although not sufficient) for improvements in living standards for most of the population. Without steady improvements, politics can become fractious and the democratic ties among the population strained; we have seen this unfolding in most Western economies since the 2008 financial crisis. Growth helps avert conflict and violence and enables redistribution (Friedman 2006). There is much debate (covered in Chapter 2) among economists as to why the apparent continuing progress in technology in the 2010s and 2020s, from advances in digital communications and AI to biomedicine, materials, energy generation, and superconductors, has not translated into faster TFP growth.

At a more profound level, the way we understand the economy and what is happening to it, whether the short-term business cycle fluctuations or the long-term trends in growth rates, depends on the data available. Economic statistics provide the lens through which we observe and interpret economic activity. The statistics collected—their categories and definitions and the way they relate to each other—reflect the underpinning conceptual structure. This in turn affects decisions made by policymakers, businesses, and individuals and so helps determine what will happen in the future, in a reflexive process. The official economic statistics available are constructed through an extensive machinery of collection and processing, shaped by an intellectual framework dating from the 1940s (as detailed in my book *GDP: A Brief but Affectionate History* [2014]). This framework, the System of National Accounts (SNA), grew out of early twentieth-century measurement efforts, and its scaffolding is Keynesian macroeconomic theory as interpreted to meet the imperatives of the wartime economy.

There is a fundamental question as to whether the SNA is still a useful framework. Consider Table 1.1, a version of which is included in Zvi's 1994 paper, showing the proportion of US GDP accounted for by each sector. He provided figures up to the year 1990; I've extended it to 2023. He designated some sectors of the economy as "reasonably measurable," including agriculture, mining, construction, and manufacturing, whereas others such as legal services and government are "hard to measure." The verdict on whether a sector is easy or hard to measure depends on the extent to which quality changes matter and thus on whether it is

TABLE 1.1. Share of Major Sectors Expressed as a Percentage of GDP, United States, 1947–2023

Sector	1947	1959	1969	1977	1990	2023
Agriculture	8.8	4.1	3.0	2.8	2.0	1.1
Mining	2.9	2.5	1.8	2.7	1.8	1.5
Manufacturing	28.1	28.6	26.9	23.6	18.4	10.9
Transportation & utilities	8.9	9.1	8.6	9.1	8.7	10.4
Of which information & telecoms services					5.3	5.5
Construction	3.9	4.8	5.1	4.8	4.4	4.0
Wholesale trade	7.1	6.9	6.7	7.0	6.5	6.3
Retail trade	11.7	9.9	9.8	9.6	9.3	5.8
FIRE	10.1	13.8	14.2	14.4	17.7	20.1
Other services	8.6	9.7	11.5	13.0	18.9	28.2
Government	8.6	10.2	12.6	12.5	12.2	11.6
"Hard to measure"	**51.3**	**55.7**	**59.7**	**61.8**	**69.1**	**76.0**
Including information & telecoms services					***74.4***	***81.5***

Sources: Griliches (1994) for first 5 columns, citing National Income and Product Accounts (1928–1982) and Survey of Current Business (May 1993); BEA (2024) for 2023 data. Notes: There have been revisions to the historical data subsequently, which are not included here but the differences are small. Data methodology breaks between 1977 and 1990; and 1990 and 2019. These too make very little difference to the percentage of GDP figures shown here.

straightforward to distinguish price and quantity; there is a spectrum, with electricity output or manufacture of standard nails being easy to measure and legal services or the amount of defence the government provides being hard to measure. His figures included information and telecommunications services in the "reasonably measurable" utilities category; many people would now consider this sector hard to measure, and the US national accounts statistics now separate them out, so this split is shown in Table 1.1. The transformation in the economy, with agriculture and manufacturing shrinking from 1947 on and finance (FIRE—finance, insurance and real estate) and other services growing, is clear. In 1947 (when modern economic measurement through the SNA was brand new) about half the economy was measurable, by 1990 less than a third, and by 2019 less than a quarter, or more likely only about a fifth. Zvi concludes in the paper: "The economy has changed [but] our data-collection efforts have not kept pace with it." Indeed, if four-fifths of the economy is hard to measure, there is a strong case for concluding that the conceptual framework is a poor fit to reality.

The central argument of this book is therefore that this 1940s measurement framework, the SNA and other standard economic statistics extending it, is no longer adequate for understanding the economy, and in fact in some ways actively hinders understanding. The structure of the leading economies has changed so much in the past nine decades that the framework is a distorting lens, or even a set of blinkers. A new one is needed.

What Has Gone Wrong with Economic Measurement?

A lag between the structure of the economy and the picture painted by economic statistics is inevitable, but sometimes the gap becomes so stark as to require a paradigm shift. As an analogy, consider the 1885 *Annual Abstract of Statistics for the United Kingdom* (I have a facsimile edition published in 1985). It consists of two hundred pages mostly packed with tables about agricultural production and trade—imports and exports of maize, barley, wheat, and oats, exports of spices, spirits, tea, and molasses from the colonies—and also finance and taxes. There are just fifteen pages covering mines, railways, cotton, and steam, the iconic aspects of the Industrial Revolution which had, by then, been underway for almost a century. So acute was the gap between official statistics and reality that by the late nineteenth century, there were numerous parliamentary investigations into the economy, reporting in what were known as "Blue Books." Eli Cook (2017) describes these as "moral statistics"; they were not collected regularly but spoke to pressing political concerns such as urban poverty or the prevalence of disease in grimy industrial cities. We are at a similar point now. The elastic relationship between the statistics and the economy they represent has stretched to breaking point.

Some shortcomings in our statistical understanding reflect long-standing critiques and are by now well known (summarised in Stiglitz et al. 2009). For instance, it is widely appreciated that the current framework omits many valuable activities, such as unpaid care, as well as failing to sufficiently measure innovations that transform quality of life, such as new medicines. Importantly, it fails to record environmental damage and externalities. It has therefore long had its critics, and the criticisms have grown in volume and salience over time. What has become known as the Beyond GDP movement has real momentum and is starting to be reflected in official statistics. The official statistical definitions are determined through a United Nations (UN) process involving expert statisticians (mainly from the rich countries) and are updated every ten to twenty years. The last set of revisions was released in 2008, SNA08, and the next is due to be published in 2025. SNA25 will incorporate UN definitions already released for measuring aspects of the environment previously overlooked in economic statistics—known by the acronym SEEA, the System of Environmental-Economic Accounting. The Beyond GDP debate largely focuses on the omission of nature from official statistics, although without natural resources there would be no economy and no life. SNA25 will include modest improvements in other statistics, such as those tackling aspects of the digital economy and those addressing the omission of unpaid household and voluntary activities, from GDP. Chapters 3 to 5 cover digitalisation, and Chapter 8 will return to the issue of non-market environmental or household activities and how to consider societal progress in the round.

Although welcome, the SNA25 improvements will be incremental. Other issues are not being addressed in the current round of revisions, such as the measurement of unpaid household or voluntary activity. GDP is often described as a measure of all marketed economic activity involving monetary transactions and has also been described as the measurement of the production of goods and services within the context of formally organised employment, or in other words, the economic activities that involve payment of tax and other interactions with the government (Vanoli 2005). However, GDP includes government spending, by definition not part of the market economy. In any case, this seemingly clean demarcation has eroded over time. For instance, GDP has been redefined to include estimates of illegal and informal activities as long as they involve monetary transactions. Statistical agencies have had to get creative in estimating this activity, which is by definition not reported to the authorities. Other important components are simply imputed, and this proportion has been increasing over time. Imputation is an immediate de facto admission that something is hard to measure. One large component is the rent that owner-occupiers are imagined as paying themselves, along with other imputations (Assa and Kvangraven 2021). So GDP is an idea whose initially clean theoretical lines (marketed monetary transactions) have become increasingly barnacled with increments and exceptions as the economy has become increasingly complex since the 1940s.

Table 1.2 shows how much of UK GDP in 2019 (before the pandemic affected the figures) was not in the market or had to be measured by imputation. Government activity is a large category. It was originally included in GDP after some debate, not only because it featured in Keynes's theory of aggregate demand but also because during the Second World War, those working on measurement did not want to show high government spending on military activities as having a negative effect on the economy (Lacey 2011, Keynes 1989, 1940). Imputed rent for owner-occupied housing was included from the start so that shifts in housing tenure between renting and owning (or different ownership structures across countries when comparing their economies) would not affect total output (Studenski 1958). A third large component is *FISIM*: financial intermediation services indirectly measured, introduced in SNA93 and extended in SNA08. This is a measure of financial activity whose price is formed by a spread between buy and sell sides— so it also includes speculation, as became all too evident in 2008. In the final quarter of that year, as global financial markets melted and huge taxpayer bailouts were required, this measure meant the finance sector made what was at that time its biggest-ever contribution to UK GDP. As Christophers (2013) points out, the method of measuring the finance sector has changed with every revision of the SNA in such a way as to increase the apparent size of its contribution to the economy. Smaller imputations were added in 1993 and 2008 for non-marketed activities, such as weapons systems and research and development (R&D) spending (Assa and Kvangraven 2021). All these changes reflect successive decisions made concerning the definition of GDP and other parts of the SNA. Too little has been written about the technical

TABLE 1.2. Imputations/Non-Market Components Expressed as a Percentage of GDP, UK, 2019

Imputed category	% of GDP
General government	45
Imputed rent	10
FISIM	7
R&D	1
Weapons systems	0.25

Source: ONS database. *Notes:* current prices; figures are rounded.

debates concerning changing statistical definitions of "the economy" or the international process through which expert consensus is reached and implemented.

Beyond these long-standing concerns—some of them debated since the very introduction of the SNA—there are several newer concerns. Many of these derive from the way digital technologies have been changing economic activity. A metaphor I used in my first book, *The Weightless World* (1997), was the literally decreasing mass of the economy, in the United Kingdom and other advanced economies. Figure 1.2 shows the material footprint of the United Kingdom's economy in millions of tonnes per pound of GDP (these figures do take account of material used in imports). With some reversals, there is a clear downward trend.

This reflects the broad shift in advanced economies from manufacturing to services, including those services embedded in or bundled with physical goods. As Table 1.1 shows for the United States, the share in GDP of services such as finance, law, consultancy and the like in the "hard to measure" category has grown. So too has the proportion of the value of manufactured items accounted for by intangibles and services, a process sometimes referred to as *servitisation*. Some firms will sell services to monitor, maintain, and repair their products; for example, the major UK engineering company Rolls-Royce makes almost two-thirds of its revenues from selling such services linked to its engines (see Chapter 3). The quality of many manufactured products has improved, reflecting their

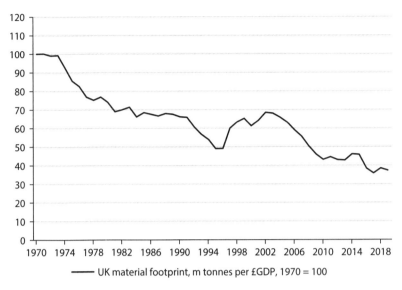

FIGURE 1.2. Weightlessness: the material footprint of the UK economy.
Source: Author's construction based on ONS data (2005, 2024b).

design and engineering, as has the quality of after-sales services, including software-enabled ones. For instance, newer cars have better fuel efficiency, more safety features, and built-in software for steering or navigation, and these design and operating improvements have formed a growing share of their value. Clothing is often made with higher-performance fabrics while brands attract a high premium reflecting design or quality (and status), while at the same time basic clothing has fallen substantially in price thanks to low-cost imports. Large companies that sell physical goods, such as Nike or Apple, or for that matter many auto, pharmaceutical, and engineering companies, increasingly do not manufacture the products they sell; they design, market, and sell the products but may contract out the manufacturing and assembly across the globe (Coyle and Nguyen 2022). Chapter 6 looks at this phenomenon of production in global value chains. The phenomenon of the increasing weightlessness or intangibility of economic value is a symbol of the substantial structural change the economy has undergone. Yet economic statistics do not record intangible value very well (Haskel and Westlake 2018).

Another major question is how best to measure the role played by the "free" digital goods and services so many of us use so often. One proposal is to treat them as a kind of barter involving consumers trading their attention to advertising in return for a free service, while advertisers pay the tech companies using the ad-funded business model (Nakamura et al. 2017); this would be another imputation. Another proposal is to estimate the monetary value consumers place on free goods using surveys and to add this to GDP (Brynjolfsson et al. 2019a, 2019b). A related proposal is to use similar estimates to again create an imputation that would form part of GDP (Schreyer 2022).

Other aspects of the progressive digitalisation of the economy pose yet more statistical challenges. For example, labour market statistics in most countries do not record gig employment well as the existing framework was designed to measure conventional jobs (Coyle 2017c), although many statistical agencies are now updating their surveys. However, while progress is being made on collecting data on these non-standard modes of employment, the economy continues to change. Hybrid work, partly online from home, and four-day weeks (rather than five-day) are emerging features of some labour markets (such as those of the United States, the United Kingdom, Canada, and Australia). New types of jobs appear frequently and do not fit easily into the categories set out in the Standard Occupational Classification used in official statistics; this system includes many detailed categories of manufacturing jobs, although this sector accounts for only about one-tenth of GDP in the Organisation for Economic Co-operation and Development (OECD) economies and an even smaller share of employment; yet it includes very little on the proliferation of types of jobs in services, including digital-related work. There are multiple categories of painter, for example, but none to record specific digital jobs, such as prompt engineer. Chapters 3 to 5 discuss further these aspects of the increasing digitalisation and weightlessness of the economy.

One inherent challenge in interpreting standard statistics that is made much harder by innovation and digitalisation is turning the nominal measures of activities—the number of dollars or pounds spent on investment or revenues earned by businesses, for example—into "real" terms or volume terms measures. This is accomplished by deflating the nominal activity by a relevant price index. The purpose is to abstract from inflation to get a measure of economic activity that shows whether there is "real" progress: Is economic welfare increasing? Yet, as Thomas Schelling (1958) observed, "What we call 'real' magnitudes are not completely real; only the money magnitudes are real. The 'real' ones are hypothetical." Price index theory derives from the underlying concept of individual utility maximisation. A deflator is an attempt to answer the question: What part of any increase in nominal activity we observe is due to increases in prices without any corresponding increase in utility? In a simple textbook economy, with standard goods of unchanging quality, revenues can be divided by volume of sales. No economy is this simple, however. It is extremely complex at the best of times to weight together multiple products into price indices, and all the more difficult when improvements in the quality of goods and services, or in variety, new goods, and shifts in people's tastes pose immense challenges for the concept of a utility-constant price index (Coyle 2024b). Think about comparing living standards over any length of time. How can we compare the utility of a population in an era of smartphones and personalised genomic medicine with that of an era—when I was doing my PhD—when cell phones and MRI scanners were just being introduced? Or still less with 1945, when less than half the US population had a telephone at all and antibiotics were the new wonder drug? What's more, as so-called real terms GDP growth is the standard metric of progress, it is not surprising that measured prices and inflation are politically contested (Stapleford 2009). Chapter 7 discusses the nearly intractable price index problems, which are more pressing during an era of technological and structural change, raising some profound questions about economic welfare.

Yet another set of issues concerns the spatial aspect of economic measurement. Nation-states collect official statistics based on the national territory and its regional or local administrative subdivisions. The digital economy has reinforced agglomeration economies, suggesting city regions have become an important natural economic geography. Often the relevant statistics for these areas can be constructed from existing data, perhaps with some effort to aggregate up from microdata. However, digital activities that cross national borders and the extensive global production chains, often involving transfers of unmeasured intangibles and data, make existing trade statistics far from adequate (see Chapter 6). Similarly, global challenges such as the climate and biodiversity crises require appropriate cross-national statistics for international policy action. There is no global government, but there is a need for global governance, informed by relevant statistics.

The terrain covered by the measurement challenges in the twenty-first-century economy is thus a broad one, ranging from starting to record the social and not just the private costs that economic activity imposes on nature, through the multiple digital reorganisations of employment, production, and consumption (both in the market and outside it), to the hypothetical concept of "real" output. The breadth of the issues, along with the difficulty of resolving them in a way that preserves the existing statistical framework, is daunting. It is one of the reasons I conclude that the framework is redundant, like the ever-more complex orbits in Ptolemaic astronomy as its practitioners struggled to fit new observations into the existing theory.

The rest of this book explores in detail why the economy has become harder to measure and makes the case for a new framework. The rest of this chapter sets out two reasons why it matters that we still measure activity using a framework that is flawed beyond easy repair: the way measurement feeds back into what is being measured through the decisions it informs, and the growing use in today's digital society of data and statistics for making important decisions.

Political Arithmetick

The statistical lens, the way economic activity is measured and therefore interpreted by governments and others, has varied greatly over time (Coyle 2014). One early framework for a synoptic view of society was William Petty's *Political Arithmetick* (1690). Here I am holding the copy in Chetham's Library in Manchester that was read by Karl Marx and Friedrich Engels when they worked there in the summer of 1845, as they drafted what subsequently became *The Communist Manifesto* (1848).

IMAGE 1.2. Holding a copy of William Petty's *Political Arithmetick* (1690) at Chetham's Library, Manchester. © Diane Coyle.

Petty's ambition was to measure the prosperity of the United Kingdom at a time when the prospect of war with France made an estimate of potential tax revenues timely. He introduced the concept of national income and wealth and saw land and labour, not gold, as the true source of the country's prosperity. The title he chose for his book is apt: statistics and their categorisation are indeed political. They are the frame into which the multiplicity of actions by individuals, businesses, other organisations, and governments are assembled to create a coherent picture. The outlines of the picture are determined by the ideas and theories prevalent at the time, and by the course of events. Petty's framework was succeeded by others, including those of Charles Davenant, who defined the exercise of collecting national statistics as "the art of reasoning by figures upon things relating to government" (1698), and of the physiocrats, whose model of the economy centred on the importance of agriculture. During the eighteenth and nineteenth centuries, the concept of economic life as a separate domain from other parts of life started to emerge (Hirschman 2016). The development of modern national statistics, with pioneers such as Colin Clark and Simon Kuznets, dates from the 1930s, when the distinct concept of the economy came into being (Mitchell 1998, Karabell 2014). Statistics were also a locus of political contention in Weimar Germany throughout its economic up-heavals of the 1920s and 1930s; 1925 saw the formation of the Reich's Statistical Office (Statistisches Reichsamt) (Tooze 2001). What governments needed from statistics in this period before the Second World War was to understand and try to manage the aggregate phenomena of hyperinflation (in central Europe) and the Great Depression (across the industrial countries), as the expansion of the franchise in the early twentieth century led to growing pressure for political leaders to take action in mitigating economic crisis. The decade profoundly influenced Keynes, leading to his *General Theory of Employment, Interest, and Money*, whose theoretical framework still forms the basis for modern economic statistics. But wartime needs then became paramount; Keynes's pamphlet *How to Pay for the War* (1940) catalysed the original version of today's SNA in a pan-Atlantic effort.

Why does this matter? This potted history of national income accounting emphasises that there is no single, natural way to classify and measure economic phenomena or the prevailing definition of the economy. The framework used meets the needs of its time, within the mental constructs of its time. The very idea of the economy as a distinct domain of national life dates from a specific period and instantiates a particular "well-defined conceptual and theoretical understanding of macroeconomic behaviour" (Ward 2004, p76). Statistics in the twentieth century became the systematic collection of quantitative information needed by the state (Desrosières 1998). This process occurred in all the industrialised countries as a key part of their becoming modern states. Desrosières writes: "It is difficult to think simultaneously that the objects being measured really do exist and that this is only a convention" (p1). Yet this is the case. Phenomena such as prices being charged and products being sold exist, but the categories and classification frameworks underpinning the collection, aggregation, and organisation of official statistics are devised to serve the purposes of the state, for macroeconomic or for social policies. Theodore Porter (1995) described the use of statistics to create state authority: "Quantification is a way of making decisions without seeming to decide" (p8), characterising it as a "social technology" intended to build trust in authority. Similarly, in his classic book *Seeing Like a State* (1998), James Scott argues that the measurements created for the purposes of government to give order to messy reality affect decisions and consequently influence that reality—generally for the worse, by ignoring important differences. In any case the invented classifications become "real." GDP and other economic statistics are entities "that hover between the realms of the invented and the discovered" (Daston 2000). "Official" statistics come to define the public sphere that structures political debate. The statistical framework breaks down when there is a significant change in the economic structure—as in the 1840s, or in the 1920s and 1930s (Desrosières, p252). At such times there seem to be multiple anomalies in existing statistics, until a new synthesis of economic theory and statistical classifications occurs.

An example of the social nature of statistics is the evolution of official data on ethnicity. Statistics on ethnicity in countries like the United States and United Kingdom have become far more detailed over time, often now with ten or twelve options to categorise people rather than two or three as in earlier periods of data collection. This reflects in part the increased diversity of Western societies and a desire to monitor socioeconomic inequalities—and in part is a political choice. For in France it is forbidden to collect data on individuals' ethnicity on the (admirable) principle that all are equal citizens of the Republic (National Institute of Statistics and Economic Studies 2016). Needless to say, there is no substantive "natural" difference between people of different ethnicities; another type of government could decide to collect statistics based on height categories, say. Statistics on race are needed only in a society where race matters as a source of identity, inequality, and policy. The question is what decision-makers will do with the data, or what they will do if they do not have the data. As discussed later in this chapter, automated decision procedures informed by data on ethnicity may have consequences that run counter to benign modern intentions to use the data to understand and thus help mitigate racial inequalities.

There is an important literature on the social construction of statistics, although it is not one that many economists know well. Yet they should. Being socially constructed, the statistics at the same time both enable and constrain economic research. When the modern national income accounts were still relatively new in the early postwar decades, leading economists—including many future Nobel Prize winners— worked on the empirics of growth. This was possible thanks to the availability for the first time of GDP and other national accounts data over many years for an increasing number of countries. The data enabled the first empirically informed theories of economic development and growth. For example, Simon Kuznets, who had worked on economic measurement since the 1930s, was one economist who used the statistics to do this kind of research (Kuznets 1955), as was Robert Solow (1957). Kuznets hypothesised that low-income economies would initially experience increasing income inequality, but at a certain stage in their development inequality would start to decline as growth continued. Solow's model of growth depending on capital, labour, and "technical progress"—the "residual"—became the workhorse theory of growth for thirty years. Thus the data available determines what can be known and shapes theorising about the economy. But theories also determine what data is collected: GDP data are needed for economists to try to analyse growth. The fundamental point about economic (or any social) statistics is that the phenomenon or behaviour they measure is a social construct, not simply a natural object. There is no economic equivalent to the true speed of light or the boiling point of a fluid at a given altitude. GDP is an idea, not a thing. Specifically, it is Keynes's idea, that $Y = C + I + G + (X - M)$ (an ex ante theoretical equality constructed as an ex post accounting identity in the SNA).

Statistics largely determine theories and beliefs about how the economy functions and so are used to inform decisions, along with other criteria such as political or ethical beliefs. These decisions then affect economic outcomes—sometimes in self-fulfilling or self-averting ways (Coyle 2022). Statistics form the basis of narratives about the economy, constructed and disputed by governors and governed (Shiller 2019; Tuckett et al. 2020). This is not an automatic or predetermined process, of course. People often have conflicting interpretations of the same economic statistics: Is a modest quarterly increase in GDP a sign of a thriving or a weakening economy? If the statistic is published during an election campaign, both interpretations will find advocates (Coyle

2017a). Politics or ideology will inform people's views. Events also change the economic narratives, with different statistics having greater salience at different times. When unemployment is high, the monthly and weekly jobless figures will be in focus. In eras of fixed exchange rates, the balance of payments statistics will be most important. As I write, both productivity and inflation statistics are making headline news, for all the wrong reasons.

Even so, there is a political economy feedback loop. Politics determine how the economy is measured—the lens through which economic outcomes are interpreted—and the statistics in turn affect political decisions (Coyle 2017b). This process takes place in the context of a political philosophy that derives authority from economic theory. Since 1980 this context has been the free market philosophy first advocated by the Thatcher and Reagan governments, drawing on the economics profession's intellectual reaction to the economic stagflation of the 1970s, with its turn to monetarism, the efficient markets hypothesis, and rational expectations. Given the successive crises of the past fifteen years (the 2008 financial crisis, the pandemic, the Russian invasion of Ukraine and subsequent inflation, extreme weather events across the globe), it seems possible that the prevailing public philosophy about the operation of the economy will change, perhaps substantially. The return of an explicit industrial policy in many countries seems to signal that this is underway. And meanwhile, there have been significant shifts in the centre of gravity in academic economic research, which has long left behind the high-water mark of free market economics (Coyle 2007, 2022). So not only is the structure of the economy changing thanks to digitalisation, but these shifts combined with the crises are altering the political context; the decisions facing governments and others therefore need different measures.

Automating Data-Driven Decision-Making

Like most of my fellow PhD students in the 1980s, I didn't think much (if at all) about where the statistics I used for my dissertation came from or how they had been constructed. We took the data as givens, as the word suggests. We downloaded what we needed in those pre-internet days either from storage media such as magnetic tapes or via a dedicated wired connection to data suppliers. Now that it is easy to access so many economic statistics by simple download, there is less attention than ever paid to how this data is constructed; yet the process is extremely complicated. Simple revisions due to new data arriving, never mind subtle methodological changes, can entirely overturn the results of empirical research or change the narrative about a country's economic growth performance. Nevertheless, teaching students even the basics about the national accounts and price indices has fallen into neglect. Similarly, few seem to be taught (as I was so long ago) to start an empirical project by looking at a simple visualisation of one's data to spot outliers and errors. This is a paradox as there is a surge of interest among economists in constructing new types of data from web scraping, mobile phone records, satellite data, social media, or text analysis, and those engaged in this novel data construction are generally extremely careful about the characteristics of the data they are creating. For as they recognise, data is made, not given. Yet, with honourable exceptions, many researchers simply download standard economic statistics and apply estimation techniques with no thought as to whether their data can bear the conceptual weight they are imposing. Far more attention is paid to the sophisticated statistical theory involved in developing estimators or tests, despite the much greater empirical significance of simple measurement uncertainty—like arguing about the best nozzle to use for the icing on a cake when you don't know whether the cake has been baked using one egg or four. There also seems to be an odd but real phenomenon of the mere appearance of numbers on a computer screen making people forget that economic statistics involve substantial margins of error.

In being so cavalier, such economists are ignoring some early cautions about how much weight could be placed on economic statistics. One book pointing out the immense uncertainties involved was Oskar Morgenstern's *On the Accuracy of Economic Observations* (1950, 1963). He noted that there are several sources of measurement error, including ambiguous definitions, inaccurate collection of data, sampling error, and so on. He also criticised empirical economists for paying little attention to how the data they use was constructed. Nevertheless, most subsequent economic research and policy analysis has continued to pay inadequate attention to the inherent uncertainty in economic measurement. The more research I have done on economic statistics, appreciating the practical challenges and inherent conceptual challenges, the less certain I am that we know anything solid about today's economy.

Yet the need to consider carefully what statistics, or "data," are measuring is greater than ever: What is the underlying concept, how closely aligned are the statistics gathered to the concept, how much measurement error is there? The reason for this need for enhanced care is that many governments and businesses are adopting machine learning (ML) and more sophisticated generative AI systems to make decisions that have a potentially large impact on people's lives. These automated decision systems are encoded versions of *homo economicus*, the perfectly rational (given an objective function and specified information set) maximisers of economic textbooks. Some of the concerns about data use in algorithmic decision-making are obvious. Data bias is one: data about people who live in a structurally unequal society will capture these inequalities. If the hope is that decisions now are less unfair, less biased than those which built the current social structures, then existing data needs to be used with extreme care. There are many examples of problematic data bias. In her book *Weapons of Math Destruction* (2016), Cathy O'Neil reports examples such as an algorithm for ranking customers contacting call centres by their likely profitability, or ranking prisoners by their supposed reoffending risk for release. The biased data problem is not easy to solve—after all, how could one build the data representation of a counterfactual unbiased society?—but at least it is known.

Related problems are perhaps less widely appreciated. One arises when algorithms substitute for human judgments in arenas of conflicting objectives. An AI or ML system needs its reward or loss function to be specified and coded. But there are arenas such as criminal justice or welfare benefits where policymakers may have objectives or values that are fundamentally opposed to each other. One response in computer science to a variety of objectives is to combine them with appropriate weights in a single objective function, but this assumes an absence of pure conflicts of interest. For example, one could not encode the United Kingdom's Brexit decision in an objective function weighting Leave 52% and Remain 48%. In criminal justice, people can have profoundly different views about the purpose of punishment: Is it for rehabilitation or for retribution? In much of the debate about technologies such as facial recognition or monitoring social media, the conflict is posed as an irreconcilable choice between security and freedom (although this framing also presumes a level of technological effectiveness that is unproven). A human debate can nevertheless settle on a practical measure, such as five years of jail time for a robbery, or the use of facial recognition technology in some specified high-risk situations, without having to resolve debate on values—these are known as *incompletely theorised agreements* (Coyle and Weller 2020).

There are deeper questions still about objective functions, questions about the meaning of fairness, or societally desirable outcomes. Algorithms are increasingly used (especially in the United States) for decisions such as about which prisoners to parole, with the objective in the latter case being to minimise the rate of recidivism. There is some evidence that algorithmic decision rules are more likely to incorrectly predict that Black prisoners will reoffend, recommending that a higher proportion of this group are kept imprisoned—there are more false positives for this group too (Ludwig and Mullainathan 2021). On the other hand, the use of such an algorithm reduces the number of people kept in jail as it is a more accurate predictor overall, and this increases the absolute number of Black prisoners who are paroled (Kleinberg et al. 2018). Is it fairer to use the algorithmic decision or not? A similar question arises regarding the use of ethnicity data in ranking patients for treatment for kidney illness. When a standard algorithm in use in the United States and elsewhere is altered by removing the data recording patients' ethnicity, some categories of people (Black and Hispanic) jump a significant number of places in the priority ranking for treatment (Diao et al. 2021). This is counterintuitive as it would seem that knowing that somebody comes from an ethnic category more likely to have low income or a background of poor health ought to make them more likely to get treated sooner. But, as in the parole example, the question is whether the algorithm should be optimising for patient outcomes given that some have already-compromised health status (because they are Black) or instead for patient outcomes regardless of their socioeconomic status (purely as equal citizens). It depends on the objective function.

The use of ML systems, especially in areas such as policing, criminal justice, welfare, and housing, raises profound questions of what it means to say society is getting better—in economic terminology, what is happening to social welfare. Many of the debates in computer science about questions such as data bias and the "alignment problem" (how well does what the machine is optimising for align with the actually desired outcome, given the data and code it deploys) pose urgent questions in welfare economics that have not been considered by the economics mainstream since the late 1970s (Coyle and Fabian et al. 2023). The need to revisit welfare economics is all the more urgent given that automated decision systems implement feedback loops that—like a river eroding an ever-deeper canyon through the rock—reinforce the social inequities reflected in the data that feeds the algorithms (O'Neil 2016, Thompson 2022).

Conclusion

Economists often, rightly, advocate for evidence-based policy. In general, most governments do not evaluate the impact of their policies or apply lessons from experience; politics and ideologies more often overrule evidence. Nevertheless, in some countries the use of frameworks such as cost-benefit analysis is legally required for some government decisions, while the use of automated decision procedures is increasing rapidly, often in the interests of making the public sector more efficient. But the more policy decisions are "evidence based" and the more this process is codified—either informally or literally through an algorithmic process—the more careful we all need to be about the statistics or data forming the evidential base.

Statistics matter. They have great weight in influencing public debate and political outcomes. They can help guide better economic policies. They also involve questions of freedom, justice, life, and death. This book is concerned with the statistics intended to measure what is happening in the economy, and it starts from the presumption that the conceptual framework underpinning today's statistics is redundant. The prevailing statistical lens distorts perceptions and is leading to bad decisions and outcomes. Four-fifths of the economy is considered hard to measure because the data collected is being interpreted through the lens of a framework developed at a time when the key economic problems were different, when a lack of physical rather than natural capital was the binding constraint on growth, material production was dominant and intangible value was low, and the pressing economic policy challenge was demand management.

This chapter has described the shortcomings of existing economic statistics and made the case for a paradigm shift in the measurement framework. It has argued that the case is urgent for two reasons: first, that measurement shapes reality as well as describing it, so mismeasurement leads to poor decisions and has negative consequences; and second, because of the rapidly increasing use of data to make decisions. But what measurements does society need now to understand itself and achieve the right kind of economic growth for the benefit of all?

To begin to tackle this fundamental question, the following chapters diagnose in detail the failures of the current framework. Chapter 2 sets the scene by describing the disappearance of meaningful growth in productivity—that residual—across the OECD countries during the past twenty years. It does not argue that the slowdown is a mirage due to mismeasurement but rather that the role of digital innovation is at the heart of productivity growth and its absence, and this has consequences for what statistics are needed for economic policy and business decisions. Chapters 3 to 5 then look in detail at measurement challenges due to digitalisation: the dematerialisation of economic value, the disintermediation of activities and business model changes, and the provision of free products. Chapter 6 follows up with a focus on globalisation (itself possible thanks to digitalisation) and the impossibility of understanding flows of value across borders. Chapter 7 discusses price indices, and why the changes due to digital have exacerbated long-standing dilemmas in calculating price indices and thus "real" economic growth. After setting out the many difficult measurement questions, I do not offer easy solutions to them, although many researchers are working on all the issues raised here. However, Chapters 8 and 9 propose a path forward that will enable policymakers and the public meanwhile to evaluate the progress of the economy. Chapter 8 sets out the comprehensive wealth framework giving a broad perspective on the constituents of economic welfare, embedding sustainability, and enabling non-market values to be incorporated. It offers a different picture into which pieces of the puzzle discussed earlier can fit. Chapter 9 draws together the threads. After discussing why some alternative proposals from the Beyond GDP debate are insufficient, it sets out the agenda for the essential paradigm shift in how we measure and therefore understand and shape the economy and our societies.

2

Productivity without Products

IF THERE IS A SINGLE MEASURE economists rely on to gauge economic progress, it is productivity growth. As Paul Krugman put it in an often-repeated comment, "Productivity isn't everything, but, in the long run, it is *almost* everything. A country's ability to improve its standard of living over time depends almost entirely on its ability to raise its output per worker" (Krugman 1990). Its importance explains why it has become the focus of much policy attention, because productivity growth has slowed across the OECD since the mid-2000s. There are variations: as I write, US productivity growth is looking healthy again, whereas the United Kingdom's has almost flatlined since 2008, in a clear departure from the earlier trend (Figure 2.1). But economists have not reached a settled view on the explanation for the slowdown, particularly when new technological innovations are in the news all the time. Technology is central to the standard story of economic progress, as is evident from historical accounts of the Industrial Revolution, which saw the dawn of modern economic growth driven by significant innovations in steam power, mining, rail and telegraph, cotton and agriculture. So it is a puzzle that now, when advances in AI and robotics are surging ahead, and on top of the pandemic-induced shift to digital and platform business models, the economy does not seem to be progressing. Given the importance of productivity to economists' standard concept of progress, this chapter sets out the debate about the productivity slowdown and its related diagnoses in order to map a route into the digital economy phenomena discussed in more detail in the following few chapters.

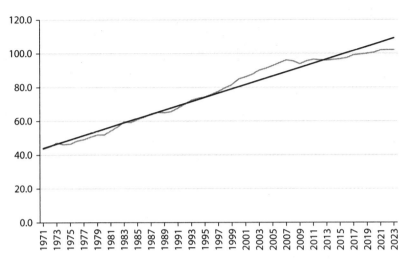

FIGURE 2.1. UK labour productivity. *Source:* ONS (2024c). *Note:* GDP per hour worked, 1970 = 100. Dark line shows long-run trend.

Economists—and politicians—talk about productivity all the time, but (as so often with economic language) other people understand it in a more informal way. It is one of the many words (such as "rational," "efficient," or "capital") that has a technical meaning in economics that differs, perhaps subtly, from normal usage, and much misunderstanding can leach into the gap. The measure reported in the media and discussed online is usually labour productivity, or output per worker or hour worked, as in Figure 2.1. To the public, the word may imply people working harder or better: people need to shape up and spend less time scrolling through social media. But although many people will have in mind employers wanting to save money by squeezing more out of their employees, cost cutting, and job losses, labour productivity growth over any moderately sustained period requires additional capital and other inputs. A construction worker is made more productive by working with more powerful and sophisticated tools, not by being shouted at to dig harder and faster with a spade. In a wonderful article, Mancur Olson (1996) pointed out that an immigrant to Germany from Haiti becomes more productive overnight as a janitor (compared with compatriots who did not migrate) simply thanks to access to better cleaning equipment (capital), the organisation of work, public capital (such as transportation networks), and the political-economic environment (loosely speaking, institutions).

To the economist, though, productivity is more generally the economic value produced given all the resources used. TFP is the additional output produced with the available inputs (capital, labour, energy, and materials), both output and inputs being adjusted for inflation. Ideally, they would be adjusted for quality change too. TFP captures new ideas and inventions and better ways of organising production, or "technology" as a shorthand. It is the gold standard measure but quickly gets complicated to define and measure. As well as TFP being less intuitive than labour productivity, many non-economists struggle with the deflation of nominal into real variables in the economists' concept, which does indeed introduce a lot of complexity. People with business experience do not understand why productivity is superior to simpler measures such as profits or value added (revenues less costs). This is a conversation I have often had with David Sainsbury, a brilliant former science minister in the United Kingdom. In his book (*Windows of Opportunity*, 2020), he argues that economists need a new approach to growth and should focus on the competitive advantage of firms: "In a competitive market economy, firms compete by trying to gain a competitive advantage over their rivals, as this is what enables them to grow and enhance their profitability" (p30). He adds: "A nation's standard of living in the long term depends on the ability of its firms to attain a high and rising level of value added per capita" (p35). Many would agree with his view that what matters for an economy's prosperity is that its businesses are competitive in domestic and export markets by adding value, selling goods and services others want to buy, thus earning profits and being able to pay their employees well. This view echoes much of the management literature such as Michael Porter's classic (1990) *The Competitive Advantage of Nations*.

Productivity as economists understand it encompasses those success measures that businesses prioritise, but it goes beyond them by taking into account the prices received for output and paid for inputs, and thus capturing relative values. It is the determinant of the real level of living standards a country can attain over time, using the concept of a production function or relationship between inputs and outputs to take into account changes in relative prices that reflect shifts in technology or how production is organised. In general (although not in recent times in all OECD countries) median (labour) incomes adjusted for inflation rise in line with (labour) productivity. The story of modern, post-Malthusian economic growth since the nineteenth century is indeed one of productivity growth. The story of the twenty-first century, unfortunately, is one of its absence. As politicians well appreciate the need for living standards to start rising again, productivity—along with its measurement—has become a focus of policy debate.

With many possible contributory causes, the "productivity puzzle" is without doubt a genuine phenomenon, even though it raises significant measurement questions. Potential culprits include multiple economic shocks (the 2008 financial crisis, COVID, the Russian invasion of Ukraine, inflation, Middle East conflict); debt overhangs from the financial crisis leaving unproductive zombie firms; reduced entry and increased concentration in many markets; high levels of income inequality; and ageing populations. There are also two possible, mutually exclusive causes that are a focus of debate in the academic literature on productivity: a substantive decline in the economic value of innovation and in the productivity of scientific research itself, or alternatively long lags in the adoption of new technologies before they deliver economically valuable outputs.

In the pessimists' corner about the impact of technology, one leading voice is Robert Gordon, who argues in his magisterial economic history of the United States (2016) that the kinds of innovation happening now bear no comparison in their significance to the innovations of the early twentieth century. Then, people's lives were improved by indoor sanitation and public water and sewage systems, by the arrival of electricity in the home and the factory, by motorised transportation. He counterposes these to recent innovations such as social media or incremental improvements in transport:

> Not only has the measured record of growth been slower since 1970 than before, but . . . the unmeasured improvements in the quality of everyday life created by [the latest technologies] are less significant than the more profound set of unmeasured benefits of the earlier

industrial revolution. . . . The rate of advance of labor productivity and TFP over the next quarter century will resemble the slow pace of 2004–15, not the faster growth rate of 1994–2004, much less the even faster growth rate achieved long ago during 1920–70. (Gordon 2016, p566–567)

Even when it comes to digital technologies themselves, he adds, the pace of innovation has slowed because Moore's Law had come to its end; he wrote the book long before generative AI appeared on the scene. Another influential contribution to productivity pessimism is due to Bloom et al. (2020), who looked at the diminishing rate of innovation across a wide range of technologies. Their fundamental point is that the number of researchers in the US economy has risen steadily yet (real) GDP growth per capita has slowed, so research productivity has as a matter of arithmetic declined sharply. This is true across all the specific technologies they investigate, such as soybean and wheat output or cancer survival rates, as well as in the aggregate figures. They write: "A good example is Moore's Law. The number of researchers required today to achieve the famous doubling of computer chip density is more than 18 times larger than the number required in the early 1970s" (p1104). (More on Moore's Law later.) It is also true at the level of individual firms, with the distribution of the number of researchers employed in firms shifting to the right and the distribution of firm-level research productivity shifting to the left.

A slowdown in research productivity for any single technology is not surprising; there will always be a physical limit. However, there will then be leaps to different technology platforms rather than incremental gains in old ones, such as switching from oil lamps to electricity, valves to transistors, or adopting hybrid seeds, and one might expect these to translate into continuing underlying productivity growth in lighting or computation or nutrition. But the aggregate story seems compelling: a growing proportion of the workforce has been engaged in research, and yet we see recorded productivity growth slowing sharply.

The optimists' camp counters with a core argument concerning the adjustments needed to use new technologies and therefore the time it

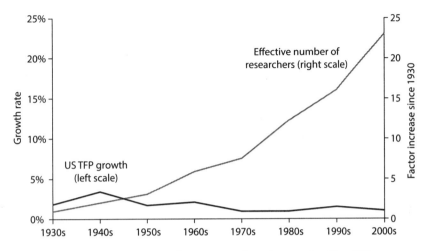

FIGURE 2.2. Aggregate data on growth and research effort, US.
Source: Bloom et al. (2020).

takes to see innovations translated into economic value. A key voice is
Erik Brynjolfsson, whose work in the dot-com boom of the 1990s demonstrated that companies adopting digital technologies do not experience productivity improvements unless they spend about ten times
more on reorganising their production processes than on buying information and communications technology (ICT) equipment (Brynjolfsson and Hitt 2000). He has recently described this as a "productivity
J curve": at the firm level, productivity first declines when new technology is adopted, before it then increases (Brynjolfsson et al. 2021). This
phenomenon of long and variable lags has also been noted often in the
economic history literature, famously so by Paul David (1990), who, in
documenting the half century it took from the invention of basic electricity technologies to the spread of electricity in factories and homes,
described the phenomenon of "technological presbyopia." In other
words, just as middle-aged people can be both shortsighted and long-
sighted simultaneously, people can simultaneously overestimate the
short-term impact of an innovation and underestimate its long-term
impact. There are by now several papers showing (for the United States,
United Kingdom, West Germany, across the OECD) that the dispersion
of productivity at the firm level is widening; the most productive firms

are the ones adopting digital technologies effectively and pulling further ahead of their competitors who have not (yet) made the necessary adjustments (e.g., Foster et al. 2021, Gal et al. 2019). This may be linked to evidence of increasing market power in many economies, with only so-called superstar firms increasing productivity and market share (Autor et al. 2020). James Bessen argues (2022) that using digital technology and the associated software has become sufficiently complex that few firms can adopt it successfully, and the more they do so, the harder it is for their competitors to catch them up. However, the evidence on the extent to which concentration has generally been increasing is not entirely clear.

A new twist is the lack of any sign (as I write this) that very recent dramatic advances in AI are having an economic impact. Much of the debate about AI, including the new frontier models, has focused on the possible labour market impact—will robots take jobs or further immiserise the middle classes? Early estimates suggest the scope of work with the potential to be performed by AI tools is extensive (e.g., Albanesi et al. 2023, Eloundou et al. 2024), although so far AI adopters have tended to expand their number of employees. It is unclear which firms are using which AI tools, and for what, though; media reports suggest it is most extensively used in professional services and in activities such as call centres. The technology carries some business risks. For example, Air Canada was held liable in a civil case for a refund policy its call centre chatbot had simply invented; the airline's argument that the bot was an autonomous agent was rejected by the court (Belanger 2024). As I write, the "hallucination" problem of generative AI (for example, making up court cases to cite as precedents in a legal document) has also not been solved, nor the many disputes concerning intellectual property rights and training data. But there may also be productivity benefits in adopting AI. One study found that its use in a call centre for a travel company had enabled the AI to codify the answers given to customers by the better agents and use these to train and improve the productivity and performance of those who were not so good (Brynjolfsson, Li, and Raymond 2023). An experiment in Boston Consulting Group on its own consultants similarly found positive productivity impacts (Dell'Acqua et al. 2024). Until more businesses adopt the latest AI tools, the impact on productivity growth will necessarily be unclear. Meanwhile, more systematic measurement of the use of AI is needed. Existing official surveys predate generative AI and often ask about the extensive margin of use only, rather than intensity or type of use. Researchers are turning to new methods, including web scraping, to gather data on use of the technology and on categories and levels of employment. But the research-based methods (e.g., Lane 2023) are time-consuming and not yet suitable for the routine production of economic statistics.

If we wait long enough (but how long?), perhaps it will become clear whether the pessimists or optimists are right. There is certainly a lot of techno-hype about AI. One can also question the economic value of many of the prominent consumer-facing digital innovations, whether social media or the kind of blocking that software companies use to extract consumer surplus, from printers that will not work if other manufacturers' ink cartridges are used to tractors that farmers thought they had purchased but are banned from repairing themselves on the ground that John Deere claims copyright over the software needed to run them. Cory Doctorow (2023) has coined the memorable term *enshittification* to capture the decline in value users are getting from digital businesses with market power. There is research suggesting people are happier if prevented from using social media (Allcott et al. 2020). And yet there is also a vast amount of innovation taking place, in digital (generative AI, robotics), in materials science (nanotechnologies, composites), in biomedicine (mRNA, genomics, biomarkers), and in manufacturing processes (additive manufacturing, biomanufacturing), as well as rapid declines in the costs of renewables generation, potentially paving the way for a switch away from the fossil fuel energy system. Some of these may be in their early stages of deployment but will eventually have a large economic impact; others may simply be difficult to measure. Perhaps fundamentally so; it might be impossible to reflect in a price index the qualitative gain from a Zoom call with a grandchild in another country, or from the impact of mRNA platforms delivering a pandemic vaccine several years faster than any previous vaccine technology.

I am on Team Optimism, but the purpose of this chapter is not to adjudicate this contest. The rest of this chapter will focus on some of the conceptual and measurement challenges in trying to understand a productivity slowdown in an 80 per cent "hard to measure" economy. As the word suggests, productivity is a measure founded on tangible *products*. Once when I was consulting for a retail bank, the CEO took me into the server room, patted a stack, and said: "This is where we make the mortgages." On another visit to the BBC's long wave broadcast transmitter at Droitwich in the middle of England, the manager pointed to one cable, saying, "That one is carrying Radio 3." So intangible services certainly require manufactured objects— material stuff is the basic platform or substrate of the weightless world. An increasing proportion of *economic value*, however, derives from the immaterial, human elements. How can a concept based on products—such as the number of cars produced given the amounts of labour hours, machines, steel, plastic, and energy used—be made meaningful when the increment in economic value even to a physical product increasingly lies in its intangible quality characteristics (safety, navigation, ease of parking, comfort, aesthetics)? To appreciate how difficult this is, let's briefly turn to the basics of measuring productivity growth.

Growth Accounting

The approach set out here is *growth accounting* based on the concept of the production function relating inputs to outputs, thus breaking down growth in output into the contributions that can be allocated to each input, and whatever is left over. It has generated a vast literature. An alternative approach is to regress TFP on some specific hypothesised drivers, such as management quality, information technology, market openness, or employees' well-being, and there is (another) large literature doing so. A challenge with regression analysis is that there is generally too little information in the data to identify separately all the potential contributors to productivity. Growth accounting has its own limitations but avoids trying to find causal explanations.

The original growth accounting literature uses a simple neoclassical production function with two factors, capital and labour, assuming a constant returns Cobb-Douglas functional form with Hicks-neutral technical change. The seminal paper underlying the now almost universally used KLEMS growth accounting approach was Jorgenson and Griliches (1967), extended in Jorgenson, Gollop, and Fraumeni (1987) and set out comprehensively in Schreyer and Pilat (2001). The Jorgenson and Griliches article starts out with the key elements of the framework:

> Measurement of total factor productivity is based on the economic theory of production. For this purpose the theory consists of a production function with constant returns to scale together with the necessary conditions for producer equilibrium. Quantities of output and input entering the production function are identified with real product and real factor input as measured for social accounting purposes. Marginal rates of substitution are identified with the corresponding price ratios. Employing data on both quantities and prices, movements along the production function may be separated from shifts in the production function. Shifts in the production function are identified with changes in total factor productivity. (1967, p249)

I have quoted this to emphasise the assumptions. One is constant returns, although increasing returns are normal in many parts of the economy and have probably been increasing in scope. Another assumption, that factor markets are competitive, means market prices of inputs of labour and other inputs can be used to make this a "social accounting" (welfare) exercise; but it may also be empirically questionable. That the variables are all expressed in real terms, deflated by relevant price indices, will also be important for measurement and interpretation. Setting this out makes clear the appeal of simple labour productivity measures. Still, given these caveats, the framework allows the identification of shifts in the production function as a change in TFP.

Having made these assumptions, the basic constructs are simple. Gross output Y is produced using factors of production capital services K, labour L, energy E, and materials M, and also given technology A.

These are flow measures, expressed as real-terms quantities per time period. H denotes the production function.

$$Y = H(K, L, E, M, A) \qquad (2.1)$$

Y here is *not* a measure of value-added output (like GDP); it is gross output without deducting the inputs used. Some productivity measures—particularly published labour productivity statistics—do use GDP, however. This is not just a technical nicety as the gap between gross output and GDP has been growing over time, with production in many countries shifting from vertically integrated firms to production networks where the central large firms contract out more of their needed supplies rather than producing them internally. The reason for this shift is (presumably) the positive productivity gain, so using a gross output measure makes sense. Yet it might be difficult in practice to capture accurately the relevant input and output prices when relative prices are changing rapidly, and when the contracting out is often to another country so involving measurement of imported components and their prices too. (Alternatively, a structural shift of this kind could be thought of as a "technology" involving a process innovation, although it may not be possible to distinguish these empirically.) On the other hand, as is well known, using value-added measures like GDP eliminates double-counting between sectors; in the gross output approach, aggregate TFP growth is *not* equal to the sum of sectoral-level TFP growth. While the tidy appeal of components that sum to the aggregate is obvious, production functions do not produce value added but rather output, so the underlying theory points to the gross output approach.

In the KLEMS diagnostic process, it is sectors or firms that are often of interest, so the variables in (2.1) will be indexed by sector/firm j and also by time period t. Rates of growth in aggregate inputs and output are weighted averages of their individual components, with the weights given by relative shares of each component in the total. The construction of weights is another important technicality, discussed shortly. To progress with measurement, the relationship between output and inputs needs to be further specified, so more assumptions come into play. If we assume technology is Hicks-neutral (that is, increasing the marginal productivity of all inputs equally), we can rewrite (2.1) as:

$$Y = A - F(K, L, E, M) \tag{2.2}$$

Then differentiating with respect to time and using log rates of change gives a standard expression for TFP growth:

$$d \ln A/dt = d \ln Y/dt - s_K \, d \ln K/dt - s_L \, d \ln L/dt - s_M \, d \ln M/dt \tag{2.3}$$

If value-added measures are used, there is a similar equation with the weights s being the factor shares in value added, but this will overstate the rate of TFP growth by a factor of the inverse of the share of value added in gross output; as this has been declining, the degree of overstatement will have increased. Schreyer and Pilat (2001) point out the implication when it comes to *labour* productivity measures:

> Growth in value-added-based labour productivity depends on shifts in capital intensity (the amount of capital available per unit of labour) and [TFP] growth. When measured as gross output per unit of labour input, labour productivity growth also depends on how the ratio of intermediate inputs to labour changes. A process of outsourcing, for example, implies substitution of primary factors of production, including labour, for intermediate inputs. Everything else equal, gross output-based labour productivity rises as a consequence of outsourcing and falls when in-house production replaces purchases of intermediate inputs, despite the fact that such changes need not reflect changes in the individual characteristics of the workforce, nor shifts in technology or efficiency. (2001, p135)

Value-added labor productivity, on the other hand, is not affected by shifts in the degree of vertical integration.

These subtleties are well known among growth accounting cognoscenti but not so familiar to others. Yet the assumptions and choices can make a substantial difference to the productivity growth measures, and hence to the story told about an economy's success. For example, the US Bureau of Labor Statistics (BLS) publishes value-added measures while the World KLEMS database publishes gross output-based

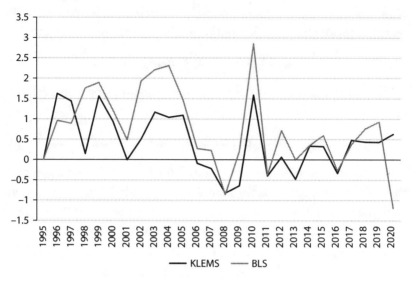

FIGURE 2.3. Two measures of US TFP growth: BLS (value added)
and KLEMS (gross output). *Sources:* BLS; KLEMS latest databases, 2024.

measures. The two are shown in Figure 2.3. The broad pattern is similar, but there are some significant divergences, sometimes enough to alter the productivity narrative; just look at the early 2000s.

There are of course many other practical measurement complexities. The calculation needs to take account of quality change in inputs and output. Much of this is handled (in theory—less so in practice; see Chapter 7) through quality-adjusting deflators, but the labor input is generally adjusted for changes in the skill composition of the workforce and measured as hours worked to take account of part-time work and trends in working time. The capital input term is the (physical) service that firms derive from their purchased capital and needs to be estimated, often done by assuming the flow is a proportion of the existing stock, adjusted for its age and for depreciation. Ideally, the calculation should take account of changes in capacity utilisation, which vary significantly over the business cycle; both labour and capital will be used less in a downturn, so the input measures ought to be adjusted downwards, reducing productivity compared with if no adjustment is made. Increasingly, intangible capital is being introduced into the calculation, and estimates for these services are also needed (Roth 2022, Corrado et al. 2022). The appropriate price of labour is the (adjusted) wage, and of capital the user cost. The aggregates for inputs and output will be constructed as index numbers from lower-level data, so there are also choices to be made about weights and formulae for these.

Whatever the choices, the aggregate slowdown in productivity growth since the mid-2000s is undeniable. But the range of assumptions and measurement strategies involved helps explain why reaching a settled consensus on the causes of the slowdown has proven difficult.

Productivity Diagnostics

One way to try to understand the prevailing productivity puzzle is to look at the contribution to the aggregate of different sectors of the economy: Is the problem widespread across the economy or concentrated in certain activities? There is another large literature looking at firm-level productivity, with its own data and identification challenges. Although production function theory applies to firms, and there is therefore a good reason for using this microdata, firms in given sectors do experience similar technologies, frictions, and shocks, and it turns out there is useful information in sectoral decompositions. For example, the finance sector has had the common experience of the financial crisis and subsequent regulatory changes, with people in the sector arguing that the increased regulatory burden explains its productivity slowdown. Similarly the auto sector is experiencing a transition to electric vehicles that will have specific sectoral effects.

There are some pivotal measurement choices in embarking on a sectoral diagnostic, particularly concerning the decomposition/aggregation process. Nominal output and the nominal value of inputs need to be deflated appropriately, and with particular care when relative prices between sectors are changing. If aggregate nominal output is deflated by an aggregate deflator, it will differ from the total constructed by adding up sectoral revenues deflated by sectoral price indices. The need to deflate revenues is particularly problematic in sectors where either there are no market prices (public services) or output is imputed (real estate, finance).

There is also a choice to be made about the index method used to aggregate/decompose totals. Nominal values in equations like (2.3) can be added so that the sum of the components equals the total, but the sum of deflated output in different sectors will not equal the aggregate (deflated with an aggregate price index) unless the deflators happen to be the same across sectors. (This is true of GDP as well, although it is not often acknowledged: real-terms GDP is not equal to the sum of its real-terms components, nor can the growth rates of components be added to get the growth rate of GDP [Whelan 2002].) Some decomposition methods assume that prices (and implicitly production functions) are the same across sectors to make sure the results of any decomposition do add up, but even at the sector (rather than firm) level, this seems unrealistically restrictive. The underlying question is what are the "real" units? In constructing the elements of an aggregate production function, we are dividing index numbers into amounts of dollars, euros, or pounds. One can count dollars, hours worked, or kilowatts of electricity used; but what is a "real" unit of labour or capital services, or of output of the finance sector? Economists have internalised the concept of "real" quantities by some intuitive analogy with counting bricks or cars, but it is a utility-related and rather metaphysical construct. Chapter 7 will return to this fundamental question in looking at price indices.

Finally, in the decompositions the weights used can involve either real-terms shares of output (or value added), nominal-terms shares, or alternatively employment shares. The choice affects the extent to which changes in the productivity aggregate will appear to reflect shifts between sectors with different levels and growth rates of productivity, or instead "within" sector changes, because real-terms shares will capture relative price shifts between sectors. In Coyle et al. (2023) my coauthor Jen and I compared three decomposition methods for UK data for 1998–2019, focusing on a change in labour productivity trends around 2008, as a first cut in the diagnostics (see Box 2.1 for more on the decomposition process using one possible method).

Our paper gives chapter and verse on this and some alternative decompositions we did for comparison. In all cases there are significant

Box 2.1 Decomposing productivity growth by sector

Which sectors contributed most to the United Kingdom's productivity growth slowdown around 2008, and how much difference to the diagnosis does the choice of index method make? We preferred a Tornqvist index as more appropriate to a study of sectoral difference because it allows prices to differ between sectors, although unlike the more common approaches (known as the shift share and the *generalised exactly additive decomposition*), it is not additive across sectors. This choice means we used estimates of sector-level growth in *real* gross value added (V_i) to construct an aggregate measure of real gross value added (V) as a weighted sum of log changes in industry gross value added. The algebra is shown in this box to illustrate the calculations (with full detail in the paper):

$$\Delta lnV \equiv \sum_i \bar{\omega}_i \, \Delta lnV_i \qquad (2.4)$$

with

$$\omega_i = v_i \Big/ \sum_i v_i \qquad (2.5)$$

and using

$$\bar{\omega}_i = 0.5\left(\omega_{it} + \omega_{it-1}\right) \qquad (2.6)$$

The weights ω_i are the share of sector i in *nominal* gross value added v, which we averaged (as a Divisia index $\bar{\omega}_i$) across two time periods. Aggregate total hours of work H is just the sum of industry hours (as these are "natural" units rather than constructed, conceptual ones):

$$H = \sum_i H_i \qquad (2.7)$$

Then aggregate labour productivity per hour is:

$$\Delta ln \left(V/H\right) = \Delta lnV - \Delta lnH \qquad (2.8)$$

and labour productivity growth for industry i is:

$$\Delta ln(V_i/H_i) = \Delta lnV_i - \Delta lnH_i \qquad (2.9)$$

(continued)

To define aggregate labour productivity growth from the industry data (as opposed to constructing it from the aggregate data), we took the share-weighted sum over industries i:

$$\Delta ln(V/H) \equiv \sum_i \bar{\omega}_i \Delta ln \left(\frac{V_i}{H_i} \right) \qquad (2.10)$$

The figures resulting from equations 2.8 (top down) and 2.10 (bottom up) will be different. The difference gives a whole economy reallocation term (R) (which will also incorporate the relative price shifts between sectors) as the difference between the two:

$$\Delta ln(V/H) = \sum_i \bar{\omega}_i \Delta ln(V_i/H_i) + R \qquad (2.11)$$

R measures the contribution of labour reallocation across industries, being positive (negative) when activity moves from less (more) to more (less) productive industries. We can do a further breakdown to subsectors (for example, from manufacturing to food production, pharmaceuticals, furniture-making, etc.) by breaking down each sector i into subsectors j, and similarly calculating the following:

$$\Delta ln(V_i/H_i) = \sum_{j \in i} \bar{\omega}_j \Delta ln \left(V_j/H_j \right) + R_i \qquad (2.12)$$

where

$$\omega_j = \frac{v_j}{\sum_j v_j} \qquad (2.13)$$

and

$$\bar{\omega}_j = 0.5 \left(\omega_{jt} + \omega_{jt-1} \right)$$

We found that some high-value-added sectors had contributed the most to the slowdown, including parts of manufacturing such as autos and pharmaceuticals, telecoms and ICT services, and that reallocation of labour from high- to low-value activities played a minimal role. But the choice of index method matters. The alternative *Generalised Exactly Additive Decomposition* finds a very large reallocation term, with correspondingly much less of the change being attributable to TFP trends within the individual industries. It weights sectors by their nominal shares of output. When relative prices change, the weights will diverge between the two methods, and so therefore will the results.

Based on Coyle, Mei, and Hampton 2023.

differences between sectors, both before and after the break in trend in 2008 and over the whole period to 2019. The figures (although not the broad patterns) change when the non-market/imputed sectors such as public services or real estate are omitted. The reallocation of labour between high- and low-productivity sectors had only a small impact, positive when real estate is included and negative when it is omitted; most of the change in trend after 2008 was driven by within sector productivity. Surprisingly, the biggest contributions to the slowdown post-2008 came from sectors that had experienced relatively high labour productivity growth through the whole period and have high levels of value added—success stories such as information and communications and finance in the service sector, and pharmaceuticals and auto manufacture in manufacturing. In similar results Goodridge and Haskel (2023) found that the strongest sectoral contributors to the slowdown were those with high levels of use of intangible capital, the same sectors. This was a UK study, but what about other comparable economies? The US and UK patterns are similar, but the sectoral contributions to the slowdown have a bigger variance in the United Kingdom; in particular, the negative contributions from finance and ICT in the United Kingdom are far bigger than in the United States. Other than that, there are varying patterns among fourteen countries we looked at, whose economies have a different sectoral composition. The obvious hypothesis is that there has been a broad productivity slowdown across the industrialised economies, which has played out somewhat differently depending on the country's industry structure (and other differences between countries, such as different labour market institutions). For example, manufacturing has contributed substantially to the productivity slowdown in the United States, the United Kingdom, Sweden, Greece, the Netherlands, and Austria but actually made a small positive contribution in Denmark and Italy (Coyle et al. 2023).

However, as noted in Box 2.1, the results differ if alternative decomposition methods are used. What is going on? And why does it matter? Aggregate economic statistics are constructed from individual reports of firms' revenues, wages and hours, input and product prices, and so on. The entities reporting the data or data sources may differ. The firm- or product- or worker-level data are then combined into aggregated time series using the concepts from production theory and index number theory with a swath of assumptions involved. As decompositions go back from the aggregate to the sector level, the conclusions they deliver will reflect the assumptions at least as much as any underlying reality. What's more, the results of the decomposition are snapshots period by period. In normal times, this is a kind of stop-motion photography that gives a meaningful image of change over time, but it is harder to interpret during periods of significant structural change, generally reflected in larger-than-average relative price and employment shifts.

Although the results are sensitive to how the decomposition is done, the principal conclusion I drew from our work is that it is nevertheless correct to focus on parts of manufacturing and ICT, in the United Kingdom and elsewhere, in diagnosing the productivity growth slowdown. But the phenomenon differs between the two sectors. In ICT—consisting of computer software and services and telecommunications services—the relative price contributions play a larger part, although again it varies depending on method and data (Coyle, Mei, and Hampton 2023). This points to the need for further consideration of the measurement of quality-adjusted input and output prices in the sector. Price theory and the construction of index numbers raises profound questions, discussed in Chapter 7.

Given these sector-level insights, our diagnostic journey next took us in two directions. One was to look at firm-level rather than industry-level data. Many researchers have embarked on estimating production functions using firm-level data with two questions in mind: What has happened to productivity in individual firms, and what has happened to their markups of prices over costs, which is one measure of the extent to which concentration in the economy has been increasing? There are somewhat inconsistent findings in the literature regarding the latter (e.g., De Loecker et al. 2020, Van Reenen 2018), although the balance of opinion is that concentration has generally increased. However, there is clear and mounting research evidence that the highest productivity firms are those using digital tools and that they are pulling ever-further away from the rest of the pack (Cathles et al. 2020, Tambe et al. 2020,

Coyle et al. 2020). In other words, the most productive firms not only have a higher level of productivity, but their productivity has also been growing faster than that of the rest. As a consequence, wage dispersion has also been increasing within sectors of the economy as the most productive firms in the sector can pay more. Thanks to getting more productive workers, and also probably thanks to increasing returns effects, it is likely that the top 5 per cent or 10 per cent of firms are organically increasing their market shares.

In another paper (Bournakis et al. 2024) we looked at firms within the UK manufacturing sector. There are well-known challenges in estimating production functions and TFP based on microdata when, as in the United Kingdom, the available nominal input and output data must be deflated with industry price indices rather than specific firm-level prices and quantities (Griliches and Mairesse 1995, Klette and Griliches 1996). There are other estimation problems too, including the simultaneous causality between a firm's selection of its mix of inputs and unobserved productivity shocks it experiences. We had to make some strong assumptions as well as use sector-level prices and aggregate revenues given the data limitations. Still, for manufacturing, we found a consistent fall in revenue-weighted within-firm quality-adjusted TFP that was reinforced by negative reallocation effects. For ICT, we found a small fall in within-firm quality-adjusted TFP that is more than offset by favourable reallocation effects. Again, there is a difference between the two sectors (Figure 2.4): manufacturing firms have seen a post-2008 decline in their individual TFP growth, and the whole distribution of TFP levels across firms shifted to the left across the two periods. In ICT, the distribution of TFP across firms shifted to the right instead.

This has been a brief summary of some of my work with my coauthors, as well as others, on productivity diagnostics. It skates over the surface of the intense effort by many economists in many countries to get to the bottom of the reasons for the productivity slowdown. Still, the fundamental puzzle remains. Despite having contributed to this literature, I now think the exploration of productivity at either firm or sector level will not make much progress, having spent some pages on our diagnostic journey. The reason is that the data available is being asked to bear an

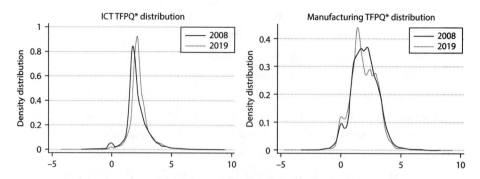

FIGURE 2.4. Distribution of TFP, UK firms in manufacturing and ICT, 2008 and 2019. *Source:* Bournakis et al. (2024). *Note:* The x-axis shows log of quality-adjusted TFP.

impossible weight. Even in countries with individual price data at the firm level, when aggregating up even just to the sector level, assumptions are needed about functional forms, returns to scale, the selection of weights to construct aggregates, while the choice of index number form also makes a difference to the conclusions. Aggregate growth accounting requires the assumption of constant returns to scale and competitive input markets; neither is valid in any industrialised economies. Production function estimation requires strong identifying assumptions, with the choices made differing between authors. A fuzzy but consistent picture emerges of increased variance in the distribution of firm-level outcomes and in "within" problems in manufacturing and ICT services at both industry and (in the case of manufacturing) firm level. But the diagnostics using the available statistics can probably go no further.

I conjecture that other methods and approaches will be needed to make progress in understanding the productivity puzzle. One core measurement question, taken up in detail later (Chapter 7), concerns the price indices used to deflate revenues and construct real-terms measures. It might be that part of the productivity puzzle is a problem of overstated deflators that lead to underestimates of the value of new and better goods and services. For example, the variety of product characteristics has increased enormously. Everyday experience makes it clear that the range of goods available in advanced economies has been increasing over time. Examples include the phenomenon of fast fashion, personalised biomedical treatments, new flavours of many food items, the number of book titles published, and many other indicators. Yet statistics on variety are not part of the standard suite of economic metrics, and it is difficult to find recent systematic data. The current balance of opinion among economists is that there is some upward bias in price indices, but the extent of the bias has probably declined over recent years and so does not help resolve the puzzle of slower productivity growth (Ahmad et al. 2017, Aghion et al. 2019, Reinsdorf and Schreyer 2020). Chapter 7 will argue, however, that there are more fundamental issues when it comes to measuring price changes, related to the restructuring of the economy as digital technology enables new business models and dissolves traditional boundaries between activities. The concept of real output and productivity growth is more mystifying the more you think about what it means.

Having said that, the productivity slowdown is a real phenomenon, not a statistical artefact. It will not be magicked away by alternative price measurements. Other perspectives on the productivity trend offer different clues about the economic concepts and measurements needed to understand it better.

Productivity of What?

Much of the discussion and analysis of productivity concerns labour productivity as it is much easier to measure and the data required is more timely. (For example, the figures in the KLEMS database often used to calculate TFP are more than three years out of date.) A different perspective is provided by looking at the productivity of other inputs, particularly natural capital. The energy efficiency of the economy is at least as important a metric as its labour efficiency. The kind of efficiency policymakers might want to prioritise is likely to change over time depending on what the binding constraint on progress is thought to be. While this might have been physical capital or labour in the mid-twentieth century, reflecting the immense damage World War 2 had inflicted on people—human capital—and on buildings and machinery, it is surely natural capital now. So rather than using the standard productivity metrics to look at progress in computing—how much computational output for the amount of labour, silicon, and machinery per chip—perhaps we should focus instead on how much output per unit of energy. Agarwala and Martin (2022) calculated the United Kingdom's environmentally adjusted productivity and report that the economy's energy productivity more than doubled between 1990 and 2019, while emissions productivity has grown 150 per cent since 1990, reflecting both the improvement in energy productivity and a reduction in the emissions intensity of energy generation. Agarwala, Burke, and Mei (2024) extended the analysis (using a comprehensive wealth framework, discussed further in Chapter 8) to calculate a measure of "total sustainable productivity" for a range of countries. The broader approach emphasises that productivity is not a technical concept but is inherently value laden; the conventional metrics embed a notion of value that may not align with current conceptions of economic progress. The term value added is frequently used in economics and also in business, but as conventionally measured it implies a definition of value. This is a normative, not a technical, concept.

Processes, Not Products

The approaches in growth accounting and productivity decompositions described so far use the idea of the production function to conceptualise changes over time in the way inputs are turned into output as technology shifts. This framing has the effect of focusing attention on new inventions, machines, or gadgets. Yet the giant leaps forward in productivity throughout the nineteenth and twentieth centuries owed much to process (rather than product) innovation—think of the assembly line or just-in-time production. These are not "technology" as we would intuitively think of it (robots, smartphones, MRI scanners) but rather ideas about organisation. Emphasising process innovation as the important driver of productivity growth points to the need for a dynamic analysis unlikely to be well captured by conventional growth accounting and decomposition exercises.

TABLE 2.1. Productivity Growth as Process Innovation

Process	Date	Key technology
American system of manufactures	early C19	machine tools
Factory system	mid–late C19	steam
Assembly line	early C20	electricity
Lean manufacturing	late C20	telecoms, early digital
Production networks	late C20–C21	ICTs
Digital platforms	early C21	AI, mechanism design

Source: Author's own.

Process innovations are often overlooked in discussions of productivity; attention is more readily captured by the excitement of scientific discovery and new devices. However, time and again since the late eighteenth century there have been significant advances in processes of production. The American system of standardised interchangeable parts in the 1800s, the factory system later that century as the Industrial Revolution got into top gear, the assembly line of the early to mid-twentieth century, and the Toyota lean production revolution of the 1970s all represent examples of the growth process. More recently, the creation of global production networks starting around 1980 and digital platform models from the 2000s have similarly reorganised the processes of production and exchange (Table 2.1).

Take the example of production networks, enabled by ICTs from the 1980s on. National economies are globalised, networked, online, involving a multitude of new devices, platforms, and products. One measure of this growing division of labour and proliferation of products is the growth of trade in intermediate goods, which has been faster than growth of trade in final (or primary) goods (see Chapter 6). Another metric is the vast increase in product variety, particularly through digital commerce and digitised goods. These phenomena illustrate Adam Smith's fundamental growth mechanism of the division of labour and specialisation, which is a description of process innovation. In his famous pin factory, production is reorganised to enable the benefits of scale. Each worker's task is simplified, and some might be automatable.

Perhaps an industry supplying new machine tools to pin factories will emerge. Perhaps the rapid expansion in pin supply and fall in price will lead to new pin-using activities. Perhaps the factory will innovate with new materials or a range of colours of pin to differentiate its product in the expanding market. Its internal economies will be dwarfed by the external economies if the virtuous circle of growth gets underway, creating new markets both upstream and downstream. In a classic 1928 paper, Allyn Young describes Smith's division of labour as a constant process of structural change in the economy, whereby innovation in the organisation of the production process leads to a constant shift of activity between firms and sectors, enabling continuing massive external economies. When the pin factory reorganises, it might outsource some parts of the process, perhaps the packaging of the thousands of pins rather than a hundred pins a day, creating a packaging sector. The massive expansion of pin production needs the market for pins to scale, so pin-using sectors are expanded or created. This is modern, process-driven growth. It is a fundamentally dynamic account, involving increasing returns to scale that cascade from one sector to another, in contrast to the conventional productivity-diagnosing approach assuming period by period constant returns as described in the previous sections. While increasing returns certainly feature prominently in economics—for example, in industrial organisation where monopolistic competition is a standard assumption, or in growth theory post-Romer (1986)—it should arguably be a standard assumption everywhere. Jennings (2023) argues that assumptions of constant or diminishing returns became common for reasons of algebraic tractability when economics formalised from the 1940s on. A lively debate during the 1920s about the nature and consequences of increasing returns fizzled out.

What would be the implications of emphasising increasing returns and dynamic sectoral shifts in analysis of the productivity puzzle? The focus would have to shift to the process dynamics in a context where individual firms' choices have an impact on their wider markets, introducing interdependencies and positive feedback loops. Furthermore, by their nature process innovations require firms to reorganise their production, never easy and probably harder than ever when intangible capital such as software (rather than, say, machine tools) is involved (Bessen 2022). One implication is that decomposition offers at best a limited perspective, whose results need to be interpreted carefully. Similarly, although economists think of the firm as the fundamental unit of analysis, this by definition obscures the Smithian dynamics just described.

Competition and the birth and death of firms takes centre stage in this dynamic account. The organisational capabilities to introduce new processes may be concentrated in the same firms that benefit from large-scale economies, superstar-type network effects, strong intellectual property protection, monopoly rents, and the consequent ability to shape regulation in their own favour. Kurz (2023) argues persuasively that productivity needs strongly enforced competition policies and appropriate IP policies to ensure the gains are shared with customers and workers rather than extracted as monopoly rents. Philippon (2019) and Eeckhout (2021) have also focused on weak competition enforcement as a key issue in recent economic performance. Incumbency power prevents the structural reorganisation that occurs as part of the growth process. Indeed, Adam Smith also emphasised the importance of competition, implying that as markets become increasingly specialised, increasing returns mean there might come a point at which they can only support a small number of firms, meaning there is a trade-off between more specialisation and more competition (Coyle 2023a). In digital markets, competition is not a static affair but rather Schumpeterian (Coyle 2019) as firms compete through what have been characterised as their "dynamic capabilities" (Teece et al. 1997); at any time there is likely to be one or a small number of dominant firms, and competition will occur when a rival develops a better product or technology to replace them. Competition analysis increasingly has to focus on the possibilities for innovation and market entry, and the barriers to entry.

Chapter 6 returns to the importance of studying production networks as digital and communication technologies have literally rewired economic relations. Another implication that I turn to next is that the economy is more than the sum of its individual parts.

Public Capital and Public Services

Kenneth Arrow (1969) pointed out that in the presence of extensive increasing returns, economic outcomes will be Pareto inefficient and indeterminate, so the standard machinery of equilibrium economic analysis is redundant. He characterised increasing returns as a form of market failure, pointing therefore to an important role for the state (or other collective decision processes such as social norms or non-state organisations) in determining resource allocation. What economic environment would enable the kind of dynamic reorganisation previously described? It would come as no surprise to anyone in business to learn that the provision of public goods from transport infrastructure and the rule of law to education and government investment in basic research will affect the productivity of their own and other individual businesses. However, we are only now emerging (and with some strong resistance) from the post-1979 public and political philosophy of market and state operating in separate and mutually exclusive domains, with markets in most contexts assumed to be the best form of collective organisation of production. Other social scientists now generally characterise this as *neoliberalism*—a term economists generally resist as it lumps together individuals with conflicting views. However, it is a convenient shorthand for the kind of economic theory that reached its heyday in the 1980s and 1990s, filtered through the political process into policy decisions that favoured markets over state and saw them as substitutes rather than complements.

Research into the productivity puzzle by and large has not paid much attention to these questions of collective organisation. The study of the economic impacts of investment in education on the one hand or infrastructure on the other, for example, has tended to be conducted in separate silos. However, both are important collectively organised forms of investment whose services underpin all other economic activity. Businesses are not going to build their own road network or set up a school system; these are types of essential public provision.

Infrastructure refers to assets with, expanding on Frischmann (2012), the following economic characteristics:

- In terms of supply, they are *long-lived assets* expected to be of use for many years and sometimes involving a high upfront cost of investment so *marginal costs of supply are low.*
- They are *non-rival* (up to the scale where congestion occurs).
- They tend to provide *generic capital services* that can be used as inputs into a wide range of other activities.
- The assets are *collective,* with a presumption that access to them is either universal or does not depend on personal relationships or identity.
- On the demand side, demand for their use is *derived,* with their economic value created by downstream activities that require them as inputs.
- Relatedly, as they involve spillovers or externalities (often due to network effects), there will be non-linearities in demand when *tipping points* are reached.

The understanding of what composes society's infrastructure has also increasingly included social infrastructure. In social sectors (such as health care, education, justice) there are significant externalities and hence whose provision is generally in large part organised, regulated, and/or provided by the state (Coyle 2020). Following Fransen et al. (2018), Corrado, Hulten, and Sichel (2005), and O'Mahony and Samek (2021), the definition of social infrastructure includes both *tangible assets* (such as hospital buildings, MRI scanners, ambulance fleets, research or diagnostic laboratories) and *intangible assets* (such as research and development, health software, management capabilities, or other organisationally embedded knowledge). Some definitions focus on the built environment of publicly accessible places where people can come together (e.g., Kleinberg et al. 2018). However, other definitions might also include or alternatively focus on networks of relationships and social capital, including in the household or community (e.g., Kelsey and Kenny 2021). The common thread is that they are collectively organised investments delivering capital services over time as inputs into other production activities or directly to consumers and citizens.

Unfortunately, most countries have poor data even on standard physical infrastructure, either the flow of new investment or the stock and
its depreciation. The measurement challenge is complicated by the fact
that infrastructure is definitionally a fuzzy concept, incompletely
measured in national accounts and other data (Grice 2016). It can be
financed, owned, and operated by either public or private sector, and
the state-market boundary with regard to infrastructure has shifted
considerably—in both directions—over time. The boundary between
infrastructure and other capital projects can be debated; national accounts measures do include, for instance, physical assets relating to
transport, energy, water and waste, communications, and flood defences. Conversely, not all public sector capital expenditure is spent on
such infrastructure. Maintenance spending on structures such as roads
or rails is vital to sustain infrastructure capital services but is poorly
measured, if at all. Current technological changes—such as digital twins
and the embedding of sensors in structures (Zomer et al. 2020)—are
also changing capital services, maintenance needs, and infrastructure
value chains, leading to sectoral shifts in activity.

To take the US figures, public expenditure on non-defense physical
capital was estimated to be $110 billion in 2018, in current dollars, of
which $63.9 billion was for transportation infrastructure; this transpor-
tation infrastructure investment had been declining as a share of GDP
since the 1960s. So too had investment in water infrastructure. However,
there are no figures for maintenance spend, and in addition constructing price indices to deflate the nominal figures is challenging, even for
the market sector, given the need to account for quality change; for instance, "smart" highway technology can reduce congestion and journey
times with no new carriageway built. Given the data issues, it is not
surprising that there is little clear empirical evidence that infrastructure
has a positive impact on growth (and implicitly productivity). The mac-
roeconometric evidence is inconclusive (Välilä 2020). There is great
heterogeneity between countries and across types of infrastructure.
There has been some focus on the impact of broadband internet and
mobile telephony on growth, generally found to be positive. Similarly,
some work has focused on transportation (Donaldson 2018, Gibbons

et al. 2018). Unfortunately, the availability of data on infrastructure is surprisingly bad, although new techniques such as using satellite imaging (Donaldson and Storeygard 2016) or mobile network coverage data (Bahia et al. 2019) are starting to help fill some gaps. These new data types provide physical data, although they cannot account for the fact that the capacity of an existing physical network can be increased by "soft" innovations such as data compression in telecoms networks or higher capacity utilisation in transport networks. Yet without infrastructure, there is no economic activity.

When it comes to public services, a major focus in economic research has been the link between investment in education and growth or productivity. Human capital estimates form the greater part of a nation's economic assets, according to the World Bank's (and other) estimates of national comprehensive wealth (see Chapter 8). Health status is starting to be explored for inclusion in human capital statistics, perhaps prompted by the experience of the pandemic (see e.g., O'Mahony and Samek 2021). Less attention has been paid to the measurement of public services and public service productivity, which is of course hard to disentangle from the question of public service outcomes. A major contribution to this measurement question, in particular accounting for quality improvements, was the 2005 Atkinson Review in the United Kingdom.

Prior to this—and in many cases still—some public service outputs were measured as the cost of inputs, defining productivity to be zero. For services such as defence or the legal system, it is challenging to think of an alternative approach, although even in such cases there has been substantial technological change; for example, has the digitisation of court records or use of AI in creating legal summaries or in sentencing decisions made any difference to productivity? It would be slightly surprising if it had not. This conundrum reflects a debate early in the days of developing the national accounts about whether government spending should all be included in GDP. Simon Kuznets, who advocated for a more explicit economic welfare approach to aggregate measurement instead of the activity-oriented approach adopted, termed some categories of government (and private) expenditure as "regrettable necessities"

(Kuznets 1973, Kane 2012). Nevertheless, they form part of the essential soft infrastructure for the economy to operate at all. Indeed, it seems plausible that as the structure of the economy and society becomes more complex in how people interact with each other and undertake economic exchanges, more of this kind of collective provision will be needed. For example, there is much current discussion about the need for countries to develop data or digital public infrastructures, through the government-organised (often privately provided) assembly of a technology stack comprising non-rival and open standard infrastructure, data, and software, which is not demanded directly but for which there is substantial derived demand.

Other services often provided by the public sector—such as health and education—are quality adjusted in some countries, including the United Kingdom. Whether the provider is public or private, this is fraught with measurement challenge. However, to alleviate the so-called Baumol cost disease whereby labour-intensive services account for a growing proportion of spending as incomes rise (Baumol 1967), some productivity growth in these kinds of hard-to-measure services is desirable. There has been immense technical progress in health but at the same time huge growth in demand, partly demographic as populations age but partly driven by the expansion of the possible. Health outcomes are also affected by many variables not related to production of health services, such as air quality or family income. When health services are mainly paid for by the state, there has been more focus on cost-cutting opportunities rather than investment in health as infrastructure or opportunities to improve human capital, to the detriment of productivity (Coyle 2023b, 2024a).

Apart from their own productivity, a key unanswered question is the extent to which collective services and infrastructure, public and private, affect the productivity of the rest of the economy. It is unanswered partly due to data gaps, but also due to the limitations of the conventional approaches to productivity diagnostics. Growth accounting and decompositions cannot by construction address the extent to which collective provision matters, any more than they take account of the inherently dynamic, increasing returns character of the economy. Both are external to the firm or the sector. The standard approaches lie firmly in the tradition of methodological individualism of economics and do not allow for the attribution of value in the presence of spillovers or externalities—this is true of increasing returns, which are assumed away, and of collective capital in the form of infrastructure. Yet both are pervasive in the economy and will certainly play a role in explaining productivity trends. For all the detailed empirical work (including mine) looking intently at productivity of firms or industries, a perfectly reasonable hypothesis would be that a more extensive scope of increasing returns leading to market concentration and the steady deterioration of infrastructure in the OECD economies (as postwar investments depreciate or literally decay) both play an important role in explaining the productivity puzzle.

Time

This chapter is going to end with what might seem like a corner turn, but in fact it relates directly to this discussion of dynamic change. I observed that process innovations have been important drivers of productivity gains. The economy experiences continual dynamic restructuring, driven by the adoption of innovations and reorganisation of production processes, sometimes—as now—particularly intense. This puts time at the heart of the issue. For most of the process innovations that have occurred through capitalist history have been time-saving innovations: the production of many more pins in one day, the journey time saved by switching from sailing ships to steamships, the time saved by just-in-time logistics in lean production, the time saved by keyhole surgery on outpatients rather than several days' stay in hospital. Production takes time, and the element of time is one driver of increasing returns to the extent that a faster rate of throughput enables greater scale (Alchian 1958). Moreover, time matters not only for production; consumption also takes time, whether of a physical product or (especially) a service (Steedman 2001). And unlike the budget constraint in the optimisation problem of a firm or household, the time constraint is a strict equality. We cannot extend our twenty-four hours a day, and we must also spend all twenty-four; they cannot be saved for another day.

Leonard Nakamura and I (Coyle and Nakamura 2022) have therefore proposed using time spent as a metric of productivity on the supply side and of individual economic welfare in terms of consumer demand. People's use of time either at work or in consumption and leisure has been changed to a startling degree by digital technologies. In consumption and leisure, for many digital goods and services the monetary price of consumption is often zero, but time and attention are required. In both the United States and the United Kingdom, the average person is estimated to spend the equivalent of a day a week online.

Labour productivity through this lens would be the ratio of Becker's (1965) "full income" (time and earned income in monetary terms) to non-sleeping hours. One could argue for limiting the calculation to working hours, but thanks to digitisation there has also been significant shifting of activities across the production boundary—that is between paid and unpaid working hours. Activities that were market based have become part of household production. For example, many people now do their banking or travel transactions online, replacing traveling to and queuing in the high street and so saving time, but also substituting for some marketed activities of banks and travel agencies (see Chapter 4 for more on this). This is the opposite of the shift from household to market that occurred in the 1950s and 1960s as household consumption technologies made it possible for second earners (mainly women) to work in paid employment. Such shifts across the production boundary can have large effects on measured productivity based on the market economy that does not take account of time use (Coyle 2019).

As in previous waves of process innovation, digital technology is also transforming the time required to produce: that is, it offers process improvements. Digitisation of more service sectors such as law (summarising vast bodies of documentation) or parts of medicine (telehealth, scrutiny of scans, etc.) is now underway and could in principle be expected to improve productivity through speeding up activities currently done by humans. This is similar to the previous automation of routine tasks in manufacturing. There is as yet little indication that conventionally measured productivity in services is improving due to the adoption of digital technologies, and indeed some digitally intensive services such as finance have been notably poor productivity performers. However, the measurement challenges when it comes to service sector productivity are considerable, as there is often no standard unit of volume and adjusting for quality is daunting: the quantity of management consultancy can hardly be measured by the length of slide decks, and its quality is unobservable.

At the same time, some productivity gains made by companies through automating services have simply transferred time input requirements to households. Examples include the use of call centres, which require customers to spend more time navigating menus to get the service they need, or automated checkout machines, which have largely substituted unpaid household labour for paid store workers. This has been referred to as a "time tax" (Lowry 2021), a problem not yet solved by new generative AI services, although we can hope.

These considerations are summarised in Table 2.2 (from my paper with Leonard). The first vertical division is the conventional production boundary between GDP and household production, and the second is the boundary between productive activities and leisure/consumption, while the horizontal division distinguishes been routine activities that can be automated and non-routine activities. In the former case, welfare gains result from technological innovations enabling the activities to be carried out more quickly. In the latter case, the economic welfare results from the scope to spend more time and deliver a higher-quality service (more personalised or tailored to individual need, for example). Some examples (in bold text) indicate ongoing changes due to digital innovations. In different ways, they may help explain why conventional productivity growth figures present only a partial picture of economic progress. For example, in professional services such as accountancy and law, machine learning means routine tasks such as elements of audit or discovery can be automated and carried out much faster than previously. This is a process innovation enabling the firm to reduce costs; customers should get a better (faster) service, and perhaps pay less for it as well (although this may be hindered by information asymmetries and markups). There will be general equilibrium effects too, through accountancy and legal services as an intermediate input to other sectors,

TABLE 2.2. A Time-Based Approach to Productivity

	Market production	Home production	Leisure/consumption
Routine	Routine manufacturing Routine services, e.g., payroll processing, checkouts, tax preparation	Cleaning, driving; **domestic robots, self-driving cars may automate some**	Daily run, personal care, eating (largely non-automatable because inalienable although some market purchases possible, e.g., nail bars, hairdryers)
Non-routine	Medicine, legal, consultancy; **elements of these becoming routinised by technology** Travel agency, banking; **increasingly moving into online home production** Non-routine manufacturing Car repair, driving, plumbing, decorating; **technology automating some elements**	Cooking, gardening (may also be purchased in the market) Creative activities, e.g., vlogs, open-source software (some people will seek to monetise these) Car repair, driving, plumbing, decorating (may also be purchased in the market)	Cooking, gardening (inherently enjoyable for some people) Creative activities, e.g., vlogs, open-source software (done for enjoyment) Theatre, concerts, sport, socialising, eating out

Source: Author's own.

and through the shifting tasks, pay, and employment of lawyers and accountants (which could decline, like drivers of horse-drawn carriages, or increase, like bank employees in the face of ATMs, depending on changes in demand for the sectors' services and the reallocation of tasks). The process innovations underway in such sectors are unlikely to be captured directly in GDP or conventional productivity calculations, as this would require a quality adjustment to the sector deflators to turn the time-saving improvements into output metrics. The fact that the process innovations enabled by digital manifest themselves as time saved rather than any other reduced input per unit of output means the productivity gains they enable are not captured when the time required to produce is omitted from the calculation.

On the consumer side, the time-based perspective calls for the "full-income" perspective on consumption, including the shadow value of time. This may be either because consumption is paid for with an implicit barter transaction of attention for services (Nakamura et al. 2017), or because consumption products are part of a subscription bundle and the relevant cost the consumer faces in choosing what and how much to consume is the shadow value of time. Competition is literally competition for people's attention and time (Goolsbee and Klenow 2006). When it comes to valuation of households' full income, there are two possibilities. One, proposed by Becker (1965), is to view the shadow value of unpaid time as equal to the market wage, representing the opportunity cost of leisure or of household work, as the United Kingdom's Office for National Statistics (ONS) does. Another is to view the shadow value of time as equal to the market price of household chores, the wage rate of household workers, as used by the US Bureau of Economic Analysis. These produce different results, as in recent decades the wage rate of household workers has fallen relative to the average wage. Leonard and I argue that both may be incomplete, and there is a case for also considering people's well-being in the time they spend in different activities. Some people might get intrinsic pleasure from their work, for instance.

A further issue is that a key supposition of standard measures of inflation and productivity is that the utility of a precisely defined market good remains fixed over time. But as Hulten and Nakamura (2020) point out, the utility of a market good to the consumer is in fact affected by changes in household consumption technology; the household "production function" of turning products into welfare can shift. Moreover, innovations will change the expected utility of goods. For example, the knowledge of professionals may improve over time, so a given price needs to adjust for the quality improvement. Similarly, online restaurant ratings and reviews may improve a consumer's ability to better match their tastes to dining options. Taking this idea forward requires better data on individuals' time use, in particular their time online. Time use surveys ask people about their lives as consumers. But to understand productivity in services information on time use at work is needed now. ONS has pioneered a time use survey of public sector workers (ONS 2024a); it would be fascinating to see this at a more granular level and applied to private sector services too. We would also want to know the shadow value of people's time, and there is scope for innovative approaches to this, such as using data on pay rates from online labour platforms.

What else does a time perspective imply for productivity? It is well understood that some countries have taken their productivity gains in increased leisure time, and for the most part average hours worked decline as countries get richer (Jones and Klenow 2016). But does the focus on time saving through process innovations help understand and address the productivity puzzle? Perhaps not, but this is open territory, particularly for Zvi's "hard to measure" parts of the modern economy.

Conclusion

Productivity is at the heart of economic progress: Why do economies grow, and what makes people better off? This chapter has taken this central question of productivity to start to uncover some of the limitations of existing concepts and statistics. There has been a striking slowdown in productivity growth in many economies during the past twenty years. While there are many contributors to productivity outcomes, this slowdown can be fairly described as a puzzle at a time when there are many and dramatic innovations. Traditional statistically based approaches, growth accounting and productivity decompositions, give snapshots that fail to capture big changes and involve assumptions that are not appropriate for a context—like now—of significant dynamic structural change, including changes in the relative prices of products and services.

This puts the spotlight instead on dynamics, and on process innovations. Indeed, one way to think about the optimistic view of new technologies and productivity, the J-curve perspective, is that digital and AI will bring about process improvements, but as this involves significant organisational change, it will take time. I highlighted Adam Smith's account of progress towards what he termed "universal opulence" as a description of increasing specialisation going hand in hand with increasing returns to scale as markets restructure and grow. This classic account of growth depending on economies of scale also points us to thinking about the importance of non-market activities and infrastructure. Moreover, thinking about processes implies a need to understand better that time use in production and work on the one hand and consumption and leisure on the other in effect defines productivity growth: process improvements speed up the production of output, while people's enjoyment of available consumption and leisure activities improves the quality of that output or the utility gained.

The focus in the next few chapters moves on in greater detail to the challenges of measuring change in an increasingly digitalised economy, which has been at the core of my work since the mid-1990s—almost since the birth of the World Wide Web, beginning with the "weightlessness" of my 1997 book.

3

Dematerialisation

"SOLUTIONS" ARE EVERYWHERE.

Once you notice, it seems that every business is in the business of offering solutions rather than old-fashioned goods and services. With a brief search online it's possible to find ads for office furniture solutions, insulation solutions, flower solutions, creative gardening solutions, and even "functional kebab solutions." What do these offers mean? It is that they will provide a *bundle* of goods and services: office planning, furniture sales, delivery, installation, and after-sales service, for example. This was always the case to some extent. If you bought a dozen desks and office chairs from a supplier in the past, you would expect them to source the items from a manufacturer and deliver them to you. But the wraparound "solutions" are newer: the office planning and the follow-up maintenance and repair, for example. Similarly with construction materials; where a contractor would previously have simply bought rolls of insulating material from a depot, now they can get tailored advice from the manufacturer depending on whether it is a new build or retro-fitting, and what is needed to meet current building regulations. When I was involved in a competition inquiry into a merger in the Rockwool fibre insulating material industry in the mid-2000s, I was amused by the acquirer's claim to be offering insulation solutions, but they were ahead of their time.

This bundling of solutions around simpler products or services is part of the phenomenon of weightlessness, dematerialisation, described previously. The reason for bundling is that the additional services account for a growing proportion of added value in the economy. This chapter explores the implications of this increasing dematerialisation of economic value for how to understand the changing structure of production, and hence the limitations of current statistics. It covers three phenomena: manufacturers that do not make anything, manufacturers producing services rather than (or as well as) physical goods, and the shift to a subscription-based production model. These phenomena are the result of the tide of dematerialisation of value sweeping over manufacturing, and the ways manufacturers are responding.

The conventional model is a company that does its own design and R&D, makes the products from bought-in materials and components, and sells them either to other businesses or (for consumer products) to a wholesaler. Yet this structure is decreasingly standard. Among the highest-profile examples of alternative structures are the manufacturers that do not make anything, and those that do still make things but integrate their manufacture with services. These phenomena have the unlovely names of *factoryless goods production* and *servitisation*, respectively. In the first category, Apple products are fabulously successful. Apple is (as I write) a $2.73 trillion market capitalisation company based in Cupertino, California. Although it certainly sells material products, physical assets account for only about a quarter of the total assets on its 2022 balance sheet. Apple's reported net profit margin that year was 25 per cent. The iPhone has replaced the jumbo jet as the most profitable product of all time. Yet, famously, Apple manufactures none of its iconic objects of desire. The manufacturing and assembly is entirely contracted out to companies such as Foxconn in China (and, as Chapter 6 will describe, many manufacturers are involved in the Apple supply chain). Similarly, Nike does not manufacture any of the shoes it designs, brands, and sells. These consumer-facing examples are well known, but the phenomenon is more widespread. Recently a focus has been on semiconductor manufacture, as American chip firms are mostly "fabless," instead designing sophisticated chips which are subsequently manufactured by (often) Taiwan Semiconductor Manufacturing Company (TSMC) (Miller 2022).

A distinct type of business but in the same category of non-textbook organisation is a servitised manufacturer. Often producing technically advanced products, these companies not only design and manufacture but also sell the products directly and offer follow-up services. A well-known example is Rolls-Royce, which manufactures sophisticated turbine engines yet makes two-thirds of its revenues (and profits) from after-sales monitoring of its installed engines and other related services. In both cases, the focus on higher-value upstream or downstream activities involves the creation of intangible assets such as R&D, patented designs, brand value, or the organisational capital created by managing complicated global production chains.

How have these alternative forms of production come about? The presence of *global value chains* (GVCs) (or *global production networks*, GPNs, as they are also called, to emphasise that there need not be a simple linear structure) is a striking feature of modern production—although it may be reversing slightly given new geopolitical tensions. These value chains require the reorganisation and reallocation of steps in the production process to "tasks" (Acemoglu and Autor 2011, Baldwin and Robert-Nicoud 2014, Timmer et al. 2014). Which firm in the network does which task generally depends on their specific capabilities (e.g., Pisano 2017, Teece et al. 1997). The phenomenon has spread since the 1980s to such an extent that around two-thirds of global trade in goods consists of intermediates rather than finished items.

These now-widespread corporate strategies of unbundling some activities and bundling others are not well measured in available statistics, which is problematic for analysing the boundaries of the firm and creation of value added, of productivity and employment, or even for assessing the often-discussed decline of manufacturing. There are also various labels involved, which can be confusing: contracting out, offshoring, contract manufacturing, toll processing, and merchanting, as well as factoryless production and servitisation. But in any case, the phenomena make the traditional distinction between manufacturing and services not only meaningless but actively unhelpful for understanding the economy. Some of the issues raised—the implications of global production networks for trade data and the inclusion of intangibles in the national accounts—will be covered in later chapters. This chapter focuses on the production structures summarised in Figure 3.1

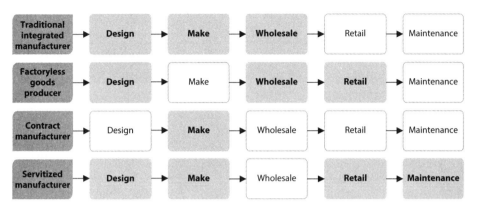

FIGURE 3.1. Alternative production structures.
Source: Coyle and Nguyen (2022).

that reflect the choices afforded by digital technologies to allow firms to focus on core competences. Traditional integrated manufacture is giving way to servitised manufacture and the combination of *factoryless goods producers* (FGPs) with contract manufacturers.

To make this clear, the production of any final product involves a series of stages. The first, upstream (labelled "design" in the figure), will involve activities such as R&D, industrial design, prototype engineering, market research, and production specification. The "make" production stage may itself involve a series of processes and the co-ordination of all the materials and components needed for manufacture. Wholesale distribution and retail sale will require setting prices and marketing. Once purchased, products may subsequently need monitoring and maintenance or repair. Underpinning the chain or network will be logistics and information systems, increasingly sophisticated. Businesses can make a range of choices about which activities to undertake in-house and which to contract out, and also about where activities should occur. These business decisions about in-house versus contracted out and about locations will also encompass choices about the mix of labour and capital used, and the technologies of production and distribution.

The array of possible choices facing businesses is a function of digitisation and communications technologies. Multinationals contracting out parts of their production existed long before the digital era, of course, and the postwar rise in intermediate goods as a share of global trade had begun a decade before the ICT revolution got into full swing in the late 1980s. Some companies have long outsourced part of their manufacturing process (Penrose 1959, Williamson 2008). The large and long-standing literatures in both economics and management on both the firm's make-or-buy decision and the strategic choices facing multinationals are testament to this. However, coinciding with trade deals and reductions in shipping costs that made locations such as Mexico's maquiladoras or Shenzhen in China viable as offshore manufacturing centres, digitisation and cheap, fast communications reduced coordination costs and information asymmetries. This altered the make-or-buy calculation and has made possible the fragmentation and reallocation of tasks within the sequence of production activities; Richard Baldwin has described these as "unbundlings" in trade patterns (Baldwin 2016b). There have also been new bundlings in the structural reorganisation of production. The phenomena described here accelerated from around 1990 with the spread of fast, cheap communications and digital information management. Timmer et al. (2014) found that the foreign share of final value added in manufactured goods rose between 1995 and 2008 for 85 per cent of the product categories in the World Input-Output Database, indicating quite a widespread phenomenon. But its scale is unknown.

Factoryless Goods Production

Let's start with FGPs and their counterparts, the contract manufacturers. FGPs are businesses that have made a strategic decision to get out of the handling of physical materials at scale and instead contract out the manufacture of their products to specialist producers, sometimes overseas. The FGPs have on average higher levels of productivity and wages than others in their sector as they retain the high value-added stages of production and contract out the low value-added stages; they are also larger than average (Bernard and Fort 2015, Morikawa 2016). The contract manufacturers that do the low-value production might produce for several FGPs or alternatively specialise in selling to one. In either case, the relationship has to be close in order to finalise the engineering design and ensure the FGP's specifications (concerning product quality, speed, scale, reliability, and so on) are met. Growing concern about labour and environmental standards have increased the extent to which the FGP tries to exercise control over the contract manufacturers following several reputation-harming scandals. Many say they have a close relationship with their contractors; for example, while the United Kingdom's consumer products group Dyson uses contract manufacturers in Malaysia to manufacture its electronic appliances, founder Sir James Dyson has asserted: "We are not contracting out; we are heavily involved with the manufacturers and teaching them how to make each of our products as it comes out" (Azhar 2018). The firm is, nevertheless, contracting out. Recently "manufacturing on demand" websites have emerged, acting as digital platforms that match large networks of approved manufacturers to the businesses seeking to contract out manufacturing. For example, xometry.com—a manufacturing-on-demand website—offers (as I write) instant quotes for 700,000 parts and claims a network of 4,000 vetted manufacturing partners in the United States. Another platform, fictiv.com, advertises similar services and a network of 200-plus partners (Rodriguez 2016).

Given the range of contractual arrangements, there are several definitions of FGPs. The US Office of Management and Budget (OMB 2010) says a business is an FGP if it "outsources all of the transformation steps that traditionally have been considered manufacturing, but undertakes all of the entrepreneurial steps and arranges for all required capital, labour, and material inputs required to make a good." This definition aligns with the official statistical standards (SNA08 and the Balance of Payments and International Investment Position Manual BPM6) by insisting that FGPs own the material inputs to production. Kamal, Moulton, and Ribarsky (2015) followed the OMB definition except they concluded that identifying the "ownership of material inputs" was not practical. An alternative definition is provided by the United Nations Economic Commission for Europe (UNECE) *Guide to Measuring Global Production* (UNECE 2015, p14), which focuses on the provision by FGPs of intangible inputs such as intellectual property (IP) like patents, designs, or brands, while the contract manufacturer provides capital, labour, and materials. Bayard et al. (2015) also emphasise the FGP's ownership of IP. Bernard and Fort (2015, p518) define a factory-less manufacturer as a business that "has no manufacturing establishments in the United States, but performs pre-production activities such as design and engineering itself and is involved in production activities, either directly or through purchases of contract manufacturing services (CMS)." Common to all these definitions is the emphasis on ownership of IP and specification of product design, and on the ownership and selling of the finished products. Likewise, all specify that the FGP is not involved in the material production or in owning production facilities. The definitions vary over other aspects.

Given this, it will come as no surprise to learn that there is scant official (or other) data on the scope and scale of this mode of production. Yet as the way FGPs combine inputs to produce output differs from the usual assumption of a linear chain of value added, this affects the measurement of value added and productivity, including what activity is assigned to which sectors. For one thing, some firms perceived as manufacturers may be recorded as wholesalers. For another, the business models set out in Figure 3.1 cross sectoral boundaries in different ways. The standard Standard Industrial Classification/North American Industry Classification System (SIC/NAICS) classifications of industries are not business-model invariant; for example, the construction value chain includes design and engineering as a separate upstream sector, while in autos it is integrated with production. This complicates comparisons between firms in different sectors engaged in similar final production activities. Offshored contracted-out manufacturing also has implications for the interpretation of balance of payments statistics as inputs and intermediates cross national borders with varying ownership and recording practices—an issue postponed until Chapter 6.

Estimates of the extent of factoryless production therefore for now largely come from the research literature (although in the United Kingdom the ONS will reclassify FGPs from wholesaling into manufacturing in the next update of the statistical classifications). For example, Bayard, Byrne, and Smith (2015) looked at company reports for S&P 500 firms. In 2012 around 46 per cent of S&P 500 firms reported the use of some contract manufacturing (up from 30 per cent in 2002), and a fifth of these firms exclusively relied on contract manufacturers (16 per cent in 2002). It appeared to be an important production model in pharmaceuticals, apparel, toys and games, electronic components, and ICT equipment. These authors reckoned that failure to account for the phenomenon led to an underestimate of 5 to 20 per cent in the size of US manufacturing value added. Bernard and Fort (2015) estimated that reclassifying FGPs from wholesaling into manufacturing would have increased measured US manufacturing employment by 3–14 per cent in 2007 (although the US employees of these firms were obviously not all engaged in traditional manual jobs); by that year, measured manufacturing employment had declined by over 20 per cent since 1990, with the decline particularly steep from 2001. Morikawa (2016) estimated that the number of manufacturing plants in Japan was being underestimated by 3–18 per cent in 2018.

Some sectors rely more heavily on FGPs and contracting manufacturing. Pharmaceuticals is one. Bernard and Fort found the sector accounted for 24 per cent of total US FGPs that they identified as being recorded in the wholesaling sector. Bayard, Byrne, and Smith (2015) showed that around 70 per cent of US pharmaceutical companies in 2012 used some contract manufacturing (up from 48 per cent in 2002). Much of the literature (as so often in economics) looks at the United States. My coauthor David Nguyen and I (2022) looked at the United Kingdom. The latest available UK pharma company reports we read gave a range of explanations for using contract manufacturers, such as avoiding risky capital investment, having flexibility when future demand is uncertain, achieving cost savings as contract manufacturers can specialise, and focusing on their own strategic goals and R&D. Many of the listed companies both produce their ownbrand products and act as contract manufacturers for other companies. For example, on its website GlaxoSmithKline lists capabilities in contract manufacturing of antibiotics, foams, liquids, and active pharmaceutical ingredients; it also reports its use of contract manufacturers for a wide range of products such as antigens, intermediates, commodities, and manufacturing components. In our paper David and I looked at pharmaceuticals and auto manufacture as case studies. One of the leading contract manufacturers in the automotive industry is the Canadian firm Magna International, hardly a household name. Yet since 1979 it has produced more than three hundred thousand Mercedes-Benz G-Class cars using a dedicated workforce in its plant in Graz, for example, and has also made cars for BMW and Jaguar. In the case of autos, Bayard, Byrne, and Smith estimated that around 22 per cent of transport equipment manufacturers within the S&P 500 were using contract manufacturers. The trend towards FGPs in auto manufacture seems likely to continue the more the value added in a vehicle depends on its engineering and software, something the transition to electric vehicles will accelerate.

David and I also used web-scraped data from the whole universe of US and UK company websites (not just listed companies) to construct some more recent estimates of the scope of contract manufacturing. (We used glass.ai's unsupervised crawler rather than relying on keywords.) Not all companies will mention their production arrangements on their website; we only captured those that do and so probably underestimate the scope of the phenomenon. Manual checks suggested we were mainly capturing contract manufacturers posting their offer in their online shop windows. We identified 491 in the United Kingdom and 2,534 in the United States. Table 3.1 shows what proportion of businesses in different sectors could be identified, for all where this exceeded 1 per cent (with the sectors being classified by AI rather than by formal SIC/NAICS codes). Our US results are similar to the figures based on keyword searches of company reports in Bayard et al. (2015) except that they find considerably more contract manufacturing in food and beverages.

The papers cited here estimate the scope of FGP activity, but nobody has been able to estimate the scale of such activity. Those figures would need the official business surveys to be revamped to include appropriate questions about the revenues and costs involved. It is therefore not possible to understand the fundamental changes since 1990 in the structure

TABLE 3.1. UK and US Sectors with the Most Contract Manufacturing

	UK Sector	Share	US Sector	Share
1	Chemicals	18%	Electrical & Electronic Manufacturing	14%
2	Life Sciences & Pharmaceuticals	18%	Life Sciences & Pharmaceuticals	11%
			Plastics	10%
3	Biotechnology	15%	Medical Devices	9%
4	Electrical & Electronic Manufacturing	13%	Chemicals	8%
			Machinery	7%
5	Mechanical & Industrial Engineering	9%	Semiconductors & Electronic Systems	7%
			Biotechnology	6%
6	Medical Devices	7%	Mechanical & Industrial Engineering	6%
7	Cosmetics & Toiletries	3%	Industrial Automation	3%
8	Machinery	3%	Outsourcing & Offshoring	3%
9	Textiles	3%	Aviation, Aerospace, & Defence	3%
10	Plastics	2%	Cosmetics & Toiletries	2%
11	Venture Capital & Private Equity	2%	Mining & Minerals	2%
12	Outsourcing & Offshoring	1%	Logistics & Supply Chain	1%
13	Logistics & Supply Chain	1%	Food & Beverages	1%
14	Packaging & Print	1%	Investment Banking & Advisory	1%
15	Food & Beverages	1%	Computer Hardware	1%
			Packaging & Print	1%
			Venture Capital & Private Equity	1%
			Textiles	1%

Source: Coyle and Nguyen (2022), based on Tables 3 and 4.

of production in Western economies without better data on these shifting business choices about the production process and its location—all the more important now that locational choices are becoming an issue of geopolitical significance.

Servitisation

Even less is known about the extent of servitised manufacturing, the kind of firms that control the whole of the value chain from IP-intensive product design and development through to direct relationships with their final customers and ongoing service contracts with them—and despite the trend for "solutions" I noted at the start of this chapter, there is not a large academic literature on the phenomenon. My introduction to the concept came on a 2012 visit to Rolls-Royce's aeroengine factory in Derby, in the English Midlands, one of the heartlands of manufacturing in the United Kingdom. The site is enormous—we had to drive around it. The huge turbines and engines being made there are amazingly impressive, of a scale, sophistication, and beauty that make you marvel at the capabilities of humankind. The wind tunnel testing was exhilarating. And then at the end of the visit we went to the building where installed Rolls-Royce engines on aeroplanes are being monitored in real time as the vehicles fly around the world. This mundane operations room with rows of people sitting at computer screens—like pretty much any other workplace you can visit these days—is key to the company's overall performance, tracking about 3,500 installed engines. The service is known as "power by the hour" (Likins 2017)—and has also been described as "Engines as a Service." Instead of customers buying an aircraft engine outright and separately arranging maintenance and support, they enter into a long-term agreement with Rolls-Royce. Under this agreement, the customer pays a fixed fee based on the number of engine flight hours or cycles. The buyers have reduced operational risks and more predictable costs, spending less on engine parts inventory, repair facilities, technicians, and engine liability insurance. For its part Rolls-Royce has an ongoing revenue stream. It can also benefit from economies of scale through its detailed know-how, investments in infrastructure, and extensive monitoring of engine performance, making it harder for specialist service providers to compete (Smith 2013).

Another example is Philips, the Dutch electronics manufacturer. In 2015 they announced a deal to provide Schiphol airport with Light as a Service: in this example Philips retains ownership of the bulbs and fittings, monitors and ensures the lights work, and will replace and recycle them at the end of their life. Maintenance costs are minimised, the lightbulbs are low-energy LEDs, and the estimated life of the fixtures is seventy-five years. Schiphol has lower costs—no maintenance to worry about—and can claim to be a circular economy exemplar. Frank van der

IMAGE 3.1. Rolls-Royce's aeroengine factory, Derby, October 26, 2012.
© Diane Coyle.

Vloed, general manager of Philips Lighting Benelux, stated in the press release, "We believe that more and more forward-thinking businesses will move to a Light as a Service model. After all, most of us are used to this kind of model—for example I drink water but I don't have a reservoir in my basement. Many people are used to pay-as-you-go models" (Philips 2015). The arrangement is still marketed by the Philips subsidiary (now known as Signify) as a "solution." I return to the "as-a-service" business model presently.

Beyond the examples, what about more systematic data? There is little. Some studies approach the task through keyword searches. Neely et al.

(2009, 2011) use a database of global listed companies to identify manufacturers with more than one hundred employees, searching for terms that explicitly mention non-manufacturing activities such as consultancy, financial services, design, or maintenance—and of course "solutions." They found that around 30 per cent could be classified as servitised, a level that was stable between 2007 and 2011 (although the extent of servitisation among Chinese companies had increased from 1 per cent in 2007 to 19 per cent in 2011). Also using keyword search, Mastrogiacomo et al. (2019) place the figure at 38 per cent in 2018, not too dissimilar. They also report the revenue split between services and manufactures; this has also remained relatively stable for their sample of firms. The proportion of servitised firms was highest in the United States and United Kingdom (53 per cent and 56 per cent, respectively), but they report a 38 per cent figure for China in 2018. The propensity was highest among the largest firms and in two sectors, manufacturers of computer, optical, and electrical equipment and of machinery and equipment. The most frequently offered services were maintenance and support (more than 33 per cent), followed by retail and distribution (around 20 per cent) and design and development (15 per cent). Dachs et al. (2014) and Crozet and Milet (2017) both use survey data covering manufacturing firms and get higher estimates of the extent of servitisation. The former's paper uses the European Manufacturing Survey, which asks firms in ten European countries whether they provide services; they found that in all the countries 80–90 per cent of the firms said yes. However, the intensity in terms of the revenue share for services is under 20 per cent in most countries. Crozet and Milet (2017) use French survey data; 75 per cent of French firms sell some services but derive only 18 per cent of their revenues this way.

From this limited evidence base, it seems likely that somewhere up to a half of manufacturing firms in the OECD economies sell some services. The examples of Rolls-Royce and Philips suggest it is a transaction that can benefit both parties: a (probably) higher margin and more stable revenue stream for the seller, which is able to leverage its know-how and capabilities and capture economies of scale in the services offered; and a reduction in risks, costs, and organisational demands for the buyer. It therefore seems to offer genuine efficiency gains, with the caveat that the close relationship involved may reduce competition over time. This caveat is more troubling in the consumer context—the servitisation literature has largely concerned business-to-business transactions because relatively few manufacturers sell directly to final customers (the exceptions being the prominent consumer FGPs like Apple or Nike). But before turning to the wider as-a-service phenomenon, it is worth pondering why better measures of the FGP and servitisation phenomena are important.

Where Does the Economic Value Lie?

Digitisation has made communications faster and cheaper and has increased the flow of information available to decision-takers. The previous chapter described the possibilities this has afforded for faster productivity growth among the minority of businesses able to adapt their organisational and decision-making structures. The phenomena described in this chapter are part of that reorganisation.

FGPs and servitised manufacturers alike have a more complicated set of internal structures and contractual relationships to manage. Both have made a strategic reorientation from lower- to higher-value activities; digitisation has been a key driver. FGPs have shifted away from conventional integrated manufacturing, having a tighter boundary of their firm and more external contractual relationships, enabled by the ICT revolution. When useful information is more easily accessed, there is less need for hierarchical decision-making with knowledge concentrated at the centre; more communication is needed when production is decentralised, but the costs of communication have fallen too (Garicano 2000, Bloom et al. 2014). The classic make-or-buy tensions when there is asymmetric information, so familiar from industrial organisation economics, have not vanished; they are manifest in the close attention firms like Apple or Dyson pay to their suppliers. But the scope of the information asymmetries is somewhat reduced or offset by other advantages.

Rather than unbundling, or contracting out production activities, servitised manufacturers have done the opposite, adding to the range of tasks undertaken inside the boundaries of the firm. This has been enabled by the scope for digitised monitoring and communications (think of engines in flight transmitting continuously to Derby) and by the reduced transactions costs involved in co-ordinating a wider range of activities, such as the office solutions business running from office design through logistics to repair maintenance services—not quite desks as a service but almost.

The affordances of the technologies have not only restructured production in both ways, depending on what firms identify as their strategic advantages, but have also shifted the capture of value added. The implications for productivity, business organisation, and the nature of jobs are far-reaching, while the distinction between goods and services is increasingly unclear (Zysman et al. 2013). The growing dispersion of productivity within sectors at firm level, described in the previous chapter, and the likely corresponding increases in market share of the most productive ones have been widely noted. It has been characterised as a "superstar" phenomenon (although the incentives in question are very different from those described in the original superstar economics of Sherwin Rosen [1981]). The shifts among firms that are in the same production networks or supply chains are less well documented—not so much superstars as different types of sun and solar system.

Applying the production network lens highlights changes in the generation and capture of economic value, which can be contested. One example is found in construction. Large-scale projects are increasingly being digitised. My coauthor Rehema Msulwa and I looked at infrastructure projects that are generally production networks around either a construction major or a large engineering consultancy (Coyle and Msulwa 2024). The ambition is a *digital twin* for major projects end to end. At present, routine parts of the upstream design and development of blueprints are contracted out to service firms in countries such as Brazil, India, and Poland. A digital blueprint (a Building Information Management or BIM system) is used to organise activity on the construction site—increasingly with the manufacture of components carried out off-site—which is a complicated task co-ordinating multiple subcontractors. In major projects the built structure will contain digital elements, such as sensors or digital signalling, and these will generate continuous flows of information once the structure is being used, enabling preventive maintenance and reducing closures or repairs. The terms on which the information is available is a contractual matter between the principal firm and its suppliers or customers. In principle, although the entire end-to-end process can have a digital twin, consistent from initial design through operation, these are still rare. Not only are there technical issues such as lack of common data standards and interoperability, but also unresolved questions about how to assign value through contractual arrangements. Every firm in the production network, and final customers too, ought to be able to benefit from the efficiency gains from the use of information to co-ordinate and cut costs. However, the market power lies with the large companies at the hub of the network.

A similar example, although rarely considered in this context, is the net neutrality debate. Here the infrastructure providers—both telcos and internet service providers (ISPs)—complain that they are bearing the costs of hugely increased demand for online content (mainly video) without enjoying adequate revenue increases. In the United Kingdom, the regulator Ofcom's (n.d.) definition of net neutrality suggests that it is fundamentally about freedom: "What is net neutrality? Net neutrality, also known as 'open internet,' is the principle that you control what you see and do online, not the broadband provider that connects you to the internet. It's about people being free to access all legal internet content equally, without broadband providers interfering." Fine words, but the issue is money. Growing demand for broadband capacity is driven by people watching videos. Video accounted for two-thirds of internet traffic by volume in 2022, with six companies accounting for half of this (Amazon, Apple, Google, Meta, Microsoft, and Netflix) and two for 30 per cent (Google and Netflix). The businesses running the network over which this content is provided suggest that not receiving more of the revenue will impede their ability to invest in more capacity and to innovate in future. Over the years they have campaigned for the ability to charge different rates for different types of data flowing through the cables, or to charge more for access to a "fast lane." When the US Federal Communications Commission in 2014 proposed a ruling that would permit some discrimination among types of content, it received 21.9 million comments from users inspired by a segment by satirist John Oliver on his TV show, so they ditched the idea. Nevertheless, although there are still legal cases pending in the United States, broadband providers are now able to apply different charges for different services. Similarly in the United Kingdom, Ofcom recently held a consultation on the future of net neutrality, concluding that while the neutrality principle remains important, it is okay to charge customers for premium or specialised services.[1] Providing different service versions is now common in many countries, and experiences vary across countries. The capture of value is nevertheless a contested matter, and a larger share of the revenues tends to go where the market power lies (Sandvine 2023).

Cloud Computing

A third example is a particular infrastructure: data centres. Cloud computing has grown extraordinarily rapidly although—surprise—there is a paucity of reliable statistics, albeit evidence from various industry reports. Businesses and consumers who use the cloud, for anything from Gmail or storing photos to advanced AI applications, generally think of it as hiring access to software. Indeed the jargon of cloud computing speaks of Software as a Service, Platform as a Service, or Infrastructure as a Service (where the latter refers also to software applications and systems). These software-related services are, though, bundled with massive amounts of hardware, the major physical infrastructure of data centres and their multiple racks of servers and other equipment.

Cloud computing presents some immediate measurement questions. It has been a compelling service because it not only gives business users flexibility but can also cut their costs dramatically. I first became aware of it in a job where the head of R&D told me, as we chatted on the way to the station, that he had been able to stop making internal business cases to invest in new racks of servers and instead just put the use of Amazon Web Services (AWS) servers on his credit card. His costs had dropped from around £10,000 a month to a tenner (although I suspect use later ballooned, sending costs up again). Like my colleague, rather than investing in their own servers and software and hiring IT experts,

---

1. https://www.ofcom.org.uk/consultations-and-statements/category-1/net-neutrality -review

companies using cloud services can rely on secure and high-quality alternatives. (Personal users pay almost nothing; services like Gmail and Google Docs or iCloud are free or very low cost up to a point.) However, this means there has been to some extent a switch from companies investing in ICT equipment and software to purchasing intermediate services that are not (yet) capitalised in their accounts and consequently in the national accounts. The switch has therefore taken corporate expenditure that added to GDP and subtracted it instead. There will have been additional investment hardware in data centres but at lower cost. The net effect on measured GDP is likely negative for now, and this will understate TFP growth for a period (see Box 3.1 for more detail).

Unfortunately, there is little official data collection concerning this pervasive business use of the cloud (UN Statistics Division 2023). The United Kingdom has a digital economy survey (now being updated) collecting extensive margin data—what proportion of businesses (of different sizes) use basic cloud services, such as storage, hosting, email, and customer relationship management (CRM) software. The proportions rise over time and with size of business; in 2021 it was a fifth to a quarter of all businesses for these applications. The survey does not ask for amounts spent on cloud services. The US Bureau of Economic Analysis (BEA) includes cloud companies (based on legally required Securities and Exchange Commission [SEC] filings) as part of a "priced digital services category," estimating their 2021 gross output at $187 billion or 5 per cent of digital economy activities; the figure had grown 20 per cent compared with 2020 (Highfill and Surfield 2022).

There are relatively few cloud service providers, unsurprisingly given the scale of investment required for a data centre. AWS dominates the market in the United States and everywhere else (and indeed founded it in 2006 by opening a previously internal function to external customers). It is followed by Microsoft's Azure and Google (along with AWS known as *hyperscalers*), then some much smaller providers including Alibaba, IBM, Salesforce, Oracle, and Tencent. A summary by the UN task force looking at updating the SNA in 2025 for the digital economy proposes this definition: "Cloud computing services consist of computing, data storage, software, and related IT services accessed remotely

Box 3.1 Cloud computing use and productivity measurement

To see the productivity measurement implications of a switch from investment in computer servers to purchases of cloud services as an intermediate, consider a simple production function, similar to the one set out in Chapter 2:

$$Y + zC = f(A, K, L, N) \qquad (3.1)$$

where Y is output, C is cloud capital with price z, A is total factor productivity, K is other capital, L is labour, and N is unmeasured intangible capital, with rental prices r, w, and h, respectively. The familiar measured TFP will be

$$S' = dY/y - (rK/Y * dK/K) - (wL/y * dL/L) \qquad (3.2)$$

which will differ from the "true" residual by

$$(zC/Y * dC/C) - (hN/Y * dN/N) \qquad (3.3)$$

This will be negative—that is, measured TFP growth will understate the "true" rate—if the growth rate of investment in cloud capital (weighted by its output share) is greater than the (weighted) growth rate of the stock of the capital services. This is likely to be the case early in the adoption of the new cloud model. There will also be implications for understanding sectoral trends, for the importance of cloud service purchases as an intermediate good by businesses implies the need for careful double deflation to calculate the real gross value added: if the intermediate consumption deflator is lower than the output deflator currently applied in many national statistics, there is a downward bias in gross value added estimates, which scales with the nominal amount of intermediate consumption and the difference between the two deflators. The bias will be the nominal amount of intermediate consumption multiplied by $(P_o - P_{IC})/(P_o * P_{IC})$, where P_o is the output deflator and P_{IC} the intermediate consumption deflator.

over a network, supplied on demand and with measured resource usage" (UN Digitalisation Task Team 2023, p3; https://unstats.un.org /unsD/nationalaccount/snaupdate/dztt.asp). Cloud services cross national borders, so the trade statistics will be affected, although it is not at all clear how to estimate the scale of data transfers given that most of it occurs within the giant cloud providers. More countries are legally mandating *data localisation*, that is, data storage within national borders; but for many countries this raises the costs so significantly it is not clear how comprehensively it is observed in practice. The UN task force also recommends more harmonisation in the classification of different cloud services, which proliferate on the providers' websites.

However, even if data collection on nominal revenues or on data volumes proved possible, there is a challenge in constructing a price index. This is needed not only to measure the cloud sector itself but also to calculate an accurate intermediates deflator that feeds through to other sectoral output estimates and price indices across the whole economy: In other words, what is happening to the prices that cloud users are paying? It is a complicated task, as the cloud providers offer hundreds of different services that change frequently and whose quality is constantly upgraded. There are many new products introduced. Pricing structures include both fixed upfront fees and pay-as-you-go. The unit basis of pricing can change—for example, switching from per hour to per minute. Two academic papers to date as I write (Coyle and Nguyen 2018, Byrne et al. 2018) have addressed the question, both simplifying the problem by selecting popular basic services and scraping price data from the AWS website via the Wayback Machine. While prices and some product quality data can be obtained this way, there is no data made available by the cloud companies on the quantity of usage of each service, information which is used to construct weights in a standard price index. Indeed, when David Nguyen and I interviewed some of the companies' executives to understand the business better, they did not have a way to conceptualise the volume of the services they provide. For the United States, Byrne, Corrado, and Sichel (2018) selected compute, database, and storage services from 2009 to 2016 and found double-digit price declines for most of the period and the services, with an acceleration from 2014 when Microsoft and Google entered the market. For the United Kingdom, David and I found even faster price declines for the period 2010 to 2018, with the same 2014 acceleration in pace. Both papers make some quality adjustments (the former using hedonic regressions, the latter a product substitution approach) and find an even faster price decline when quality is taken into account.

For all these measurement challenges, the cloud example seems to be one where the as-a-service restructuring of production, the contracting out of activities within the firm to an external supplier, does seem to have generated shared economic value. The caveat is that the economy's reliance on a small number of large tech providers is as concentrated in cloud services as in other digital markets, with AWS having about a one-third and the top three having about a two-thirds market share globally. Both academic studies just cited found that the decline in prices calculated had slowed after the steep initial post–new entry drop in 2014. A mid-2023 market study by the United Kingdom's regulator (Ofcom 2023a, b) concluded that there needed to be a full competition inquiry (underway as I write) because of practices such as charging customers exit fees to leave or additional fees if they use more than one provider, and limiting the interoperability of services. Around the same time the Federal Trade Commission (FTC) announced (FTC 2023) they were consulting users about whether the business practices of cloud providers were limiting competition or compromising data security.

All this hints that many of the benefits of the digital transformation of production are, in different ways, mainly accruing to larger producers, which are organising production so they can focus on the high-value activities. There is potential for mutual benefit among all participants in a production network and also for the final customers because of genuine increases in efficiency thanks to digital affordances. These reduce costs, including transactions costs. Market power is the fly in the ointment. It complicates economic measurement not only because we lack adequate statistics to track the phenomena of digitised production but also because it makes the concept of a deflator problematic. Unbundling and rebundling is playing havoc with deflators in any case, which are in effect a way of trying to isolate real economic value.

Everything as a Service

Servitisation as described earlier in this chapter is a frame for conceptualising manufactures as a service. It is a broader phenomenon, however. The cloud example shows that services can be offered as a service too—the alternative term of the *subscription economy* might sound more natural in this case. There are also some ways in which consumer economy is shifting towards this model. As one marketing pitch puts it, "In the old world (let's call it the Product Economy) it was all about things. Acquiring new customers, shipping commodities, billing for one-time transactions. But in this new era, it's all about relationships. More and more customers are becoming subscribers because subscription experiences built around services meet consumers' needs better than the static offerings or a single product" (Zuora n.d.). The fragmentation of production into networks of suppliers evident in both FGP-centred networks and servitisation can be seen simply as a further extension of the basic division of labor and specialisation of activities identified by Adam Smith in 1776—the principal driver of economic growth albeit with the consequence of potential implications for competition and dependence (Coyle 2024b). They can also be seen as extensions of the phenomenon of leasing, the separation of ownership and use that had already been increasing somewhat over time. But it raises new questions about ownership and power, with examples both benign and malign.

A benign example is what was briefly described (and probably hyped) as the sharing economy. This was the emergence of a business model (sometimes non-profit) that provided consumers with asset services without the need to purchase the asset. Airbnb is one example. It has morphed into a large accommodation platform but was originally envisaged as a homespun way of matching people who had spare rooms or apartments looking to earn from spare capacity with travelers wanting a place to stay short-term with different characteristics (including lower price) than a conventional hotel room. Uber was initially touted as a similar model (although prompting scepticism from the start). There are many examples of smaller businesses true to the original philosophy of asset sharing for mutual benefit, including ride-sharing proper, platforms sharing gardening or DIY tools, driveways for car parking, or even pet sharing. A fleet of services has slowly built around these, providing insurance and financial services, for example—including some big players such as Stripe. Businesses of this kind are providing the matching efficiencies and gains from variety enabled by the digital platform model. The sharing economy concept generated a small literature identifying such efficiencies (e.g., Sundararajan 2016) along with its claimed potential environmental benefits.

Less benign are examples where the customers do not know that when they purchase a product, the bundle of rights associated with the transaction is not what they expected. The reason is that products with integral software and data have been servitised: the owner of a John Deere tractor or GM car, for example, has bought a physical object consisting of metals and plastics but cannot use it without the integrated software and data, IP products whose ownership is retained by the vendor. The claims by John Deere, for example, mean that farmers who bought costly equipment have been prevented from trying to repair the vehicles by software locks that stop them from working at all; they are required to take them to a specialist dealer and perhaps have to wait several days for the repair. John Deere claims copyright over the software and will not make the code available to others. The issue is being contested in US courts, with John Deere's assertions giving rise to a "right-to-repair" movement. Some US states have passed right-to-repair laws, while the Department of Justice (DoJ) is also pursuing action.

A DoJ (2022) filing states in one of the John Deere cases: "Increasingly, product manufacturers have made products harder to fix and maintain. For example, manufacturers have (1) hindered access to internal components; (2) monopolized parts, manuals, and diagnostic tools; and (3) used software to impede repairs with substantially identical aftermarket parts." It notes that the practice extends to autos and medical equipment. In fact, there are many examples of corporations using software and IP claims to limit competition and extract more money from customers. Activist Cory Doctorow (2023) has colourfully entitled the practice as an example of enshittification, the progressive worsening of things that used to work well through the exploitation of

market power by an intermediary platform that can progressively capture value from all sides of the market. HP can brick software to prevent
buyers of its printers from using ink cartridges from other manufacturers; they are locked into its ink subscription service if they ever signed
up (Harding 2023). (When I searched online to check details of this
story, Google served me the ad in Figure 3.2; the lock-in is not mentioned upfront.) Tesla can rig the range-estimating software in its cars
(Shirouzu and Stecklow 2023). Volkswagen refused to help police track
a stolen vehicle with a toddler in it because the owner had not renewed
her subscription to its tracking software (Brodkin 2023). An early example was Amazon deleting e-books (Orwell's *1984* to be specific) its
customers had purchased on their Kindles on claimed copyright
grounds (although later replacing the copies following its loss of a lawsuit, Newman 2009). Video game companies use digital rights management (DRM) software supposedly to prevent piracy, but also diminish
the performance of some games and consoles (Potoroaca 2023). In all
these examples, legal and practical ownership of the physical object is
not effective ownership because of the bundled software and the asser-
tion of intellectual property rights. Practices such as these have led to a
broader debate about the overextension of IP law and likewise ownership claims over data. But no wonder the enshittification nomenclature
is catching on. In all these malign examples, economic value is being
withheld from consumers by companies with market power.

The as-a-service or subscription models do offer user advantages
such as flexibility and lower costs, and in addition access to economies
of scale, improved range and variety, and distinctive capabilities on the
part of specialist providers. They involve a close and continuing relationship between customer and provider, which can be beneficial. The
contracts can be structured to create mutual benefit, with lower costs
and insurance against breakdown for customers and a steady revenue
stream and access to economies of scale for producers. When these are
high-trust relationships, the advantages of the model are clear. However,
the dependence can turn sour, and is increasingly doing so as companies
exploit their market power. Digital has expanded the scope for exploitation through the link between physical products and software, which is

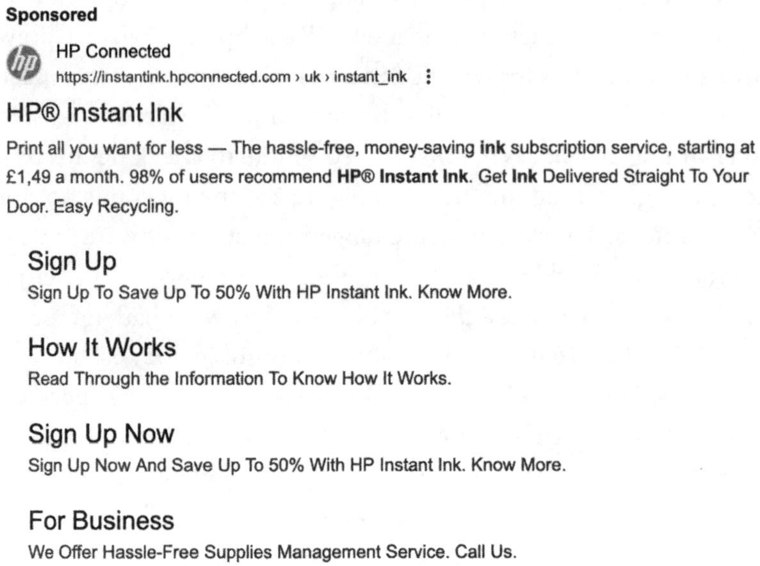

FIGURE 3.2. HP Instant Ink ad on Google. *Source:* Screen grab,
accessed July 17, 2024, London.

legally protected by copyright and technically easily enforceable
through DRM mechanisms. There are four reasons why this has implications for measurement.

First, there is a fundamental need to measure the scope of the various
phenomena (FGPs, servitisation, digital platform business models) for
economic policy purposes, not least competition policy, but also trade
policy and supply side interventions. The active current debate about
industrial policy in the advanced economies will be hindered by the
absence of adequate statistics about the reshaped structure of the economy since 1990.

Second, having clear constructs concerning what it is people are buying is essential: What is the product? This determines the creation of
data on quantities and prices. The bundle of attributes being purchased
is often different than in the past. Inflation has almost certainly been
lower than measured in current statistics for some goods and services,
but perhaps higher than measured if we think in terms of servitised

purchases or consumers trapped by technology. There is an additional consumer protection aspect.

Third, one of the aims of aggregate economic statistics is for the purposes of a welfare assessment. It is well known that real GDP is a flawed economic welfare measure (some people claim it was never intended to be one, but as soon as nominal GDP is deflated with a constant-utility price index it becomes one de facto—see Coyle [2014] for a discussion). To improve welfare-relevant measurement of the economy, a better understanding of the distribution of economic value in production networks and on platforms is needed.

Fourth, the products discussed in this chapter are examples of the dematerialisation of economic value and involve intangibles. The economic importance of intangibles is unmissable (Haskel and Westlake 2018, Bontadini et al. 2023), but they pose distinctive statistical challenges. Not only is the necessary data gathering absent, but the concepts and definitions are not settled. What's more, there are lingering questions such as how to capitalise intangibles, or what their depreciation rate is. Chapter 5 looks specifically at data as an asset and considers intangible assets in the context of what a full national balance sheet will consist of.

Conclusion

This chapter has focused on the digitally driven restructuring of production as manufacturers seek to capture the increasingly intangible value generated in the advanced economies. There is greater value in producing and selling services (or "solutions") linked to material products than there is in manufacturing them. The resulting shifts, including the emergence of FGPs and servitised manufacturing, and also the growing as-a-service phenomenon, can mutually benefit producer and customer. But these services also provide opportunities for the stronger parties to capture a disproportionate share of the value created. There are both benign and malign aspects of dematerialisation. It is hard to believe that the progressive degradation of consumer experience—the enshittification—will be allowed to continue.

In any case, industrial policy, as well as competition and consumer protection policies, would benefit from better data on all the phenomena described in this chapter. Industrial policies, particularly in the United States, are concerned with reviving national manufacturing bases and understandably so, but they will misfire if policymakers do not appreciate that the distinction between manufacturing and services is not what it used to be. A lot of policy attention focuses on the decline in the role of manufacturing, and rightly so. In the United States the manufacturing value-added share of the economy was down to 11 per cent in 2023 and in the United Kingdom to just 8 per cent. Even in Germany and Japan the shares are only 18 per cent and 19 per cent, respectively. But these figures use the classifications inherited from the 1940s, while policymakers should appreciate that the manufacturing-services distinction is increasingly meaningless. The question they need to keep in focus is who is benefiting from the dematerialisation of economic value and the resulting changes in production structures. Are national firms (wherever they are classified) able to provide "solutions," capturing value downstream or occupying higher-value activities upstream? Are their customers or consumers benefiting from the value added or instead being exploited because these production structures have led to increased market power and lock-in?

The next chapter turns to another shift, in the production boundary between formal production and household and voluntary activities. There, too, questions of who benefits come to the fore.

4

(Dis)intermediation

IN FEBRUARY 2020, a month ahead of the first COVID lockdown as it turned out, David Nguyen and I put into the field a stated preference survey asking a representative sample of ten thousand Britons with internet access how much they valued online grocery shopping, along with twenty-nine other "free" goods, online and offline. We had been testing the questionnaire for about a year, interested in getting some UK evidence alongside the burgeoning US-based literature on how to value free digital goods, and also interested in probing the limitations of the method. The median stated value for online grocery shopping was £10 a month. By May 2020, events had provided us with a natural experiment. When we repeated the survey during the first COVID lockdown in the United Kingdom, the median stated value had risen to £50 a month. The means were much higher: for some people the ability to shop online was very much more valuable. The proportion of people doing their shopping online climbed from 46 per cent to 54 per cent in three months, but the available slots were restricted to vulnerable customers; if they had not been rationed, that proportion might have been higher: the appropriately distanced queue for my local supermarket in the warm sunshine of that strange, silent spring was hundreds of meters long, winding down the street, over the railway bridge, past the station entrance, and around another corner. If I had been presented with our own survey, standing in line for well over an hour, £50 would have seemed reasonable.

There will be more about that study in the next chapter, but it prompted me to reflect on how much the experience of shopping for groceries has changed over the years. This basic human experience has seen significant periods of innovation, including the first department stores in the late nineteenth century, the arrival of supermarkets mid-twentieth century (my small hometown in Lancashire got its first in the early 1970s), and the introduction of linear barcodes (Universal Product Codes) starting in US stores in 1974. Retailing has been a vector of digitisation and driver of productivity growth since the first dot-com boom of the 1990s. A well-known McKinsey Global Institute study from 2002 estimated that from 1995 to 2000, a quarter of US labor productivity growth was attributable to the retail industry, and almost a sixth of that just to Walmart thanks to its combination of organisational change and investments in technology to improve logistics and stockkeeping. The focus on Walmart has since been queried (Freeman et al. 2011), but retailing undoubtedly was a key sector in taking US productivity growth to an annual 2.5 per cent during that half decade (Van Ark 2010). Digital and communication technologies have revolutionised retail logistics, in fashion and consumer goods of all kinds as well as groceries.

Just ponder the changes over five decades. There are fewer, larger supermarket chains able to take advantage of economies of scale in their purchases and operations. Food price inflation in the United States remained in the range of 0–5 per cent for most of the period 1982–2021, after the inflationary shocks of the late 1970s, although it has shot up more recently (peaking briefly at about 11 per cent). The variety of goods available expanded (more on this in Chapter 7). The spread of barcodes and investment in checkout scanners reduced the amount of time shoppers had to stand in line to pay, while also greatly improving retail logistics and reducing the amount of stock required. The need for humans to work at checkouts has been further reduced by self-scanning by shoppers as they walk around the store putting items in their trolley, and by the introduction of self-serve automatic checkouts. This saves shoppers even more time (at least once you adjust to the machine's quirks about where exactly to put your shopping bag). It saves stores money as they are replacing paid labour with capital services and unpaid labour: yours and mine. Stores like the recently introduced Amazon Go shops further substitute some physical capital but mainly software to eliminate the checkout experience entirely: "Come in, take what you want, and just walk out," enthuses the website. Humans still have to stack the shelves, but part of the labour required has been substituted out. It remains to be seen how much this will spread (our local Amazon Go store has already closed). And then there's online shopping, which requires me to pay a fee to have other humans doing the picking and delivery for me, but there is no scanning and queueing on my part at all. This is enabled by digitised logistics and increasingly automated picking in warehouses, pioneered by Amazon but being adopted far more widely.

What does this trajectory of broadly substituting capital (physical and intangible) for paid labour do to our understanding of economic change? Paid labor productivity as measured will have increased thanks to capital deepening. Value added and total factor productivity growth are probably higher. On the paid-for time-saving productivity metric (Chapter 2), the changes look positive. But there is an unmeasured input: the shopper's unpaid labor. The "true" productivity gain will be lower. The focus of this chapter is on processes of disintermediation by digital platforms and their implications for interpreting economic statistics and assessing the pace of progress.

Digitisation has been shifting a range of activities previously involving market transactions across the production boundary, out of the market and into the household, or combining household and marketed activities. Other examples apart from doing your own grocery checkout include online travel booking, banking, financial day trading, estate agency, and online search; some sharing economy activities involving using the services of household capital assets; and some provision of household labor providing free digital public goods such as open-source software or entertaining videos. In a 2019 article I labelled the first set of these "do-it-yourself" digital activities *digital intermediation services* and pointed out that—although we do not know the full scale—many of them have grown in usage. In any case they do not need to be large to have a noticeable impact on measured GDP and productivity growth. No less an authority than Gary Becker (1965) pointed out that shifts in activity across the production boundary make standard measures of the

IMAGE 4.1. Steve Jobs unveils the first iPhone, San Francisco, January 9, 2007.
© Rory Cellan-Jones.

economy harder to interpret. He gave the example of the invention of
the safety razor leading people to shave at home rather than go to the
barbershop. Barbers switched to providing haircuts instead, so their
measured productivity stayed about the same, but the (market plus
household) productivity of shaving services had been increased by the
technology. An example in the opposite direction was the increase in
the proportion of women working in paid jobs through the second half
of the twentieth century, substituting market activities (buying
microwaves and washing machines, ready meals, paid childcare) for unpaid household work. This transition substantially increased measured
total factor productivity growth in the United States from the 1970s
(Albanesi 2019).

Why might the reverse shift in activities across the production
boundary from inside GDP to outside be happening now? A large part
of the answer is what happened in 2007: the iPhone.

My husband Rory Cellan-Jones was at the launch in his capacity as
the BBC's technology correspondent and took this blurry picture of

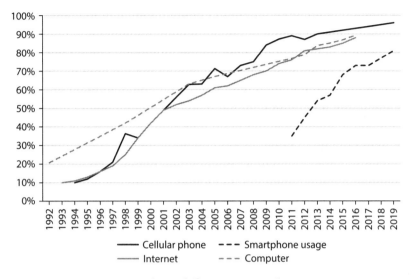

FIGURE 4.1. Smartphone diffusion compared, US, 1992–2019.
Sources: Horace Dediu; Comin and Hobijn (2004); other sources
collated by Our World in Data; Roser, Ritchie, and Mathieu (2023).

Steve Jobs as seen in Image 4.1. (For the obvious reason, he was not
taking the photo on an iPhone.) We have since grown used to being able
to take high-quality photos on the smartphones almost all of us carry
almost everywhere; it used to take a bit of skill to take good or at least
not blurred pictures even on digital cameras, but not anymore. Rory's
book *Always On* (2021) reports the way smartphones have subsequently
transformed life in the Western economies. Smartphone usage has
climbed past 80 per cent and is near universal in some countries such
as South Korea. Figure 4.1 shows the speed of its spread in the United
States compared with other recent digital technologies.

This rapid take-up in usage has depended on there being things it can
be used *for.* There were two other important innovations spreading at
about the same time. One was the accelerated rollout in mobile networks of 3G (expanding from about 2007, having been introduced in
the early 2000s) and particularly 4G (from 2011 in the United States and
2012 in the United Kingdom) and beyond. The other was the adoption
of market design techniques to build search, sorting, and matching

algorithms in apps created for the new devices and their app stores. The quality improvements have been continuous since then. For instance, the early Google Maps app was a static resource, then it integrated more information from other sources, then from search, and then real-time user-generated information (in Waze). The mobile networks are faster, and compression has improved massively. Coverage is extensive although incomplete especially in rural locations. Wi-Fi too has become widely available, in homes and offices, on public transport and in malls. I was astonished and delighted on a visit to wealthy Luxembourg to realise that state-provided free Wi-Fi was available everywhere (public transport is also all free in that epicentre of financial capitalism).

The consequence is that many of us are, indeed, always on. You can use your smartphone to read, tell the time and set an alarm, use search and social media, listen to or watch content, find routes, make travel reservations, buy tickets, check how the buses are running, read and reply to emails, take photographs, play games, go shopping. Oh, and make phone calls. And we do. The experience of daily life—how we consume and how we spend leisure time—has been transformed for the 80–90 per cent of citizens of the rich economies who have a smartphone and data plan. The combination of device, network, and applications has also led to a slower but progressive transformation in business models and production processes in many areas of economic activity. Yet this immense change since 2007 is pretty much invisible in official economic statistics. The reasons for this are the subject of this and the following chapter. One is that what we think of as the economy is defined by a production boundary excluding activities people undertake for themselves, outside paid employment, and there is much more do-it-yourself digital activity now. Another, discussed in the next chapter, is that many online services used by consumers are free—that is, have no monetary price—and there is no agreement about how to account for these in national accounts that are made to balance across output, expenditure, and income. There has also been an increase in free provision through home production of online services or content.

This chapter focuses then on the first of these, the production boundary and digitally intermediated services. The long-standing debate about whether and how to value economically valuable activities outside the market dates back before the origin of the national accounts in the early 1940s. There is little useful data on the amount of non-market activity—this is becoming a familiar refrain when it comes to digitisation—but I will present some evidence about the growing scale of digital disintermediation of marketed activities and discuss some of the measurement and conceptual implications of taking household production seriously. This includes household capital goods. Another aspect of digital intermediation models for households is the increased prevalence of contingent (or gig) employment. Finally, the chapter revisits the lens of the (household and paid) time required to produce and to consume. Gary Becker recognised the importance of taking into account time to produce. Less often acknowledged is the need for time to consume, which is becoming a more central issue given the growth in consumption of digitally mediated services (Steedman 2001).

The Production Boundary

When I embarked on this program of research over a decade ago, official statisticians would often say to me something like: GDP is just a measure of marketed economic activities and shouldn't be regarded as anything more. Of course what happens in the household is important, they would add, but it is not what we happen to measure. As described earlier, this is factually incorrect, as government activities and significant imputations are counted inside the production boundary that separates GDP (the economy) from everything else. The official handbook for the SNA08 states that production for its purposes is understood to be "a physical process, carried out under the responsibility, control and management of an institutional unit, in which labour and assets are used to transform inputs of goods and services into outputs of other goods and services." It continues:

> All goods and services produced as outputs must be such that they can be sold on markets or at least be capable of being provided by one unit to another, with or without charge. The SNA includes within

the production boundary all production actually destined for the market, whether for sale or barter. It also includes all goods or services provided free to individual households or collectively to the community by government units or NPISHs [non-profit institutions serving households]. (UN et al. 2009 D1.42)

So production counted in GDP includes:

- goods and services produced for supply to "units" other than their producers;
- own-account production of *goods* retained by their producers for final consumption or capital formation;
- own-account production of *knowledge-capturing products* retained by their producers for final consumption or capital formation (but excluding such products produced by households for their own use, e.g., family photos);
- own-account production of *housing services* by owner-occupiers;
- production of domestic and personal services by *paid domestic staff*.

The latter point gives rise to the often-cited paradox that someone marrying their paid cleaner is reducing GDP by getting the same services for free, post-ceremony.

But the SNA08 then goes on to discuss wrinkles associated with household production. Some households, particularly in low-income countries, produce goods such as food and clothes for their own use; these are included (in principle) on the alleged grounds that their producer could decide to sell them after they have been made. However, household services are excluded because "the decision to consume them within the household is made even before the service is provided." This compromise reflects an extended debate about how to account for household production, mainly then (and often still) performed by women. In Paul Studenski's detailed (1958) account of the early debates concerning the creation of the national accounts, he claimed: "Most scholars favour, in principle, the inclusion of the unpaid services of the housewife in national income. The difficulty, however, consists in finding a fair measure of the economic value of the housewife's services" (p177). The debate predates the modern national accounts, with Margaret Reid's 1934 classic book *The Economics of Household Production*. Reid defined household production as activities for which marketed alternatives can be substituted, introducing the third-party criterion (could somebody else do the task?): sleep therefore does not count, nor taking a shower. The failure to account in any way for home production—for all the difficulties of valuing or assigning a shadow price to it—means the importance of innovation by the household is underrated. So, for that matter, is innovation *for* the household: the late, great Hans Rosling gave a marvellous 2010 TED Talk about the importance of the washing machine for economic development, but this rarely features in lists of great tech innovations.[1] Perhaps failing to account for what happens in the household helps explain why Silicon Valley focuses on self-driving cars and cryptocurrencies rather than ironing and cleaning robotics. One reason for this may be the absence of regular economic statistics pointing to the potential scope of this market; time-use data are infrequently collected and not sufficiently detailed, although statistical agencies are improving this (Bridgman 2016). University of Kansas economist Misty Heggeness is addressing this data gap with the creation of a dataset on the "care economy," having identified the importance of the interaction between unpaid care responsibilities and the version of the economy measured by official statistics (2020).

Another omission due to the SNA's definition is accounting for leisure time. The character of leisure time is changing because of digital innovation—more streaming video and games, less stamp collecting and knitting—but the quantity of leisure time is what is important for evaluating comparative living standards. All countries apart from the United States consider fewer working hours and more leisure hours to be an improvement in their economic welfare. The current debate about the merits of a four-day working week suggest the long historical trend toward greater leisure will continue in many countries. Taking account of leisure time (as well as mortality rates and inequality) in addition to consumption, Jones and Klenow (2016) concluded the gap between western European and US living standards is considerably lower than when measured using

---

1. https://www.ted.com/talks/hans_rosling_the_magic_washing_machine?language=en

TABLE 4.1. Core National Accounts and Household Satellite, UK

In the SNA £1817.3bn				Not in the SNA £1018.9bn	
"Core" SNA		Household production for own use			
Market production + government	Voluntary production of goods	Own account production of goods (£0.2bn)	Housing services produced by owner-occupiers (£177bn)	Services produced for own use: Childcare (£320.6bn) Adult care (£56.9bn) Housing services (£149.7bn) Nutrition (£144.3bn) Clothing/laundry (£5.6bn) Transport (£235.8bn)	Voluntary services (£23.3bn)

Source: ONS (2016). Note: The figures are for 2014. This was the last full update. US BEA updates some components more frequently.

GDP per capita only; they attain 85 per cent rather than the conventionally measured 67 per cent of the US level of economic welfare.

These various considerations explain why many countries now produce household "satellite" accounts, the term for supplementary accounts that are not part of the core national accounts but provide useful information about economic activities. They combine information from periodic time-use surveys (to measure labor input) with other data sources (providing metrics of outputs). Table 4.1 indicates the scale compared with GDP—about half the size of the formally measured economy.

A key methodological decision is how to value the time spent on household activities, the alternatives being using average market wage rates; the opportunity cost of the labour time involved for specific activities; or the price of a near-market alternative. This is a complex issue when the production boundary becomes fluid, as discussed later in this chapter.

Digitally Disintermediated Activities

Household satellite accounts are a starting point for the phenomenon of production boundary crossing, but they are of limited use. They are not frequently produced and are based on time-use survey data that has only recently started to include some recording of digitised activities.

The surveys ask a sample of people to fill out online diaries recording how they spend their time on different "principal" activities (recognizing that sometimes we can do two things at once, like ironing and watching TV). The categories of these activities have been expanded recently. For instance, in the United Kingdom the new ONS survey has data on online time spent from 2020 onwards. In March 2023 people reported spending an average of 47.6 minutes a day using a computer or device. This included 15.3 minutes playing video or computer games, 11.0 checking a phone or tablet, 10.0 browsing the internet, 5.9 using social media, 3.7 on browsing for online purchases, 0.2 on creating or coding a website, 0.5 on writing online or creating content for the public, 0.1 for "assisting others online eg a forum," 1.1 minutes on other computer use, and 0.5 on the computer with "no main purpose." (These separately itemised activities add up to 48.3 minutes.) Streaming videos or TV is included in the watching TV category in the latest figures, 135.9 minutes; the survey previously reported this as a separate activity, 42.2 minutes in March 2022. Presumably it has become harder for people to distinguish *how* they are watching TV or other video content: is streaming through a smart TV set watching TV or viewing online? This is all interesting information but inadequate for understanding substitutions across the production boundary. For one thing, these time estimates are lower than reported in other sources. The United Kingdom's telecoms and online regulator Ofcom reported that "UK adult internet users spent almost four hours online a day in September 2021, with three of those hours spent on smartphones." The discrepancy is likely to be that some of the time-use survey categories (such as shopping, telephoning, and the category described as completing a document, such as a job application) are done online. But these are exactly the kind of substitutions of interest here. In a simple example, Box 4.1 sets out the logic of why technological changes will lead to shifts in activity across the production boundary.

Many activities are crossing the production boundary—writing wills is one example, formerly involving lawyers but now more likely a form downloaded off the internet. Travel agency is another example. Shifts between market activity and household activity may change the time required for a given output in subtle ways. That is, self-service gasoline stations may require some work on the part of the driver but also less

Box 4.1 Technology and the substitution of household for market production

The shift from market to household production will be more likely the higher the elasticity of substitution between market and non-market output and the lower the requirement for household capital stock (or capital to labor ratio in home production) (Greenwood et al. 2005). Suppose individual utility takes standard constant elasticity of substitution (CES) form in consumption and leisure:

$$\sum_{t=0}^{\infty} \beta^t \left[\ln c_t + \alpha \ln (1-n_t) \right] \tag{4.1}$$

where

$$c_t = \left[\mu c_{mt}^{\epsilon} + (1-\mu) c_{nt}^{\epsilon} \right]^{1/\epsilon} \tag{4.2}$$

is a mix of market consumption c_{mt} and non-market consumption c_{nt}, while n_t is the sum of time spent in market and home work, $n_t = n_{mt} + n_{nt}$. There are home and market production functions, also CES:

$$c_{nt} = k_{nt}^{\phi} \left[(1+\gamma)^t n_{nt} \right]^{1-\phi} \tag{4.3}$$

$$y_t = \left[(1+\gamma)^t n_{nt} \right]^{1-\theta} \tag{4.4}$$

respectively, where γ is an exogenous rate of technical change. It is intuitive in this very simple model that a shift into home production will be more likely to occur the larger is ϵ (substitutability between home and market consumption) and the smaller is ϕ (the share of household capital stock). So technological changes that make the two activities more similar (such as making payments via a teller using a computer compared with making them using a computer at home—or a smooth shave in either salon or home) or require less investment in domestic capital (such as the falling price of laptops and connectivity—or cheap safety razors) will encourage such a shift.

waiting for the gas station attendant to get to your car. Internet shopping implies time saved in traveling to the store and not having to wait on a queue at the cash register, but it may require more time returning purchases whose characteristics are not as expected. These shifts are still evolving. On the whole, however, it is likely that thanks to digitalisation there is a net shift from market to household time–using production such that the measured productivity of affected sectors is lower than in the counterfactual non-digital world.

Of course, there has not been complete disintermediation. Online services have generally become just another channel for many high-street intermediaries such as banks, travel agencies, or recruitment agencies. Market transactions will be taking place and will be measured. But the mix of services provided in the market has changed. Banks will be providing fewer services in their branches (which are indeed often closing) but more advisory services. Travel agency has moved online with providers offering more choice and bundled services such as insurance or tour guides. Households are carrying out some of the functions of those intermediaries themselves, purchasing household capital (such as laptops and routers) and paying broadband subscriptions. The marketed activities are therefore still significant, but the mix will have changed and so too will the implications for understanding both productivity (particularly at the sectoral level) and economic welfare.

Other sources of data help indicate the scale of the substitutions taking place. For example, the number of physical bank branches has been declining (accelerated by the recent switch away from cash). The total number of bank and building society branches in the United Kingdom fell from 13,345 in 2012 to 8,060 in 2022, a fall of 5,285 or 40 per cent (Booth 2023). The number in the United States fell from 85,000 to 71,000 over the same period, a 16 per cent decline (FDIC n.d.). The proportion of people using online banking services, however, has increased. In the United Kingdom, two-thirds of adults used online banking at least monthly before the pandemic, and now an estimated nine in ten do so. The proportion is somewhat lower in the United States, around two-thirds by 2023, but this had increased from about a half in 2019. The finance sector's slowdown in productivity growth has been one of the major contributors to the overall productivity puzzle in the United Kingdom, although the United States has seen a smaller slowdown in its productivity growth. Perhaps unmeasured disintermediation is part of the story? Just as with Becker's shaving example, if the output of banking included home as well as market production, perhaps its productivity record would look much better. Online banking is more convenient, after all. The cost of dealing with paper cheques and cash has greatly reduced. Transactions occur much faster—no waiting three days for cheques to clear. There have been payments innovations such as contactless, Google Pay, and Apple Pay and innovations from companies like Stripe, Square, and Revolut. It is hard to disentangle other influences (such as increased regulation and the need for debt write-offs) in the productivity story, but on the face of it there have been tremendous productivity advances in quality-adjusted digitally enabled retail banking services, and at least part of that due to not having to line up in the bank branch or mail a cheque to make payments.

Another piece of evidence is the expansion of online shopping. In the United Kingdom online sales were just over a quarter of total retail sales in mid-2023 (having reached a temporary peak of 40 per cent during the pandemic). For supermarkets, online sales had fallen to 9 per cent of the total spent on food, lower than the pandemic peak of 12.5 per cent but steady at almost double the pre-pandemic level. The proportions are lower in the United States: e-commerce accounted for 15.4 per cent of total sales in mid-2023, a proportion that had stayed at its higher pandemic-induced level. For food and beverages the proportion was about 7 per cent. Ahuja et al. (2021) estimated that the food delivery market—all built on digital platform models matching restaurants, riders, and customers—trebled in size between 2017 and 2021, growing even faster in the United States, United Kingdom, Canada, and Australia. The rapid growth has led to the emergence of a dark kitchen phenomenon, in effect restaurants without the cost of tables, waiters, and some rent on premises. Speed is an important dimension of quality, as customers expect delivery within about thirty minutes of placing an order. Similarly, supermarket chains are deploying stores without customers as distribution centres for online delivery. Some of these have highly sophisticated robotic technology.

Household Capital

Digital intermediation (and other DIY digital activities discussed further in Chapter 5) require investment in domestic capital equipment, with the traditional domestic appliances like washing machines and stoves joined in most homes by an array of digital connected gadgets. There may be more digitally networked devices in our future as the population ages and more people need to be cared for in their homes, creating a market for domestic robotics in future, even if the technology is not available yet. The existence of sharing economy platforms that involve transactions (or barter) of services using assets such as tools, spare rooms, and cars also highlights the increased interest in measures of consumer capital goods.

The extent of the shift to consumer activities mediated through domestic capital and online services is substantial (Byrne and Corrado 2019). Figure 4.2 (their Figure 1) shows how many of these have been adopted since the mid-2000s. The content services consumed via these devices are often not captured in the national accounts, and they have substituted for paid-for physical predecessors such as DVDs, cameras, radio sets, and so on. Many of the apps on smartphones—launched, remember, only in mid-2007—have replaced prior separate purchases. The services they provide might be counted elsewhere in the national accounts—for instance, as part of the revenues of app stores or of paid-for app providers—but much is currently uncounted. Data usage, representing the use of online services by businesses and consumers, has grown exponentially since the mid-2000s. There is a sequence of economic transactions that current statistics only partially capture. The next chapter looks more closely at the options for measuring the consumption of free (in monetary terms) services. Chapter 7 looks at the need for an appropriate price index to capture the economic value. Here, as it is relevant to the home production issue more broadly, the focus is on the services provided by consumer capital goods.

As Figure 4.2 shows, there are a growing number of these networked devices, not just smartphones and laptops, but also smart thermostats, smart speakers, smart doorbells, robot vacuum cleaners, and so on. These have been rapidly growing markets according to industry data,

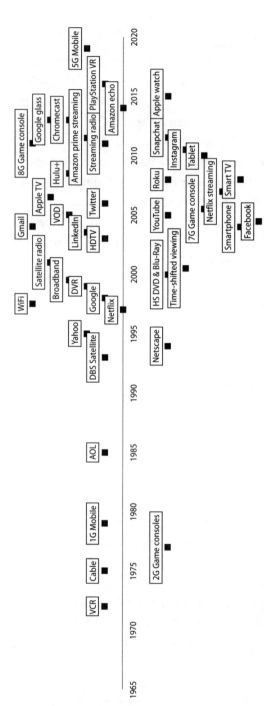

FIGURE 4.2. Timeline of innovation in consumer content delivery. *Source:* Byrne and Corrado (2019).

although it is not clear how widespread they will eventually become. Byrne and Corrado (2019) consider consumer purchases of devices and their use of both free and paid-for network services as bundles (bundles again!). The demand for household capital—the devices—is a derived demand as people want the services they can access through them. To complicate the analysis, there has been considerable quality change. For example, fixed and mobile broadband speeds, compression, and reliability have improved, devices have more features and capabilities, and the services themselves have grown more varied and sophisticated.

The usual framework for imputing the value of the capital services provided by already-purchased consumer durables applies a discount and depreciation rate to the price of purchasing new capital equipment (Christensen and Jorgenson 1973). The intensity of usage (in effect a capacity utilisation rate) also needs to be taken into account. Byrne and Corrado apply this analysis to fourteen types of consumer durable goods, using expenditure data from the US national income and product accounts for each and applying assumed depreciation rates and measures of usage. Unsurprisingly, they find the services provided by these goods increased steadily from the 1980s, accelerating from 2007: "Real [capital] services from use of connected digital systems grow very strongly, averaging 26.0 percent per year for the full period of the study" (p20). If these services were to be allowed across the production boundary to be made visible in GDP, then along with estimates of consumer services from accessing digital content, they estimate it would have added 0.44 percentage points a year to US real GDP growth (which was 3 per cent a year on average, according to BEA figures) from 2007 to 2017. This is a large increment to post-2007 growth. Their method also shows GDP growth accelerating noticeably after 2007, rather than decelerating as in the official figures, due to both the expansion of the production boundary and the use of a quality-adjusted price index for the consumption bundle.

At the same time that some household durable goods are becoming more significant economically, there are some countervailing trends that stand to reduce household capital. Participation in the sharing economy, discussed in the last chapter, is one. The scale of sharing of domestic capital goods is unknown, although probably small. For instance, the United Kingdom's National Travel Survey shows a clear decline in car ownership—and this is not because of marvellous improvements in public transport but almost entirely because ownership of second cars is plummeting (Department for Transport 2022). Still, there is a lively car club and car-sharing market in the United Kingdom. However, car sharing is not a phenomenon in the United States due to its strong car culture, longer distances, and absence of public transport alternatives. Yet future trends may point to more renting of external capital services, such as autonomous vehicles if these take off at scale, or likewise access to 3D printing machines. Business models of this kind are as-a-service subscription offers for households rather than those provided to companies as described in the previous chapter.

Gig Work

There is another aspect to digital disintermediation: as the digital platform business model has become more widespread, so have non-standard modes of work, often collected under the (disparaging) heading of gig work. The equivalent of gig work used to be the norm before the Industrial Revolution introduced the factory system and the mid-twentieth century brought mass employment in standard jobs. Historians have studied the way time monitoring became systematic as employment was formalised away from cottage industry (including much home production of food and clothes), and as technologies such as the telegraph and railways demanded consistent timekeeping across locations. The opportunities for the recent shift away from the mass, formal employment model were created by the combination of labor market deregulation and anti-union laws with digital technologies and their scope for organising and monitoring work differently. There are several current models of flexible or non-standard work. Traditional self-employment, including people working as sole traders, grew until the pandemic struck, when being outside welfare safety nets suddenly seemed non-viable and self-employment plunged. For example, in the United States the number of companies with zero employees, which the Census calls "nonemployers," climbed from about 18.7 million in 2003 to 23 million in 2013 (National Academies of Sciences, Engineering, and Medicine 2017). Newer modes include freelance work, always common in some sectors such as the creative industries, now extended to people like crafters, coders, and even managers through digital matching platforms such as Upwork and Taskrabbit—these two specialising in, respectively, white-collar and blue-collar skills. Potentially more exploitative are modern forms of casualised labour markets, offering short-term or zero-hours contracts, probably paying minimum wage and offering poor job quality.

In principle digital platforms offer a new way of addressing the fundamental problem of economic organisation, namely how to co-ordinate the supply and demand of many individuals in the absence of full information. Traditional markets co-ordinate using location, as in an old-fashioned marketplace, or time, as in financial market auctions. Platforms achieve improved co-ordination using technology. Participants do not need to be co-located, and while individual transactions happen very quickly, they do not all need to occur at the same time. There is thus a dramatic reduction in search costs and improved matching. But the pure efficiency gains that are possible in principle can be largely captured by the platform if there are neither incentives nor enforcement mechanisms to share them with those on both sides of the market. This is one reason why monopsony power in the labour market (as well as monopoly power in product markets) has become a hot issue in competition policy again, after many decades. There is some evidence that digital platforms are able to exercise monopoly power in both local and national labor markets. One recent (Araki et al. 2023) comprehensive cross-OECD study used harmonised online vacancy data to calculate employer shares in specific locations and industries, concluding that "8 per cent of workers in the fourteen countries considered are in labor markets that are at least moderately concentrated—according to the definition frequently used by antitrust authorities in the context of selling markets—and 11 per cent are in highly concentrated markets" (Araki et al. p342). Rural areas and some jobs such as health professionals stood out. This is one example in a growing literature identifying increased monopsony power in labour markets (e.g., Dube et al. 2020, Sokolova and Sorenson 2021).

It will come as no surprise to learn that there are no entirely adequate statistics providing a definitive picture of these labour market dimensions of digital disintermediation, although again this is starting to change as updated surveys are rolled out by statistical agencies, specifically asking about these modes of work. For now, however, estimates of the scale need to be pieced together or deduced from surveys. In the United Kingdom, self-employment rose steeply up to 2020, peaking at about 15 per cent of total employment. A 2021 survey for the United Kingdom's Trades Union Congress found three in twenty (14.7 per cent) of working adults surveyed worked via gig economy platforms at least once a week, compared with 5.8 per cent in 2016 and 11.8 per cent in 2019. In April 2020, 23 per cent of employed workers had variable schedules; for more than half of these workers, their employer controlled their hours and schedules (Adams-Prassl et al. 2021). Recent ONS data from the Labour Force Survey indicate that 3.6 per cent of the workforce was on a zero-hours contract in 2023, up from 0.8 per cent in 2000. For the United States, a 2019 study found a "modest upward trend in the share of the US workforce in alternative work arrangements during the 2000s" based on available data but reckoned the phenomena were being under-recorded by surveys (Katz and Krueger 2019). A 2022 survey by McKinsey reported a steep increase: 36 percent of employed respondents identified as independent workers. It had been 27 per cent in the 2016 survey. These bits of evidence suggest that in both countries the proportion of the workforce in, broadly speaking, a contingent arrangement of some kind is a fifth to a third. Some new US Census Bureau evidence derived from mining other survey data reported 490,000 platform workers compared with 367,000 in 2018 (Gayfield and Laughlin 2023). More than 60 per cent were ride-share drivers and almost 14 per cent were food delivery riders. Across the European Union, one survey showed the proportion of people who had ever done some work via digital platforms ranged from 10 to 18 per cent, although smaller proportions made much of their income that way (Urzi Brancati et al. 2020).

As digital platforms have no business if they cannot attract enough suppliers or workers (because the value they create lies in the matching process between supplier and consumer), they need to offer more attractive work opportunities than the outside options in the labor market. Some of the survey evidence indicates that the contingent workforce contains two groups, those who value the flexibility and are content with what they earn, and those who cannot find anything better (Adams-Prassl et al. 2022). The former tend to be high-skilled, the latter low-skilled. For some people in deregulated labor markets or poor areas, the outside options may be unattractive. What's more, the debate about contingent work in the context of the growth of the digital platforms offers both a need and an opportunity to re-evaluate the way the state delivers social and employment protection to individuals. Welfare systems are structured around the idea of a long-term main job, so those working in more contingent ways are less well protected than others against economic risks (Coyle 2017c). But, to state the obvious, without new official survey data, forming effective policies will not be possible.

The prevalence of contingent work is another phenomenon that makes measurement and understanding of investment in domestic capital goods important. Such workers often have to invest in their own equipment. If they are formally self-employed or a sole trader, this expenditure will be reported (to reclaim tax) and in principle captured in investment statistics. But a Deliveroo rider or ride-share driver for Lyft will often use their own vehicle, and carpenters or photographers selling their services via digital platforms will buy their own equipment. It is not clear to what extent any of these capital purchases are being measured. Incomes might not even be fully declared as there will be some overlap with the informal economy. The bigger platforms are careful to regulate suppliers' activity so that the law is observed, and they increasingly provide financing deals for vehicles or equipment, insurance, and so on. But for now, the overall scale is a bit of a mystery. What does seem clear is that there will be less investment by individuals than in the counterfactual world of formally organised employment. This is equally true of investment in human capital. "If [the individuals] do not take the personal initiative to undergo training, or upgrade the equipment they use, these investments will not occur. One would there-fore expect that levels of human, physical and intangible capital in the economy will be lower than would otherwise be expected" (Adams-Prassl et al. 2021, p16).

Hybrid and Remote Work

Most people reading this will have experienced the hours in online calls, meetings, and lectures that characterised work and life during the pan-demic. I loathe online meetings thanks to this, while acknowledging how convenient they can be. But many people now prefer remote or hybrid work, and Stanford economist Nick Bloom and others argue that, if well managed, hybrid arrangements can increase individual and firm-level productivity, although it is still too early to evaluate the longer-term effects on learning within organisations and corporate cul-ture (Bloom et al. 2023). Some people did some work from home (WFH) long before 2020. A US Census Bureau study in 2013 declared that it was "on the rise," increasing by over a third to 13.4 million workers spending at least a day a week at home, mainly in the private sector, and mainly managerial and professional staff. The fastest increase had been in computing, engineering, and science. Between 2019 and 2023 there was a fivefold increase, with 40 per cent of the US workforce working from home at least one day a week by the end of that period (Barrero et al. 2023). They are better paid on average than the 60 per cent who have to work on-site. The pattern is similar in the United Kingdom, where working from home is as common as in the United States, despite people typically having smaller homes. The data sources are periodic surveys and supplementary alternatives such as Google mobility data. The pandemic clearly had a big impact, but progress in the technology had already driven a growing trend that has continued; much as some of us hate Teams, Zoom, and the like, it has provided flexibility, saved travel time, and enabled different modes of working.

The new technology-enabled flexibility also complicates the valua-tion of leisure and household time, as alluded to earlier. This is not con-stant through the day, but the demarcation is clearer when an individual faces a choice between an hour of overtime in paid work in the factory and an hour cooking a meal and watching TV at home. Those who work from home have a constant labour/home production/leisure trade-off instead.

There is a continuing debate about the implications of the trend, and indeed to what extent it will persist. This includes disagreement about the consequences for productivity (concisely summarised by *The Economist*, 2023). While employees think WFH makes them more productive, employers think the opposite. There are some research findings indicating productivity benefits for WFH. It certainly enhances employee well-being and saves commuting time, some of which is given to employers who do not pay extra for it, and some kept by the employee. It is unclear, however, how WFH will affect learning (especially on the part of new employees) and organisational culture over time. WFH may eventually merge into the newer phenomenon of the four-day week, being trialled by some organisations. Unfortunately—surprise—there is not yet any regular, systematic tracking of the data, which makes these debates inconclusive. In this case, too, there are interesting implications for understanding investment in domestic capital equipment: Is it being undertaken by workers or their employers? Is there more or less than previously—for example, are workstations and chairs being doubled up, one at home and one in the office? Or are firms cutting back on having office spaces and if so, to what extent?

Time as an Input and Output

This brings the discussion back to time as a metric. One of the consequences of digital disintermediation of the offline world is time saving, such as the avoidance of queues in shops and bank branches. Time saving is also an important feature of hybrid work, the saving coming from reduced commuting time. But the shifts are also time-using. Consuming services via the ubiquitous devices involves spending time, substituting for other leisure or home production activities. The economic tradition founded by Gary Becker's introduction of time to produce has not been matched by the same interest in time to consume.

There has, however, been the coinage of the term *attention economy*, which draws on a rich psychological literature concerning cognitive limits. Herbert Simon's (1971) aphorism is often quoted: "What information consumes is rather obvious: it consumes the attention of its recipients. Hence a wealth of information creates a poverty of attention, and a need to allocate that attention efficiently among the overabundance of information sources that might consume it." He pointed out that the information science measure of information content, the bit, would not do as a measure because "bit capacity is not invariant." That is, human understanding depends on how the bits are packaged (or encoded), the form of the content. Rather, "scarcity of attention in an information-rich world can be measured in terms of a human executive's time." (This was written in an era when computers were purely business machines.) The human decision-maker bears the costs of the abundance of information, in having to spend time deciding what to pay attention to and then paying the attention. Hence one proposal for addressing some of the problems posed by digital platforms in the information age is for the platforms to pay their users for their time (Arrieta-Ibarra et al. 2018). The brilliant essay from which Simon's famous quotation is taken points to a non-human solution to the world of information abundance: knowing that something cannot all happen in our heads but must involve being able to store and access information elsewhere, he went on to advocate for research in artificial intelligence.

The 2001 book *The Attention Economy* by business scholars Thomas Davenport and John Beck brought the idea back into the mainstream. Some economic research has started to look at the implications. Indeed, an early contribution was Sherwin Rosen's 1981 article on superstar economics, where one of the mechanisms that lead to disproportionate (relative to their talent) rewards to star sportspeople or actors is an audience's inability to sample all the possibilities, so taking the shortcut of relying on other people's assessment and opting for the most popular. A recent focus has been social media and its competition for attention with traditional media (DellaVigna and La Ferrara 2015, Cagé et al. 2020). Another has been the net impact on consumer welfare of time online, with the presumption that people save time. Households have new kinds of online activities for which there were previously no (or only a few) market intermediaries. An example is online searches that were not previously possible, such as looking for films or restaurants before going out or locating suppliers of specific items. This could be a large effect; Varian (2016) estimates that the value to US consumers of time saved through using online search rather than going to a library or another alternative is approximately $65 billion annually. Brynjolfsson and Oh (2012) concluded there was an annual consumer surplus gain of around $21 billion between 2003 and 2010 created by free websites, equal to 0.17 per cent of average annual GDP. Most of this gain was due to time saving. There is also an extensive literature in transport economics about how to value time saving, key to transport cost-benefit analysis, which would be applicable to any data on how much time people save from using digitally intermediated services (see ITF 2019 for a survey). However, there is more reference to the attention economy in both the management and psychology literatures than in economics.

Becker (1965) introduced the time spent in production, either in the paid labor market or in household production, into microeconomic theory. Time is also needed to consume: consumption of physical products takes time in any case, but spending time (and attention) is intrinsic to the consumption of services, including digitally mediated ones. The only systematic analysis I am aware of is Ian Steedman's 2001 book, *Consumption Takes Time*. The book makes the compelling point that textbook consumer theory is simply incorrect in omitting time needed to consume. The feasible consumption set is not the space of all commodity bundles, not even those that lie inside the budget constraint. It is in fact only the set of combinations that exactly requires twenty-four hours a day (or whatever is left after sleep) and also satisfies the budget constraint. There is no free disposal of time; everybody has to spend all twenty-four hours rather than carrying some over to another day. This combined constraint of time and money has significant implications for consumer theory. For example, small changes in income or relative prices could have large non-marginal effects on consumption of different goods depending on the amount of time needed to consume each good. Non-satiation—an assumption often questioned at the start of introductory microeconomics courses but then forgotten—becomes even less plausible when thinking about consumption as part of an exhaustive set of activities in a given time period; unless consumption becomes infinitely fast, the consumption set must be bounded. The introduction of time into a joint-choice problem also underlines the importance of using rules of thumb or satisficing in decision-making, as well as of the location of people's activities and transport between them.

Time saving, to create more time for activities that provide more value, is at the heart of progress for both consumers and producers. The absence of time-use data with sufficient detail and regularity is an omission from economic statistics—and from economic models of production and consumption. In contrast to the monetary budget constraint, the time budget constraint is an absolute equality. We wake up pondering what we are going to do today, not what we are going to spend today.

Conclusion

It is impossible at present to say anything definitive about shifts in how people are spending their time, or the scale and consequences of the broader phenomenon of digital disintermediation of the physical. We do know how pervasive the changes have been just from the everyday experience of being always on, and we do appreciate the social gradients to these phenomena, benefitting the most those with higher education and professional jobs. But we need to know much more. Among the gaps in the landscape of economic statistics and concepts are more frequent and granular time-use data including on all digitally mediated activities (WFH work, home production such as online banking, leisure); better data on purchases of household capital and personal purchases of capital equipment for work; better data on gig and related modes of work; and more thought about the implications of taking seriously time to consume.

The reason for filling in the gaps is the need for a fuller understanding of how well the economy is doing. The lack of attention paid to household production since the origins of the SNA has been a distortion: activities carried out at home such as caring and cooking are economically valuable although no money changes hands. A full accounting for them would have significantly reduced measured productivity growth during the 1960s when two-earner households started to become the norm; perhaps the long cycles observed in measured productivity growth would be partly smoothed away when work and innovation on both sides of the production boundary are accounted for. Having statistics on household activities and their economic value might incentivise Silicon Valley to innovate more in the direction of washing machines and less in the direction of online delivery apps.

But there's more blurring of the distinction between the monetary economy and the time economy. The next chapter turns to other striking digital phenomena: "free" paid-for digital services, free home-produced services, user innovation, and data.

5

Free

GENERATIONS OF economics undergraduate students have been introduced to the diamond-water paradox: water is essential and diamonds not, but the diamonds have the higher market price. Adam Smith distinguished use value from exchange value. Water has high use value. But as the relative exchange values of the two are determined by conditions of supply and demand for the marginal unit produced and purchased, the price of the marginal diamond is high. As with so many of the intellectual constructs of economics, such as utility functions, indifference curves, and production possibility frontiers, students quickly internalise marginal pricing and never again question it. Yet in all my years of competition inquiries (as a member of the UK Competition Commission), when we asked the executive teams how they priced their products, the answer was usually (average) cost plus a profit margin, or alternatively "what the market will bear." You would have had to be a die-hard economic theorist in that context to believe the latter meant the market was manifesting the outcome of an Arrow-Debreu competitive general equilibrium. People running businesses do not think in terms of economic concepts such as marginal cost and often misbehave with respect to economic theory.

What the market will bear for many consumer digital services is zero. We have come to expect them to be free. What does it mean to define an economy based on exchange values when for so many useful—indeed increasingly essential—products the (monetary) market price is zero? This chapter is about the difficulties "free" production and consumption

pose for a conceptual and measurement framework built around the idea
that the economy is defined by monetary transactions.

How free services came to be normal is not entirely clear, but it seems
to have been introduced to grow usage in the early days of the web
because even small charges choked off usage in these nascent markets
(Odlyzko 2001). The pattern of customers paying a fixed monthly fee
for unlimited usage was familiar in the United States from the telephone
service, where local calls were free and unlimited once the standing
charge was paid. Perhaps it was not obvious to potential users why the
new technology could be useful. Whatever the reason, "free" was a compelling consumer proposition. Early online services that succeeded in
growing were all free to consumers, and this pricing stuck. But attracting
consumers was not the only challenge for new online businesses. The
emerging platform models needed users on both sides, supply and
demand, somebody to provide the content or information that would
attract consumers; the sides have to be in appropriate balance or the
platform will fail (now known in the literature as the "chicken and egg"
problem). Naturally the platforms providing such services also need to
earn revenues. Some charge a commission or subscription, others sell
advertising. As the classic early papers by Jean-Charles Rochet and Jean
Tirole (2003, 2006) showed, pricing on each side depends on the relative elasticities of supply and demand. Typically these are such that the
suppliers pay a fee and the users use for free as the demand elasticity
is greater than the supply elasticity. Or—as is now well known—the
platforms have advertisers on one side and make their money from advertising revenues. To make this pay, they track consumer data and sell
consumer attention to the advertisers.

A pioneering 1999 book on how to run internet businesses was *Information Rules* by Carl Shapiro and Hal Varian—the latter is still chief
economist at Alphabet and a key architect of the Google ad-based business model. I remember hearing him give a talk in Toulouse years ago,
explaining how the company priced each pixel on the screen through
its auction mechanism. The book pointed out the inherently high-fixed,
low-marginal cost structure of information businesses. Much of the cost
is in developing software and reaching critical scale in the first place.

Many traditional business activities involve economies of scale too, but the difference between fixed and marginal cost is extreme in the case of information businesses; the cost of production of the marginal Boeing aircraft is far higher than that of producing a marginal Google search or Facebook "like." For many digital services, marginal cost is effectively zero, so a zero price would represent efficient pricing. *Information Rules* drew some key lessons that still form the basis of successful platform strategies: try to gain first-mover advantage, scale up as fast as possible to attain the network benefits that cement your lead, price discriminate as much as possible by personalisation, and learn all you can about your customers from their behaviour in order to sell advertising. (The book also, presciently, warns that the dynamics of digital businesses will lead to market concentration and attract the interest of antitrust enforcers. If only those enforcers had paid attention when it was published rather than twenty years later.) The alternative model is to sell monthly or annual subscriptions, but as the authors noted even in 1999, that would mean a far lower number of users. Many companies that try "freemium" offers (such as Spotify for music streaming) even now find that most consumers will rather put up with advertising than pay. Business users are more likely to pay subscriptions, but even those platforms with a subscription option (such as Dropbox, Slack, or Canva) have many more free than paying users.

The world of digital services is therefore one where price on the consumer side is often effectively zero yet—as this chapter will describe— the use value is positive, and in some cases high. What is the scale of the free digital goods phenomenon? We freely use search, email, social media, and more, as if we were turning on the tap in the confident expectation of running water, bathing in an environment of Wi-Fi or 5G and endless free content, and are massively frustrated if we cannot get what we want at the end of a click. There have been several different proposals about how to measure these free digital services. This poses a problem for GDP and the national accounts because the absence of a price puts a zero in the expenditure side of the accounts, whereas in the familiar circular flow conception the output, income, and expenditure sides of the national accounts should be equal. Ignoring a ubiquitous phenomenon does not seem a satisfactory approach, however. In the absence of any consensus about what to do, the SNA25 revision will encourage official statisticians to create "satellite" digital accounts rather than integrating free digital services into the core accounts.

This is only the first of the measurement challenges posed by free services, though. Following on from the household production discussion in the previous chapter, there has been an explosion of household and voluntary production of online products, spanning entertaining pet videos and TikTok dances all the way to sophisticated open-source software. One important category is user innovation, the informal or household creation of innovative products shared freely and sometimes developed into new enterprises in the formal economy. Examples range from designs for medical devices to sports equipment innovations. Another free product with distinctive economic characteristics is data—the digital records of activities, purchases, ideas, behaviours. It has become a fundamental feature (or fuel) of the digital economy and is driving much policy interest and legislation. These are all partly captured in conventional statistics, through the fees suppliers pay to the digital platform firms, or the salaries paid to programmers uploading open-source code in their spare time, or the now-large data-broking market around advertising-supported digital services. But not only is there inadequate data about these free phenomena—free-to-consumer services, free production of intangible products, and free provision of data—it is also unclear how to conceptualise them.

"Free" Digital Services

There are multiple services whose users do not pay for the service directly: search, email, audio and video content, games, maps, social media, and so on. Many of us fill hours each day using them. Some aspects of the services are captured in existing economic statistics. Their providers pay staff and others have costs such as energy, servers, or building and running data centres—although these will generally be incurred and recorded in their home country's statistics, while their profits will mostly be recorded in lower-tax third countries. They receive revenue from advertising or other sources, depending on their business model choices. The customers will buy devices, pay broadband or mobile fees, and pay for electricity. But there is a key piece missing in the national accounts, the consumer transaction with the digital company.

The national accounts are in effect quadruple entry: double-entry accounting for both the seller and buyer in a transaction. As the ONS national accounts handbook explains:

> The traditional double-entry book-keeping principle, whereby a transaction gives rise to a pair of matching debit and credit entries within the accounts of each of the two parties to the transaction, is a basic axiom of economic accounting. For example, recording the sale of output requires not only an entry in the production account of the seller but also an entry of equal value, often described as the counterpart, in the seller's financial account to record the cash, or short-term financial credit, received in exchange for the output sold. As two entries are also needed for the buyer the transaction must give rise to four simultaneous entries of equal value in a system of macroeconomic accounts covering both the seller and the buyer. In general a transaction between two different institutional units always requires four equal, simultaneous entries in the accounts of the System—i.e. quadruple entry accounting—even if the transaction is a transfer and not an exchange and even if no money changes hands. These multiple entries enable the economic interactions between different institutional units and sectors to be recorded and analysed. (1.39)

A zero for one of the four entries is a problem, or conversely if an imputed value is to be introduced for the zero-priced service, it has to match the other three counterpart entries. The academic literature has responded with three broad approaches: imputing the value of the service to its users through imagining it as a barter of attention for the service, already used in the national accounts for advertising-funded TV; using stated preference methods to estimate the additional consumer welfare created and add this to GDP; and incorporating the zero price services into a price index to incorporate in the calculation of real-terms GDP. As Bourgeois (2020) notes, these are different conceptualisations and so, not surprisingly, generate different figures regarding scale; and it is early days in this research agenda.

An Imputation for Barter

The barter approach takes to heart the quadruple-entry structure and imagines the transactions taking place in the following way. The platform and its consumers barter exposure to advertising for access to content, which is an in-kind payment for the service provided. This approach is consistent with the principles of the national accounts, which already include advertising-funded services such as print and broadcast media. There is a distinction in how the transactions are mediated, but conceptually they are identical. (The fact that statisticians never used to worry about the phenomenon is testament to an intuition that the scale of use of free digital services is much larger even than attention paid to ad-funded television.)

A 2017 paper by Leonard Nakamura and BEA economists Jon Samuels and Rachel Soloveichik applied this approach to US data. They start by describing what currently happens with traditional advertising-supported media. Content such as a YouTube music video by Adele supported by an ad for Nike trainers is treated as an intermediate input of YouTube, which sells eyeballs to Nike. The cost of eyeballs is an intermediate (marketing) input for Nike. The consumer side does not feature. However, this part of Adele's output is not counted in the music industry but is part of the advertising and marketing industry. Measured output declines because a final output has become an intermediate input in the shift to online content. This caused some issues even before the internet. As the paper explains, "In the 1950s, for example, spending on real consumer recreation services rose only 2 percent per year, much slower than the overall increase in real personal consumption, because households switched from movies to television as their prime source of entertainment" (p6).

Now, in their proposed approach the authors treat the production and consumption of the "free" content as a new bartered good, with a notional sum paid by consumers to the advertiser. The new industry output is attention, and the new input is the free-to-consumers content online. They add the value consumers derive from free content to consumer expenditure and the expenditure side of the national accounts, and add to the income side of the accounts an imputed amount people are paid to pay attention. This amount is the cost of providing the services in question. The paper constructs the supply side of the free content as the costs of its production, how much the tech companies have to spend on supplying all the free products and services. A similar construct is applied to business uses of free digital services. The value of the services is added to the intermediate inputs used by business and is balanced by an imputed business output of attention paid to advertisements. "This additional business output precisely equals the additional expenditures on intermediate inputs, so measured nominal value added by industry and nominal GDP do not change in the case of business use" (p3). (However, the real value added may change if prices of the two move differently; but—as many people fail to appreciate—the national accounts only ever balance in nominal terms, not in "real" or volume terms. The intuition is that you cannot actually add up units of haircuts, cars, apples, and electricity; real GDP is an index number and its components are different index numbers. More in Chapter 7.) The calculation has to incorporate in addition the decline in some traditional ad-funded content, such as the newspapers and magazines losing out to online competitors such as Google. Taking all this together, from 1995 to 2014 all "free" content categories together raised nominal GDP growth by 0.033 of a percentage point a year and real GDP growth by 0.08 of a percentage point. This is a nice-to-have increment to growth, but these are not big numbers, which seems counterintuitive for such a salient phenomenon. A related approach was taken by van Elp and Mushkudiani (2019) for the Netherlands, which added a more substantial 1.0 to 3.4 percentage points to GDP and 2.3 to 7.8 percentage points to consumption by households in 2015. An extension (van Elp, Kuijpers, and Mushkudiani 2023) concluded the increment to GDP from the imputation was 2.3 to 4.7 percent for the years 2015 to 2019. (This paper also suggested an alternative by amending the quality-adjusted deflators.)

The appeal of the approach—certainly to national accountants—is that it is consistent with the principles and practice of the SNA. As described in Chapter 1, there are already many imputations in GDP. In the 1968 iteration of the SNA the intermediation services of the financial sector were treated as intermediate sales to an imaginary industry in a similar way (Christophers 2013). There is even precedent from a distinguished national statistician for thinking about advertising as a barter transaction: André Vanoli (2005) wrote about ad-funded television: "Everything happens as if the advertisers buy from TV enterprises entertainment services in order to remunerate in kind the 'listening' to advertising messages provided to them by households" (p163). He favoured this over earlier proposals to extend household production by including "listening to advertising" services. So this approach is a tweak to current statistical methods and does not change history, the narrative about the trajectory of the economy. However, its smallness seems to be—well, too small. Has the transformation of consumption and production to always-on life really not changed very much? And is adding further imputations to GDP the best option, or does it turn GDP into an even stranger beast?

Stated Preference Methods and Consumer Welfare

One possible reason for the divergence between these kinds of estimates and our intuition about scale is that the digital revolution in consumption has had a bigger impact on consumer welfare than it has on consumer expenditure and production. As already observed, real GDP is a measure of economic welfare (however imperfect), but it does not try to capture the entirety of consumer surplus (the whole amount above the market price and under the demand curve that consumers would have paid for the product in question). There is a growing body of empirical work suggesting that these consumer welfare gains are large, and the digital wedge between GDP and welfare is growing (Heys et al. 2019). One early example is Goolsbee and Klenow (2006), who observe that the main cost to consumers of using free online services is time, not money. The opportunity cost of time spent can be considered as the value they derive. They calculate that (as of 2005) the "true" consumer value was an order of magnitude bigger than the monetary expenditure: more than $3,000 versus $100 over twelve months for the median consumer, valuing leisure time using wage rates.

Several researchers have begun to look at alternative ways to measure the consumer welfare impact. Some focus on the increase in choice and variety, which I will also postpone until Chapter 7. A series of papers by Erik Brynjolfsson and his coauthors (2019a, 2019b, 2020) looking at aggregate effects, and many others looking at individual digital services, have taken the alternative route of stated preference surveys and discrete choice experiments to elicit estimates for consumer welfare. Stated preference approaches (asking a sample of people to state their willingness-to-accept [WTA] loss of a service or willingness to pay to access it) have a dim reputation among some economists, who strongly favour revealed preference approaches (e.g., Hausman 2012); but this is not much use in contexts where market prices or exchange values fail to capture economically important information. Survey methods could in any case be appropriate for statistical production, as conventional economic statistics are already often survey based, whereas alternative approaches to measuring digital consumer welfare tend to require econometric methods.

Survey methods can perhaps also partly capture the negative welfare effects of digital service use. Many commentators have pointed out that in any case Big Tech companies capture most of the value from use in the form of monopoly rents, or "attention rents" (O'Reilly et al. 2023). Some digital services such as social media also have directly negative welfare consequences, although the economic literature does not try to quantify the overall effect of phenomena such as disinformation and online harms, an impossible challenge. One example of a study looking at Facebook use in the United States (Allcott et al. 2020) found median annual values of using Facebook to be around $100 but also found that the WTA stated values changed when they enforced loss of access: "We find that four weeks without Facebook improves subjective well-being and substantially reduces post-experiment demand" (p672). The paper, which recruited a sample of Facebook users in 2018 from an ad on the site to survey them and monitor their usage, also reported large increases in well-being among those who stopped using Facebook. Corrigan et al. (2018) ran several auction experiments which paid people to stop using Facebook: "We consistently find the average [US] Facebook user would require more than $1,000 to deactivate their account for one year." However, these were mean values—the median was $100.

Facebook has been a particular focus of study, and much of the research refers to the United States. As mentioned in the previous chapter, David Nguyen and I looked at the United Kingdom and at a range of around thirty "free" products, including some offline ones, and also had the natural experiment of the COVID lockdowns to inform us about what happened to the stated (WTA) values when people's online behaviour was forced to change. The literature on stated preference methods emphasises the desirability of incentive compatibility. Our surveys did not have this feature—we did not pay people to actually give up each product—but it is impossible to do this at scale, and there seemed no compelling reason to expect respondents in the online panel to give strategically biased answers. Unsurprisingly, the median and mean stated values were positively correlated with usage and much higher for the almost-universally used products (search and personal email). Means were always higher than medians, as some people in each case are intensive users who place much higher value on the product. For example, the mean WTA for Facebook in our sample was just over £2,000, compared to a median of £150. The mean-median gap was lowest for the most intensely used products, online search and email—for example, a mean of well over £5,000 for search with a median of £1,500 and nearly £6,000 on average for email with a median of £3,500. Like Corrigan et al. (2018), we found that in some cases (LinkedIn, Facebook, Instagram) the WTA values for twelve months are greater than twelve times the monthly WTA; in others (public parks, Amazon, cinema, Wikipedia) the twelve-month values were less than twelve times the monthly values. With a large sample and sociodemographic data, we could explore differences between groups, which varied quite a lot depending on the product in question; but in all cases there was quite a broad distribution among respondents. A US study using stated preference methods (based on Google survey responses) to evaluate consumer valuations of a range of free digital products after the onset of COVID found median stated values ranging from $44.93 for Zoom to $8,703.30 for online search (Jamison and Wang 2021). However, their estimates are an order of magnitude higher than ours. For example, their estimate of the social media median of a $140.32 WTA loss for one month compares with our £150 median for Facebook for twelve months. This approach needs many more empirical applications in order to understand the reasons for such variation, which could be anything from sample selection to prevailing incomes.

While the studies of individual products such as Facebook are fascinating, what about the aggregate scale of change in the digital economy? Some earlier papers approached this through measuring the value of internet access to consumers. Greenstein and McDevitt (2011) and Dutz et al. (2012) used the variations in the price US consumers would pay for high-speed broadband to estimate consumer surplus. The former study estimated the consumer surplus total from 1999 to 2006 was $4.8 to $6.7 billion; the latter estimated consumer surplus at $32 billion in 2008. The series of pathbreaking studies by Erik Brynjolfsson and coauthors (2019a, 2019b, 2020) looking at the aggregate impact of free digital products used surveys and incentive-compatible online choice experiments to estimate consumer surplus for a range of digital products for the United States. They advocate for adding the aggregated consumer surplus to GDP to create GDP-B (Beyond GDP). The estimates are large, with real GDP-B accounting for just a limited range of digital products growing an annual 0.05 to 0.11 percentage points faster than published GDP from 2004 to 2017. For comparison with other studies, their median WTA for Facebook was just over $40 a month in 2017. They observed (2019b): "The estimated contribution to welfare due to Facebook in the U.S. over the period 2003–17 is $231 billion (in 2017$) which translates to $16 billion on average per year. The per user welfare gain over the period 2003–17 is $1,143. Considering that this is a single new service, this estimate is substantial." These studies conceptualise the value of free digital services as an increment to consumer welfare, a bigger area under the demand curve and above the zero market price.

Hulten and Nakamura (2022) also suggest using stated preference methods as a means of estimating their proposed E-GDP, extended GDP. This is a different conceptualisation, which treats online access as a shift in the consumption possibility frontier using Lancaster's (1966) framework. This assumes consumers have preferences over characteristics of goods rather than the goods themselves—for light rather than for light bulbs for instance. Both approaches break the direct link between resource use and consumer welfare, and argue for measurement of the latter in place of GDP.

Using Stated Preference Values in the National Accounts Framework

National accountants are somewhat cautious about approaches such as GDP-B or GDP-E (as they would be about what one might call GDP-H, adding measures of unpaid household time discussed in the previous chapter), but one intermediate approach is to integrate stated preference values for online products into the familiar accounting framework. This is a variant on stated preference methods but, instead of adding them to total GDP, uses the estimated values to plug the gap in the quadruple-entry system. One study that does so (Schreyer 2022) combines household and SNA production. Using Facebook is treated as household production of leisure services, which can be added to GDP to create a new aggregate, an "extended measure of activity" (EMA)—but GDP itself is unchanged. As Schreyer notes, the Brynjolfsson et al. methods aggregate additional activity by either treating the estimated consumer values as estimates of the wedge between actual price (zero) and the Hicksian reservation price (2019a, b) or by thinking of the additional value as an increment to total income (2020). But these additions to consumption or income require, in the logic of the accounts, an addition to production. Schreyer argues that the household is the producer as well as the consumer of the services once the revenues from advertising or other sources are accounted for. This places them outside the production boundary, not least on the grounds that the "third-party criterion" does not apply—I cannot sell my consumption of Facebook services to anybody else. But it nevertheless is a useful approach for considering the scale of the difference the free online services have made to the economy. Use of Facebook is estimated to have led to growth in the EMA for the United States 0.04 to 0.2 percentage points higher than real GDP growth for the period 2004 to 2017. (Compare the 0.05 to 0.11 increment for GDP-B previously noted.)

The paper makes a point of distinguishing between estimates of consumer *value*—its aim—and estimates of consumer *surplus*: "'consumer value' is understood as the marginal willingness to pay for or willingness to forgo one unit of a particular product—a shadow price, not to be confused with "'consumer surplus'" in the sense of a cumulative measure across all consumers' willingness to pay for the utility derived from all the units consumed. The latter is conceptually different from valuation at market prices in the national accounts and would make any comparison with GDP meaningless, whereas the former permits such comparisons, at least in principle" (p11). The distinction is between marginal and average price. For the prices used in constructing GDP are similarly conceived as marginal valuations, the price the marginal consumer will pay for the final unit of the product purchased on the (imaginary) demand curve. Consumer surplus is the amount consumers have *not* had to pay on all their intramarginal demand. The philosophy of the national accounts is to stick with conventional marginal pricing.

Adjusting Price Indices

A different approach aiming to produce measures consistent with national income accounting principles is similar to the kind of hedonic quality adjustment that statisticians apply to certain goods whose quality changes over time, such as cars in the United States or mobile phone handsets in the United Kingdom (see Chapter 7). As already noted, using a price deflator delivers in real GDP a metric that introduces some considerations of welfare changes over time, even if it is an inadequate measure of economic welfare overall. Hedonic regression to construct quality-adjusted price indices captures some additional welfare improvements. John Lourenze Poquiz (2023) used the prices of premium versions of some online products (news, video calling, and personal email) to estimate the value of the free component using hedonic regressions. He argues that this method t is familiar in national accounts terms. Other components of the national accounts, such as parts of public services, use the price of marketed substitutes where there is no direct price observable. But, like the stated preference approaches just discussed, it does capture some of the consumer welfare gain omitted from cleaving closely to national accounts principles. John's paper estimates that the value of the three free digital goods categories in the United Kingdom in 2020 was between £6.1bn and £22.7 bn, and their value was growing much faster than the measure of real consumer expenditure, in the range of 0.07 to 0.12 percentage points. This is a clever way to split the difference between the world of national accounts and the world of consumer welfare. But—like the two realms in China Miéville's novel *The City and the City*—the overlaps are unavoidable.

None of the work using stated preference approaches has been fully scaled up and is just now being applied across a number of countries by Brynjolfsson's team. Much of the evidence relates to the United States only, and to a limited range of products—with a particular focus on Facebook. What's more, it is clear that there are some issues of theory and methodology to address. One is the time discounting question mentioned earlier: Why does the twelve times the monthly figure not equal the annual figure? Another is how to classify the products, whether to use specific brands or generic terms, and when and how to add new products. To my mind, one of the most difficult issues is applying a budget constraint. In conventional consumer theory and economic statistics, there is a monetary budget constraint reflected in the data: consumer expenditure is equal to consumer incomes plus new credit. When it comes to consuming online products (and indeed all consumption, production, and leisure), there is a time budget constraint, but this is not accounted for in the stated preference values. Indeed, perhaps we should not simply assume free digital goods add to consumer welfare. Apart from considerations such as addiction or the wide range of harms from social media, Lukasz Rachel (2024) argues that consuming more free digital goods will reduce overall welfare if the value of additional leisure time spent online is exceeded by the value of less non-online output and consumption; the allocation of time between the two delivered by the market outcome may be less than optimal because the zero monetary price distorts consumer choice. Finally, if the justification for adding digital welfare to GDP is to construct a better measure of economic welfare, should we not also take into account all the other contributors to consumer welfare, ranging from the value of conventional public goods such as parks and defence to the external costs of pollution or biodiversity loss? And if so, should they be valued at marginal prices, like diamonds, or at their true shadow prices, like drinkable water? All in all, there is considerable interest in all these approaches but many unanswered questions.

User Innovation

So far this chapter has mainly focused on commercially produced free digital products. A separate issue is how to account for user-generated ones. As in the discussion of home production in the previous chapter, these will be causing some substitution of free for marketed activity and thus reducing measured output a bit below what it otherwise would have been. In the case of consumer goods, as discussed previously, it is substitution out of final demand and GDP. Now we are thinking about investment goods and innovation.

User innovation is a particular category of free production identified by some researchers as possibly significant in scale and in unrecorded value, and leading to an expansion of production and consumption possibilities rather than simply substituting for existing ones. The innovators either give away their ideas and designs or start out doing so and later commercialise some aspect of them. The concept of user innovation has had more attention in the management and science policy literatures than in economics. Eric von Hippel (1976) pioneered the literature, and he and subsequent authors have argued that it is a reasonably common phenomenon. Jason Potts (2023) has argued that it should be called "von Hippel innovation" and identifies the following characteristics:

- Innovators and users have specific tacit knowledge about the demand gap or use case.
- Innovators are not motivated by large-scale market opportunities and so can invest early or take risks.
- The need for financial investment is low.
- Innovators can make use of an ecosystem of equipment and common resources.
- There are economies from the free sharing of information (avoiding the transactions costs involved in patenting).
- Innovators generally do not seek a profit.

Skateboards are one often-cited example of such innovation, created when some users cut their roller skates into two and attached the wheels to either end of a board. Other consumer or non-professional examples cited in the literature include medical devices invented to serve markets too small to appeal to commercial investors; the mountain bike; and the zipper. For example, children who needed prosthetic limbs might have had to wait until their teens, as they were too expensive to replace frequently as they grew (Graboyes 2016). However, a South African carpenter and an American maker designed a 3D-printed prosthetic hand by email correspondence and posted the design freely online. Subsequently e-NABLE (https://enablingthefuture.org/), an online volunteer group, started in the United States and spread globally to match those who needed prosthetic upper limbs with those who could help additively print them. The cost fell from some $5,000 to tens of dollars. The website claims to have provided ten thousand to fifteen thousand recipients with limbs. The limit on further innovation is regulatory, as adding sensors or electronics would turn them into medical devices needing approval. Doctors and surgeons are often user innovators in their own fields (Hinsch et al. 2014).

The boundary between free user innovation in the household sector and user innovation by people as part of their paid work is fuzzy. And for obvious reasons it is hard to estimate either the extent of user innovation or its value. Much of the available evidence is survey based. von Hippel and coauthors have conducted household surveys in a number of countries and report the proportion of households under-taking some innovation ranging from 1.5 per cent (South Korea) to 7.3 per cent (Sweden) and 9.5 per cent (Russia) (Sichel and von Hippel 2021, von Hippel et al. 2017, von Hippel 2017). One review article con-cludes that the extent of user innovation is underestimated in policy decisions (and much academic work), leading policymakers to miss a trick because they pay too much attention to innovation in formal re-search organizations and business (Bradonjic et al. 2019). One attempt to put an aggregate figure on the scale (Pearce and Qian 2022) looks at open-source digital designs for 3D-printed products, taking the top 100 most popular designs posted on the YouMagine repository. It uses the price of similar products on Amazon to estimate how much people can save from the DIY home production: $35–40 million a year.

User innovation is unlikely to be substituting for many activities in the market, as almost by definition it targets market niches that are un-filled or commercially unattractive. Although providing free ideas, these may well be subsequently commercialised, and the activity omitted by not measuring the earliest stages is unlikely to be large in those cases. The largest effect user innovation will have is in serving niches too small to be of commercial interest, and there the main impact is an increment to economic welfare. The problem of innovation for low-value markets has had wider interest in economics in the context of pharmaceuticals or vaccines for diseases mainly affecting low-income countries, but also for huge problems such as the need for effective antibiotics in the face of antimicrobial resistance. The issue has led to policy ideas such as advance market commitments (Kremer et al. 2020). The consumer wel-fare impact of lower-profile user innovations could similarly be large indeed but has attracted no interest at all in public debates about R&D policy. How to measure innovations that might literally be life-changing is an unresolved problem.

User-Generated Digital Products

There is a torrent of other forms of free user-generated services. People post informative or amusing videos in vast quantities, upload photo-graphs and poems, devise games and put them on the app stores for free or freemium, run newsletters about their local area, write blogs, contribute to Wikipedia, and more. These "products" are part of home production and have zero price but create economic value and may substitute for market products. When my boiler flashes an error message, my first step these days is to find the YouTube videos by plumbers explaining what to do. For them, it is a form of marketing—they hope they will gain some customers, and some ask for a financial contribution if their fix worked. But it probably reduces the demand for the services of other plumbers, shifting the task from the market into home production. Other free content will substitute for either other free or paid-for leisure activities—for example, people will read the local blog or join the street WhatsApp group rather than buy a local paper. Perhaps the successful blog will eventually take advertising or sponsorship, or adopt a freemium model, perhaps even morphing into a next-gen local paper. Yet other free content will stay firmly on the household side of the production boundary but may also cause its consumers to substitute away from some sources of entertainment or information in the formal economy. A time-based accounting framework would capture these shifts, as already discussed. Meanwhile, one estimate for the United States, using a proprietary dataset collecting information from individuals' devices, concluded, "The number of American adults creating content quadrupled from 43 million in 2006 to 166 million in 2016" (Nakamura, Samuels, and Soloveichik 2017). The total US population was about 320 million then, so that's more than half of all adults, spending an average of 251 hours in that year on content creation, compared with 1,318 hours in paid work and 1,208 hours of household work.

One particularly interesting category, because the scale and impact on businesses as well as consumers are evidently large, is user-created or open-source software (OSS). There are several reasons people might engage in such prosocial behaviour (Bénabou and Tirole 2006), including reputation building, social norms, or reciprocal learning. Two studies (Nagle 2018, 2019) discuss how firms use and produce OSS. The first finds that the benefits of OSS usage are complementary with contributions to OSS, evidence of a "learning-by-contributing" mechanism where contributors crowdsource feedback on their code from more experienced contributors. The second finds that the productivity benefits of OSS usage are also positively related to the technological sophistication of the firm under consideration, proxied by industry and IT capital intensity. In any case, the social norm among coders of posting code on GitHub or other online locations is now strong. Whatever the reasons, OSS production is an important phenomenon. Free software packages such as R and Python, Apache and Linux, are increasingly widely used and are without question substitutable for paid-for alternatives (Muenchen n.d).

At the more aggregate level, Greenstein and Nagle (2014) looked at the impact of Apache OSS, estimated to be the second-largest open-source project after Linux. It is widely used in e-commerce, disproportionately so by high-traffic websites (57 per cent of the million busiest websites are hosted on Apache). The paper estimates the value of Apache software on servers in the United States to be $2 billion to $12 billion, equal to 1.3 to 8.7 per cent of the stock of prepackaged software. The paper argues that this should be seen as lower bound, because it accounts only for web servers on the public internet and not corporate intranets. Several more recent papers (European Commission 2021, Blind and Schubert 2023, Wright et al. 2023) all do similar exercises aiming to estimate the link between OSS use and macroeconomics outcomes such as growth or the number of start-ups. Hoffman, Nagle, and Zhou (2024) estimate the value of OSS from both supply side (how much would it cost to reproduce all the code once?) and the demand side (what would firms need to spend if it did not exist, and each had to rewrite the code for themselves?). The former figure is around $4 billion for the United States, the latter figure nearly $9 trillion.

An alternative approach (Robbins et al. 2018, Calderón et al. 2022, Korkmaz et al. 2024) is to use engineering characteristics to develop cost-based estimates, using thousands of lines of code contributions, complexity of code, and average labour costs for software engineers. For example, for the top four open-source packages (Python, R, Julia, and JavaScript) this sums to about $3 billion for the United States in 2017 (Robbins et al. 2018). Looking at US government use specifically, they estimate the cost of OSS at $1.1 billion, or around 2 per cent of total government investment in software. The 2020 presentation provides a cost-based estimate of the global value of public (and machine-detectable) GitHub repositories of $928 billion. Similarly, Calderón's 2022 paper estimates the value of OSS investment in the United States to be $36.2 billion in 2019, about half the officially recorded total for own account software investment.

In either method, it is clear that OSS, although outside the production boundary, is economically valuable and of significant scale. Robert Muenchen's blog post, "The Popularity of Data Science Software,"[1] tracks usage of different proprietary and open-source languages over time. Looking at metrics ranging from languages used in job adverts to Google trends, the proprietary ones are shrinking and the open-source ones expanding. The substitution affects not only measures of output or productivity but also software price indices, as discussed further in Chapter 7.

Valuing Data

There are several points in this book where a discussion of the value of data could slot in. Data is often not free, but one rationale for including it here is that the value of data collected by tech companies can be considered an alternative estimate of the scale and impact of free digital products. Another reason is that data's characteristics mean there will be a wedge between price and surplus, or between price at the margin and on average. In any case, it is at the heart of the digital economy. The cliché that data is the new oil is profoundly incorrect in one way (oil is a rival good, and one of data's key features is that it is non-rival), but it gets to the core point that data is the new fuel of the economy. To speak of the data economy or digital economy may soon sound as weird as talking about the electricity economy. Data is potential information, and digital technology has transformed the information basis of economic activity.

There are some industry estimates of the quantum of personal data collected by Big Tech, and the numbers are big. Some of the data is sold

---

1. https://r4stats.com/articles/popularity/?utm_content=cmp-true

into the data brokerage market, estimated at \$268.73 billion in 2022 according to one market research report (Maximize Market Research 2023). Some is sold in the form of marketing analytics or is monetised through selling advertising, and some is used to improve or personalise the product. The global online advertising market was \$209.9 billion in 2022. Another estimate of scale is simply to take the revenues of Google and Meta as a lower bound, as they dominate online advertising and data harvesting. Other Big Tech companies also earn money from data, but this cannot be disentangled from other revenue streams. Non-personal data is increasingly important too—think about data for construction supply chains or logistics or autonomous vehicles—although for understandable reasons much commentary focuses on the personal data issues.

It is impossible to miss the salience of discussions about data's importance to the economy, and while there is breathless hype, there is also solid evidence that using data effectively can improve productivity (Chapter 2). The SNA25 revisions will include more data assets than previously, but this will in effect count the cost of the process of digitisation, not the full economic value of the data (Ahmad and Schreyer 2016). Unsurprisingly, estimating the value of data is tricky, and there is no consensus about how to do it. Table 5.1 summarises the characteristics that determine data value, dividing them into the economic and the contextual or information based.

One immediate issue is that the private and social value will diverge. This is inherent because data is non-rival, so open access will enable more users to create more useful products and more economic value. However, the creators or controllers of data will derive more private value if they restrict access, and—as with other IP products—this may to some extent be necessary to incentivise collecting and investing in data at all; it is a classic public good. Some controllers of private data with market power will continue to collect more simply to safeguard monopoly rents—described in Furman et al. (2019) as the "data loop." So a first challenge is deciding which kind of data value is to be estimated, private/commercial or societal. There are many spillovers, with risks to privacy being the usually cited negative externality, but in general some

TABLE 5.1. Characteristics Affecting the Value of Data

Economic Lens	Information Lens
Non-rival/excludable	Subject
Externalities (positive and negative)	Generality
Increasing/decreasing returns	Temporal coverage
Option value	Quality
High fixed, low marginal costs	Sensitivity
Complementary investments	Interoperability/linkability

Source: Coyle et al. (2020).

data may add to or reduce the value of other data. With high fixed costs there will be a range of increasing returns, but beyond a certain point some data—such as personal characteristics for marketing purposes—has diminishing marginal returns. Data needs substantial complementary investments, hard and soft, to be useful. The use value of data will also be highly contextual, depending on characteristics such as its timeliness, accuracy, granularity, and so on. Depending on the data subject matter, it might depreciate either quickly or slowly, and it might or might not experience diminishing marginal returns (Coyle et al. 2020). But similar points are true of other types of assets as well.

There is no agreement about how to value data, given that the value depends on how it is used and is so heterogeneous. What's more, there are few observable exchange values for data. It is bought and sold in some markets, but prices are often non-transparent. For example, consumer credit data is a familiar category, and there are well-known companies that sell it, but they do not post prices for the individual personal data and generally sell their data analytics services rather than data per se. Similarly, it is not easy to find prices paid by or to data brokerages, nor any standard units. A key exception is financial market data, purchased in financial institutions via Bloomberg or Reuters terminals; the units of data are standardised based on underlying accounting standards or economic theories (Mackenzie 2006). A growing number of start-ups are selling data analytics based on novel data types, such as satellite or shipping data, and again the price will often be negotiated.

TABLE 5.2. Dark Web Prices for Personal Data

Type	Example	Price
Credit card data	Canada hacked credit card details with CVV	$30
Bank payments	Switzerland online banking login	$2,200
Crypto accounts	Binance verified account	$410
Social media	Hacked Gmail account	$60
Hacked services	Netflix account 1-yr subscription	$20
Scanned documents	US passports	$50
Email database dumps	10 million US email addresses	$120
Malware	UK high-quality per 1,000 installs	$1,600

Source: Adapted from https://www.privacyaffairs.com/dark-web-price-index-2023/.

Another place where you can find posted prices for personal data is the dark web. The prices for early 2023 from one dark web price index published by a cybersecurity firm are summarised in Table 5.2. The table shows just one example in each category, but the implied relative prices, for example, between countries or between bank account types, are also fascinating.

China is experimenting with several high-profile public data markets, encouraged by national initiatives to establish the required infrastructure and standards (Cloud Security Alliance 2022). The first was the Guiyang Global Big Data Exchange established in 2015, but with low reported cumulative turnover (under $80 million) as of early 2023. In 2023, however, it claimed the first transaction based on personal data (Shen 2023). The first national data exchange, in Shanghai, was established in 2021 and launched officially in 2023, with posted fees of a one-off 9,980 yuan charge and a 2.5 per cent trading value commission. Trading value was over 100 million yuan in 2022, the exchange said (Shi 2023). There are now exchanges in other locations such as Beijing, Shenzhen, and Chongqing. Other entities are also experimenting. For example, People's Data, a unit of the *People's Daily*, launched data certificates to prove ownership and trading rights of three kinds covering data ownership, data processing rights, and data product management rights (Jiang 2023). The World Economic Forum has said that other countries, such as Colombia and India, are experimenting with data exchanges too

(Zabelin et al. 2022). However, the challenges are obvious. Data is the ultimate experience good; the buyer cannot know its quality until the transaction has happened. Exchanges will need to involve not only technical standards but standards regarding classification, metadata, and various dimensions of data quality. Importantly, definitions of the volume units are needed. The number of bytes or data records is insufficient because the information content matters, so some other means of defining a unit of data is needed—such as the definition of an option price or share price in financial markets. In any case, there is not yet enough trading of data on data markets to provide a useful empirical handle on data value.

There are other approaches to valuing data using market values in some form. One is using the gap between the market capitalisation of data-intensive companies and their competitors. For example, Wendy Li and I did so for the hotel sector, taking this organisational capital as a good indicator of the value of data being collected and used (Coyle and Li 2021). The loss of the value of incumbent firms' organizational capital due to their data disadvantage (Li and Chi 2021) can be used to measure the potential size of the demand for data by such firms in the industry sectors disrupted by online platforms. That is, specifically, our measure is an estimate of how much firms should be willing to pay in order to maintain the value of their firm-specific knowledge derived from data—the method is described in Box 5.1.

We applied this approach to firm-level data in the hotel/hospitality sector and scaled up to the global level by using companies' market shares. The value of data in the sector using this method was estimated at US $43.2 billion, with a growth rate currently doubling market size every three years. Figure 5.1 illustrates the approach, showing the impact of Airbnb market entry on Marriott's market capitalisation at the firm level, and the scaled-up global data market value estimate. Ker and Mazzini (2020) use a similar idea, defining a category of "data-driven" firms and comparing their aggregate market capitalization with others.

None of this addresses the broader economic welfare question, and there are far fewer empirical approaches to measuring the social value of data—and hence of open data—in the literature. Yet such estimates

Box 5.1 Using market capitalization to estimate the value of data
---

We applied the Li and Hall (2020) depreciation model to first estimate the depreciation rates of incumbent firms' organisational capital. This requires firm-level data on sales and investments in intangible capital to identify the firm-level depreciation rates of such intangible capital. A profit-maximizing firm will invest in organisational capital such that the expected marginal benefit equals the marginal cost. That is, in each period t, a firm will choose an amount of organisational capital investment to maximise the net present value of the expected returns to organisational capital investment:

$$\max{}_{R_t} E_t[\pi_t] = -R_t + E_t\left[\sum_{j=0}^{\infty} \frac{q_{t+j+d}I(R_t)(1-\delta)^j}{(1+r)^{j+d}}\right] \qquad (5.1)$$

where R_t is the organizational capital investment amount in period t, q_t is the sales in period t, I is the profit rate due to the investment, δ is the depreciation rate of the organizational capital, and r is the cost of capital. The parameter d is the gestation lag and is assumed to be one year. The profit rate function I can be modelled as:

$$I(R_t) = I_\Omega\left[1 - \exp\left(\frac{-R_t}{\theta_t}\right)\right] \qquad (5.2)$$

where $\theta_t \equiv \theta_0 (1+G)^t$ acts as a deflator to capture trend increasing organisational capital investment. Maximising the expected return allows the estimation of the unknown parameters θ_0 and the depreciation rate δ. Then, as in Li and Chi (2021), we assume that the depreciation rates of organisational capital by incumbent firms can be maintained at prior rates if they undertake their own digital transformation. We can then use Hall's (1993) method to calculate the stocks of organisational capital based on before-entry and after-entry depreciation rates. Finally, our impact-based approach uses the difference between the two stocks as the proxy for the demand for data by disrupted firms. This difference measures the loss to these firms due to their failure to use data in order to cope with changes in competition due to the entry of an online platform.

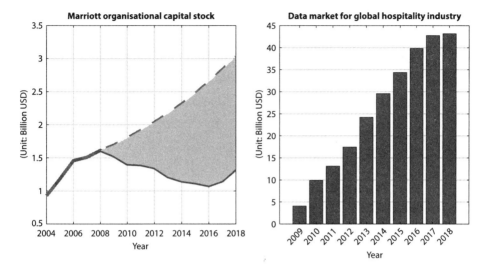

FIGURE 5.1. Marriott's organisational capital stock and the estimated data market size of the global hospitality industry. *Source:* Coyle and Li (2021).

are needed. For example, how much should public authorities invest in public or official data, or how much commercial gain should they sacrifice with a private contractor to make the data involved open? When competition authorities are considering the market power of data-based tech companies, how can they estimate the potential economic welfare gain from requiring the firms to make some data open (as in the United Kingdom's Open Banking regime)? With my coauthor Annabel Manley (2023), we surveyed the possibilities. Figure 5.2 (Figure 1 in our paper) sets out a typology of approaches to valuing data. The national accountants prefer the sum-of-costs approach at the top, and this will be adopted in the new SNA25; the top half shows other methods based on exchange values or revealed preference. The next set down shows stated preference methods; Annabel and I also experimented with discrete choice experiments under this heading (Coyle and Manley 2021). At the bottom of the chart are some firm-level approaches, one applying machine learning methods to evaluate the impact of data use on corporate outcomes such as profits (e.g., Bajari et al. 2019), the other using real options methods. With Luca Gamberi, I have also experimented with

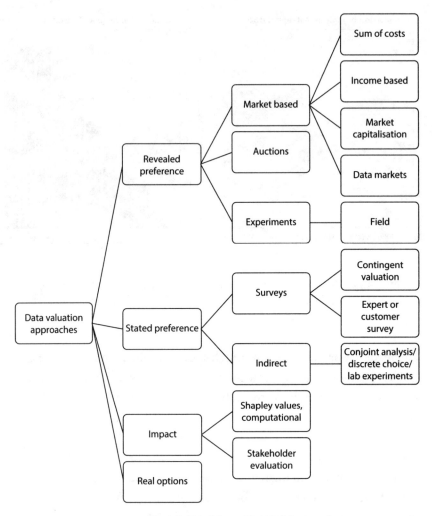

FIGURE 5.2. Typology of data valuation approaches.
Source: Coyle and Manley (2024).

the latter (Coyle and Gamberi 2024). There is a burgeoning literature on data, including some impressive economic theory (e.g., Acemoglu et al. 2022, Jones and Tonetti, 2020), but the slog of working out how to do the empirics is still novel territory. An aggregate estimate for the whole economy is a long way away. Which is striking given the widespread belief that data is of increasing economic importance, whether conceptualised as a factor of production or an intangible asset or as an increment to social welfare.

Conclusion

Why should we worry about any of the issues in this chapter? It's because "free" crystallises the paradox of a pervasive digital economy that is invisible in standard economic statistics. The most valuable businesses in the world, ever, are giving away services. They are driven by a fuel nobody knows how to value. Millions of people are giving away valuable ideas, intellectual property—while others are having it extracted with no payment by AI companies. Similarly, every action online generates data freely, from which companies collecting the data make money. Each of us knows from experience every day in life at work and at home that technology has transformed ways of doing things. Generative AI, a vast eater of data, means this transformation will continue. People spend hours a day online via digital devices for work, home, and leisure. New businesses are all digital platforms. How we engage as customers or workers with firms is mediated via digital.

But this is statistically invisible because the conceptual framework for classifying activities and collecting data dates from the 1940s. It's like trying to see in the dark using normal spectacles rather than night vision ones.

6

Borders

PEOPLE FROM MY GENERATION (late baby boomer) onwards have (at least until recently) experienced a world of expanding international links, mainly in trade, then investment, and to a lesser but increasing extent migration. This process of globalisation has been politically contentious since the late 1990s, charged with being a cause of increased inequality in OECD economies, although China's participation in world markets has clearly massively reduced inequality in the global income distribution. Globalisation has also changed in character. In the immediate postwar years trade consisted largely of commodities exports by low-income countries and trade in finished goods among the high-income economies. World Trade Organization (WTO) figures show a forty-three-fold increase in world trade volumes between 1950 and 2021. Over time, particularly since the 1980s, the share of components or intermediates in manufactures trade has risen steadily; by 2020 about two-thirds of goods traded were intermediates (Johnson and Noguera 2012). A growing proportion of the finished goods traded were being purchased through e-commerce platforms. Services trade has also increased, and a rising share of this consists of digitally enabled services.

One of the causes of the great expansion of trade is the massive reduction of transport costs: for physical shipments thanks to containerisation and cheaper air freight (Ganapati and Wong 2023, Hummels 2007), and for communication thanks to the ICT revolution. These have reinforced each other with the combination of technologies increasing efficiencies in logistics. The combination has also dramatically restructured production globally, from a world of vertically integrated manufacturing, with any inputs needing to be purchased and sourced as locally as possible, to one of dispersed global production networks with finished goods assembled from components manufactured in many countries.

I once visited an extreme version of the former type of production on a visit with some investment bankers to the newly ex-communist Hungary, in early 1991. The government had put up for sale Ganz Electric, one of the country's biggest manufacturers. It took in iron ore at one end of the vast site outside Budapest and turned out products from light bulbs to tram cars at the other end. (The collapse of the previous regime was so recent that when any of our party wanted to go to the toilet, toilet paper had to be unlocked from a cupboard by the managing director's suspicious secretary and doled out grudgingly in portions. The company was duly split up and sold off.) By contrast, the iconic example of global network production is Apple's iPhone, which requires raw materials from South America and Africa to be shipped first to Vietnam and EU countries for processing into refined materials and plastics, then to Taiwan and South Korea, where key components are manufactured, and finally to China and increasingly India for assembly. At least forty-three countries in six continents are part of the supply network. It is a similar story for Samsung phones. And the companies at the core of the smartphone networks, Apple and Samsung, are the ones that retain most of the value added (Dedrick and Kraemer 2017). The pattern of production is more common in some industries than others, including electronics and pharmaceuticals, as noted in Chapter 3 in the discussion of factoryless goods production. But it is more common than you might think for other types of goods. Around my house I quickly found toothbrushes, toys, and cosmetic products that seemed to have been assembled in one country from components produced elsewhere.

Perhaps the late-twentieth- and early-twenty-first-century era of globalisation is coming to an end—just like the late-nineteenth- and early-twentieth-century era Keynes described in a famous paragraph in *The Economic Consequences of the Peace* (1919/2013):

The inhabitant of London could order by telephone, sipping his morning tea in bed, the various products of the whole earth, in such quantity as he might see fit, and reasonably expect their early delivery upon his doorstep. . . . He could secure forthwith, if he wished it, cheap and comfortable means of transit to any country or climate without passport or other formality . . . and could then proceed abroad to foreign quarters, without knowledge of their religion, language, or customs, bearing coined wealth upon his person, and would consider himself greatly aggrieved and much surprised at the least interference. . . . But, most important of all, he regarded this state of affairs as normal, certain, and permanent, except in the direction of further improvement. (p6–7)

That era did end, in a world war, the Great Depression, and another world war, so the precedent for deglobalising is not good. Nevertheless, there is a new concern for economic resilience, post-pandemic and post-invasion of Ukraine, and for national security as US-China tensions have increased. "Reshoring" and "friend-shoring" are current buzzwords.

However, if production is restructured globally once again, it seems more likely to rewire the global production networks than simply to unpick them. The fall in transportation and communication costs has changed optimal production arrangements. Just-in-time logistics might recede to build in a buffer for resilience, but the efficiency gains of the production networks are so large that they will not be abandoned; inventory to sales ratios in manufacturing and retailing have declined substantially everywhere (from about 1.7 in the United States in 1990 to about 1.3 now). Similarly, the efficiency gains from the shift from vertical integration to outsourcing in production and a focus on services and intangibles are overwhelmingly large, so the production structures described in Chapter 3 will persist. Trade in services, especially digital services, and international e-commerce probably both have significantly further to go. But finally, there is one economic domain where we are seeing and will continue to see more rather than less vertical integration—in the digital sector itself. This chapter looks at the cross-border aspects of the digital rewiring of the economy discussed in the previous chapters.

Global Production Networks

The smartphone example highlights one of the key points about global production networks. Reduced costs have made them possible, but what has made them interesting to companies is the opportunity to focus on the high-value-added parts of the production chain, and therefore to make a higher profit margin. Intangibles are therefore a core part of the story. The hub company will need to share some of its IP, such as blueprints or patents, to enable manufacture (and may charge a fee for this, or an internal transfer price that helps with minimising tax payments). It will also derive profits from various intangible assets, such as patents or brands, whereas the manufacturing processes are low margin by comparison. In the smartphone example, Apple and Samsung are the market leaders now, but it used to be Nokia and BlackBerry until 2010, so a strong brand brings some market power but it might not last (Dedrick and Kraemer 2017). The academic literature on GVCs is surveyed in Antràs and Chor (2022) and Tahbaz-Salehi and Carvalho (2019).

One way to think of the long-term evolution of global production is in terms of Richard Baldwin's three "unbundlings" (2016a, b), as these link production patterns to steep declines in transport costs and technological change. The first unbundling was the decline in shipping costs in the early Industrial Revolution, paving the way for people in the global North to consume finished items produced elsewhere. It reached its peak as the nineteenth century turned into the twentieth. The second unbundling took place in the 1990s thanks to ICTs and led to the first wave of offshoring, and the start of today's production networks. Trade consists not only of finished items but also of components used in production. The natural lens to analyse the networks is an input-output framework. The third unbundling is yet to come, reflecting much cheaper and better telepresence enabling growing trade in services (Baldwin 2019)—discussed later in this chapter.

Making a physical product involves three main stages, as Teresa Fort (2023) has summarised: research/design, physical processing of materials, and marketing/distribution/sales. Only the second is classed as manufacturing in official statistics. Any of these stages can be carried out anywhere; even the middle stage is no longer confined to one nation, in the case of offshoring of the contracted-out tasks. Multinationals may also invest in their own manufacturing facilities overseas (through foreign direct investment) as well as or instead of contracting production to a supplier. FGPs will often be counted in the distribution sector as a wholesaler, or sometimes in professional services if their focus is on research and design (such as chip design).

The way these structures are reflected in trade data is complicated. Under current accounting standards, the FGP (the principal) is performing service activities while the foreign contract manufacturer is engaged in production (UNECE 2015). However, factoryless manufacturing can impact statistics for total exports and imports as well as the sectoral composition of trade flows (Doherty 2015). The totals can be distorted if certain flows are not captured in current business surveys conducted by national statistical institutes. Figure 6.1 presents a schematic representation of this, highlighting how specific flows may be measured in practice; it is simplified as it abstracts away from questions of transfer of ownership. It is not clear how in practice different national statistical institutes are recording this phenomenon. However, the implications are clearly important. For example, if Dyson is producing a vacuum cleaner in Malaysia and then sells it in Japan, we cannot be sure whether this is recorded as a UK goods export. If a Jaguar car is produced by a Canadian-owned plant in Austria but sold in Germany, it is similarly unclear how the statistics will record this.

There is, of course, a lack of data on global production arrangements such as factoryless production and related phenomena (merchanting, toll processing, and subcontracting). There are some useful US business surveys (Fort 2023) on such arrangements, and the import of contract manufacturing services is currently quite likely to be recorded as a resale of products (i.e., merchanting) in US data (Doherty 2015). As a result, sectors with relatively high resale figures will include some activity of FGPs. As Fort points out, the accounting conventions mean that "when US firms sell their products directly to foreign customers from their foreign suppliers or plants, those goods never cross into US commercial space. The ensuing profits are counted in US GNP [gross national

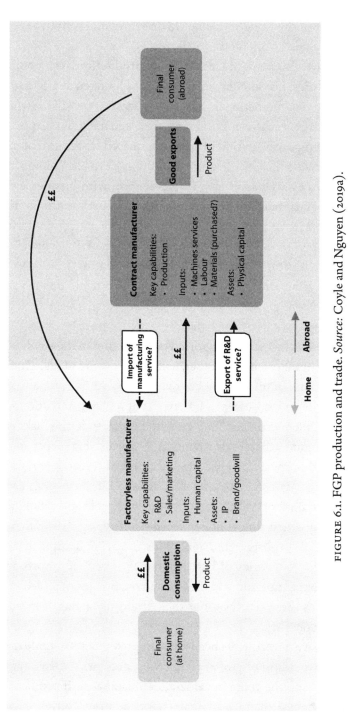

FIGURE 6.1. FGP production and trade. *Source:* Coyle and Nguyen (2019a).

product], but the value added by US designers and software engineers may be excluded from GDP" (2023, p54).

There are also some traces of global production arrangements in trade statistics. David Nguyen and I (2019b) looked at UK trade data reported in the International Trade in Services Survey (ITIS) which the ONS conducts each year. Businesses are asked for "total [export] sales during the reporting period of goods purchased for resale that have remained outside the UK." In 2018 this amounted to £10.3 billion, almost three times as high as in 2013 (ONS 2020b), with businesses in the wholesale and retail industry accounting for almost two-thirds. The survey asks for "total goods purchased [imported] for resale during the reporting period that have remained outside the UK," which is much lower. In addition to these merchanting activities, ITIS asks about "manufacturing services on goods owned by others," defined as "fees charged by foreign businesses for the processing, assembly, labelling and packing of goods overseas that are owned by your business." Around a third of the total here was reported by businesses in the wholesale and retail industry (which, remember, will include some FGPs). The use of contract manufacturing services overseas by a UK company should theoretically be recorded as a UK export of research and development services. One question in ITIS comes fairly close to this, asking businesses to report "charges or payments for the use of patents and other intellectual property that are the end result of research and development without transfer of ownership." In 2018 UK businesses exported £2.8 billion under this category, but the wholesale and retail industry officially recorded almost none, which strongly suggests underreporting. Total UK exports were £490 billion in 2018 and imports £672 billion, so these categories add up to about 3 per cent of exports and less than 0.1 per cent of imports, clearly underestimates of scale. Table 6.1 summarises these figures—but they offer only a partial lens on the phenomenon.

There have nevertheless been some improvements in trade data and the understanding of global production networks at an aggregated level thanks to the trade in value-added databases. If production involves a sequence of processes in different countries, conventional trade

TABLE 6.1. UK FGPs: Trade Statistics

	2013	2014	2015	2016	2017	2018	2019	2020
				Exports (£ million)				
Merchanting	3,585	1,395	2,241	2,691	7,223	10,330	Suppressed	6,672
Manufacturing services	2,555	2,103	2,350	2,735	3,518	2,739	2,832	3,033
Charges for IP	1,446	1,561	1,737	1,455	1,985	2,833	5,130	3,722
				Imports (£ million)				
Merchanting	437	1,099	372	345	304	401	Suppressed	1,075
Manufacturing services	760	581	627	601	925	1,256	1,165	1,433
Charges for IP	669	586	686	919	1,310	2,780	3,398	2,608

Source: Coyle and Nguyen (2019a). *Note:* updated by the author.

statistics will count the exports and imports every time. Trade in value-added statistics, by contrast, capture embedded imports in export data and thus avoid double-counting; these statistics also link exports to the ultimately importing country, if these go through other countries for further processing. The more global production networks grow as a share of world output, the bigger the gap between the two kinds of data. One source of value-added trade data is the World Input-Output Database. Long-run data is available for twenty-three countries for 1965–2000 (Timmer et al. 2015) and separately for forty-three countries for 2000–2014 (Timmer et al. 2016). The latest release was in 2016. Recent data is available in the OECD's Trade in Value-Added indicators (OECD n.d.), also constructed from supply and use (input-output) tables; the 2023 release runs up to 2020. The data-construction exercise is immense, so figures are available only with a delay. They are useful for understanding the role of trade in the economy from the national perspective, but there are policy questions for which different organisations of input-output data would be more useful—for example, analysing the impact of a unilateral tariff on a certain item requires a combined sectoral-national slice (Borin and Mancini 2019). There is also little empirical work on the links between production in GVCs and (national) economic outcomes. What does exist suggests a positive effect. For example, McNerney et al. (2022) find that longer production networks are associated with faster transmission of new technologies and faster GDP growth. One group of researchers has recently called for an international alliance to map global production networks for improved resilience to supply shocks (Pichler et al. 2023). Another recent research database captures the extent to which countries specialise in upstream or downstream stages of production in GVCs (Mancini et al. 2024).[1] Although these immense efforts are shedding light on global networks, additional data collection is needed, ideally based on automatic recording of appropriately classified transactions rather than on traditional statistical surveys. Surveys could explicitly ask firms if they do contract manufacturing or use contract manufacturers.

Why does this matter? An important reason is that supply shocks can propagate through production networks, being amplified as they cascade across the network. This has been a key lesson from several recent experiences, ranging from floods in Thailand in 2017 affecting auto production globally to various product shortages during the pandemic and as a result of the later energy shock. There turned out to have been bottlenecks in production nobody knew about (Baldwin and Freeman 2022). As Tahbaz-Salehi and Carvalho (2019) set out, understanding how global production networks contribute to macroeconomic fluctuations and inflation is important for macroeconomic policy. It is also important to be able to locate potential bottlenecks for reasons of competition policy (Coyle 2023a) and for reasons of economic security and resilience. The organisation of global production is yet another large-scale economic phenomenon over which there is too little visibility.

Digitally Enabled Services

When I sit on the shabby train from London to Cambridge early on Monday mornings, finishing my porridge before getting out my laptop, or in a coffee shop for an hour between meetings polishing off some

---

1. https://www.tradeconomics.com/position/

admin online like the crowd of others do as they hunch over tepid cap-
puccinos, it doesn't feel like living the enviable life of a digital nomad.
The cluster of ICTs—powerful laptops, 5G and Wi-Fi, data compression, cloud computing infrastructure—means that many white-collar
workers can work remotely. Many of us have done it a bit for years, but
the pandemic has given rise to the nomad phenomenon. The *Harvard
Business Review* even added its imprimatur with how-to articles, explaining the practical and legal issues (Hennigan 2023). Countries from Co-
lombia to Czechia offer digital nomad visas. One 2023 survey claimed
"a stunning 11%" of Americans describe themselves as digital nomads
(albeit saying only a little about the survey methodology) (MBO Partners). The enforced remote working in 2020–2022 clearly led to a step
change in hybrid work (see Chapter 4). To the extent this means service
delivery across national boundaries, it has implications for interpreting
trade statistics and understanding the role of services in global production networks. Digital nomadism is an individual version of trade in
digitally delivered services that was already expanding (Figure 6.2) in
Richard Baldwin's third unbundling (Baldwin 2019).

Baldwin's third unbundling separates labour services from the physical
presence of the labourers. The IT services sector in India, particularly
around Bangalore, is one example. Many Western companies outsourced activities such as their call centres or payroll processing to India
and a few other English-language places. In 2022–2023, exports of software services were valued at US\$185.5 billion (18.4 per cent year-on-year
growth). This has grown from US\$62.6 billion in 2012–2013 and
US\$108.4 billion in 2017–2018 (Reserve Bank of India 2023). The two
largest components within this are IT services (\$119.8 billion) and
business process outsourcing (BPO) services (\$51.2 billion). The major
destinations were the United States (55 per cent) and Europe (31 per
cent). Total service exports for India in 2022 were US\$309.37 billion,
while total exports were \$778.55 billion (World Bank 2023). Companies
in Brazil and Poland as well as India specialise in the design and engineering drawing stages of the construction industry (Coyle and Msulwa
2024). The business model of Big Tech in the United States and other
Western economies has involved substantial amounts of labour in

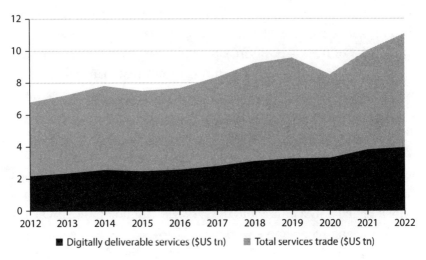

FIGURE 6.2. Global exports of services. WTO database.

low-income countries involved in tagging images and text for super-vised learning, or for content moderation, employing casual labour or even refugees in countries such as Kenya or Bulgaria (Murgia 2024). Google Translate enables the workers to work with English-language text. As in the prior waves of manufacturing outsourcing, there is a de-bate about the ethics and economics of these arrangements: Are they exploitative of people with no agency, or are they creating better-paid work in poor communities? Will they prove temporary boosts to jobs and growth or provide a pathway for low-income countries to respond to "premature deindustrialisation" (Rodrik 2016)?

Baldwin coined the ungainly term *globotics* to describe the combina-tion of globalisation and automation. Trade in services has already grown (Figure 6.2). He argues that the technological improvements (for example, in bandwidth, data compression, and improved latency) and applications such as Slack or Teams have improved enough to reduce the "transport costs" of trade in services—such as the delays that used to make video conferencing untenable. Although there are already plenty of examples of digitally enabled services trade, Baldwin's argument is that there are currently high barriers (mainly technical) with further to fall, and there is no capacity constraint given labour availability in lower-income economies, so the "globotics upheaval" could be large. Just as has been the case with global production networks, the phenomenon will have implications for the macroeconomy (for example, for how the labour market operates and hence wage inflation pressures, or for tax collection) and for questions of competition and resilience (Baldwin 2022). One uncertainty about his prediction of continuing rapid growth in this trade is the impact of AI on some of the occupations involved ("bookkeepers, forensic accountants, CV screeners, administrative assistants, online client help staff, graphic designers, copyeditors, personal assistants, corporate travel agents, software engineers, lawyers who can check contracts, financial analysts who can write reports" [Baldwin 2022, p16]), as companies might opt for 100 per cent automation rather than hybrid human plus ICTs for some of these. The counterargument is that there is still plenty of scope for outsourcing services. What is clear is that the data to track the scale and speed of change in this type of services trade is not available.

E-commerce

Production networks concern business-to-business (B2B) links, with logistics falling into the B2B category—for example, Walmart's purchases of products from non-US suppliers. This can be thought of as related to global production networks but with looser contractual arrangements, or none. But cross-border e-commerce can include business-to-consumer (B2C) sales, direct to final consumers, too. The data available on a global basis is sparse, largely comprising industry datasets. For instance, data company Statista claims retail e-commerce sales globally were about $6 trillion in 2022, although most of the total will be domestic retail e-commerce. Individual countries collect data for online sales—proportionately, China and the United Kingdom are the biggest online shopping nations. The United Kingdom's latest available figures show e-commerce sales by business (for 2019) amounted to £670 billion (30 per cent of 2019 current-price GDP), about half website sales and half electronic data interchange systems within supply chains. Big companies of over 1,000 employees accounted for over half the total.

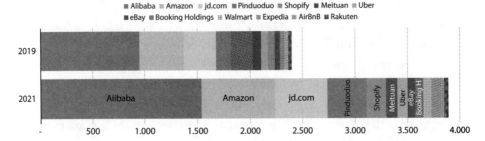

FIGURE 6.3. Gross value of sales sold through companies listed, $ billions.
Source: UNCTAD (2022).

Average weekly online retail sales in 2022 amounted to £2.2 billion, compared with a total weekly retail sales average of £8.4 billion (excluding fuel). Americans are somewhat less keen online shoppers: at the end of 2022 e-commerce sales were $253 billion in the final quarter, just under 15 per cent of the total. Figure 6.3, a UN Trade and Development (UNCTAD) chart, shows the impact of the pandemic on sales by the largest global e-commerce platforms.

The main reason for considering e-commerce as a distinct element of digital trade is that the retail sector has been a significant driver of productivity (and direct-consumer) gains at times when stores have implemented logistical improvements—like the impact of Walmart's digitised logistics in the 1990s. Walmart features again recently as a player in US online retail sales, and the only company able to give Amazon a competitive run for its money.

Data and the Cloud

All the digital phenomena discussed in these chapters depend on underpinning infrastructure, both hard and soft, and this is as good a place as any to discuss it. The physical component consists of communications networks—fixed line, wireless, and undersea cables—and data centres. The physical infrastructure is fascinating and underresearched and indeed undermeasured (like all infrastructure—see Chapter 8). One excellent resource is TeleGeography, which produces network

maps. Vili Lehdonvirta at the Oxford Internet Institute is a leading re-
searcher on internet infrastructure (2022), but it seems to be a lonely
effort. He has a new research project mapping the physical internet
globally.

The intangible component consists of the software running in the
data centres—in the cloud—and data itself. The previous chapter discussed the value of data, so here I will focus on the cloud. Again, there
is little available data, only industry estimates and forecasts. Market research firm Gartner estimated the size of the global public cloud market
at $491 billion in 2022, expected to reach $597 billion in 2023, and with
another 20 per cent–plus increment forecast for 2024. The spread of
generative AI models is widely expected to ratchet up demand for cloud
services further. For many users, their access to frontier software and AI
occurs through cloud services. A market study by the UK telecoms/
digital/broadcast regulator Ofcom (2023a, b), recommending a full
competition inquiry into the cloud market, lifts the veil a bit. As the
study begins, "'Cloud computing' is the provision of remote access to
computing resources (such as compute, storage and networking) on
demand and over a network. Cloud computing has both transformed
the way businesses and organisations of all types and sizes run their
operations and become a critical input to the digital services we all rely
on each day." So this is critical infrastructure. Amazon Web Services
(AWS) is the market leader by a country mile, followed by Microsoft's
Azure and (at a distance) Google, with a competitive fringe of smaller
players trailing far behind these hyperscalers. AWS leads everywhere,
as the cloud emerged from its decision in 2006 to offer an internal func-
tionality to outside customers. The report found that the UK market is
seeing revenues grow by 35–40 per cent a year. Each of the hyperscalers
is building its own ecosystem, from the basic networks up to the software layer, and that competition focuses on customer acquisition. For
like Hotel California, you can check out in principle, but you can never
leave—the egress fees and technical frictions make switching very un-
common. Competition concerns aside, the attractions of cloud use are
obvious—reduced in-house IT needs, both skills and equipment, access to the latest software, flexible on-demand usage. Ofcom's research

found that 82 per cent of respondents had increased their cloud use in recent years, and 79 per cent expected to continue doing so in the following eighteen months.

Different service options are available, usually divided into Infrastructure as a Service (IaaS, raw compute); Platform as a Service (PaaS, a virtual environment); and Software as a Service (SaaS, use of applications provided by the cloud provider or an independent software supplier they host). Most of the familiar uses fall into this latter category, from personal Gmail to Microsoft Office 365 to the BBC's iPlayer. The on-demand aspect of cloud computing is core to the definition, distinguishing the public cloud from a fixed-term software licence or service; so too is the network aspect because it means cloud services can be delivered remotely and sometimes from another country (UN Statistics Division 2023). Currently, statistics combine cloud services and hosting services provided by ISPs (as "data processing, hosting, and related services or data processing, hosting, application services, and other IT infrastructure provisioning services"). A more detailed breakdown would of course be desirable but would perhaps require different reporting by the hyperscalers, including revenues by country; Amazon's published results do not contain statistically useful detail, and it is unclear how the company reports to each country's statistical agencies. Figure 6.4 is Ofcom's representation of the cloud stack.

Measuring cross-border flows of cloud computing is challenging because the data centre could be overseas, and corporate customers are likely to have operations in more than one country. Purchase, production, and consumption may occur in different places. In any case, what should be measured? Monetary payments between customers and hyperscaler, if the latter would provide the data, of course. But how should the statistics track the volume flow of storage and software services that are the intermediate services creating economic value and calculate the price? It is not entirely obvious what the volume metric ought to be—surely not bytes of data? As noted earlier, a few studies have calculated the price of cloud services (Byrne, Corrado, and Sichel 2018, Coyle and Nguyen 2018, 2019b, Coyle and Hampton 2023), and a price index would enable calculation of a volume index from revenues. But the

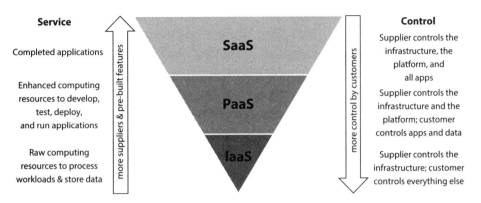

FIGURE 6.4. The cloud computing stack. *Source:* Ofcom (2023a, b).

exercise is not straightforward as the hyperscalers offer a huge variety of services, frequently introducing new options that improve quality, and do not provide information on the extent of purchases of the different services. However, new approaches offer the promise of better understanding digital flows across borders. Stojkoski et al. (2024) use the revenues of the Big Tech companies to estimate three categories: digitally delivered services (e.g., streamed movies or video games), digital "productised" services (e.g., digital advertising), and digital platform fees. These are a subset of the cross-border service flows involving digital technology—the important trade in professional services, for example, is excluded. The figures derived from corporate statements are triangulated against other data sources on the use of such services. The authors find that digital trade is large and growing more rapidly than traditional trade, and its geography differs too: "Trade in digital products follows a different geography and network structure than other forms of trade, being more concentrated in its production and more dispersed in its consumption when compared to trade of all digitally delivered services, all services, and all physical goods" (p10).

The desirability of better statistics is demonstrated by the policy trend toward data localisation, part of the general climate of increasing nationalism in economic policy, although often presented as a privacy imperative. In a 2022 report, McKinsey estimated that three-quarters of countries had such a rule (Parekh et al.). For large economies, the hyperscalers will have multiple data centres inside the relevant political boundary, so this kind of rule is largely unproblematic—there will be a few wrinkles like trying to prevent Irish data crossing the United Kingdom to get to the rest of the EU. For small economies, data localisation requirements may not be so benign—there are small, poor economies where AWS or Microsoft will never find it economically viable to build an in-country data centre, especially hot ones where electricity supply is variable and cooling requirements would be costly. A country such as Kenya can mandate where data should be stored, but this will greatly increase cloud computing costs for its companies and consumers. Furthermore, although security and privacy requirements are important, there are economic advantages from using data to serve local markets, and where the data is stored or run through software is unimportant. Wendy Li and I (2021) (as well as estimating the data market size—see Chapter 5) developed a typology of countries based on the following distinctions: whether a country is a *net (raw) data importer with existing dominant global platform companies or a data exporter*; whether it is a *developed or developing economy* (corresponding to the World Bank's definitions); whether it has a *large or small domestic market* (dependent on population and income per capita); and whether it has *other high-tech advantages,* including talent and digital infrastructure. Some of the categories have only one member; nevertheless, we think the structure helps in thinking about the potential implications of data policy measures (Table 6.2).

Thinking about the types, it becomes clear that being a data exporter need not be a disadvantage. India and Indonesia are examples of such countries. India's digital outsourcing means it both imports and exports data, though on net it is likely an exporter. It has a sophisticated high-tech industry and skilled workforce. The US and Chinese tech giants have leading market positions in India, but there are also some strong local competitors such as Jio. Indonesia is a challenging market for overseas firms. It consists of five major islands and about thirty smaller groups, a geographical feature that poses special challenges for logistics networks for e-commerce. Much of the population is still unbanked. But it has the largest e-commerce market in Southeast Asia, and the market leader is local startup Tokopedia (founded in 2010). Businesses like these examples

TABLE 6.2. Categories of Data Trading Countries

Type I	Net data importers	Large developed countries with dominant international online platforms and leading high-tech industries (US)
Type II	Net data importers	Large developing countries with dominant international online platforms and leading high-tech industries (China)
Type III	Net data exporters	Large developing countries without dominant international online platforms but with leading high-tech industries (India, Canada)
Type IV	Net data exporters	Large developing countries without dominant international online platforms and leading high-tech industries (Indonesia)
Type V	Net data exporters	Developed countries without dominant international online platforms but with leading high-tech industries and/or talent (e.g., UK, France)
Type VI	Net data exporters	Small developing countries without dominant international online platforms or high-tech talent (e.g., Kenya, Vietnam)

Source: Coyle and Li (2021).

often have attracted investment funds from the Big Tech companies, who see them as a means of market entry but—in this context—also benefit greatly from access to cloud services. Even competing in the domestic market is impossible for domestic businesses without access to the cloud. Data policies need to accommodate the role of cloud services as an important intermediate service in local production.

The Digital Stack and Digital Public Infrastructure

This perspective suggests that Western economies like the United Kingdom and France may be at a disadvantage in terms of digital trade in general, as their markets are already dominated by companies like Amazon, Alphabet, Apple, Meta, and Microsoft. In the Furman Review (Furman et al. 2019) we members of the review panel were told repeatedly by small UK tech companies that the only viable exit for their early investors was being acquired by one of the big US companies. How might the governments of such countries think about improving their national out-look for digital trade? Answering this requires an adequate understanding of the landscape globally. This is partly a matter of better statistics for value-added trade and production networks. But it also requires a systematic understanding of the technological infrastructure involved.

This chapter began by describing the evolution of global production networks in manufacturing and increasingly services, enabled by digital technologies. It turned then to the digital plumbing, the networks and the cloud, and to cross-border aspects of digitally enabled trade. They are linked through the *digital stack*—a generic term borrowed from the computing world and referring to the layers of technology needed to enable the applications and services that now characterise economic production and consumption. The physical infrastructure, including data centres and telecommunications networks, form the base, other physical investments such as servers and devices the middle, supporting operating systems and middleware next, and data and applications at the pinnacle. The stack will vary between types of activity and will require complementary infrastructure and services. But digital economic activities at some point need a digital government interface, and unsurprisingly governments lag behind the technology frontier. However, there is a growing focus on the digital government stack, including digital payments systems and central bank digital currencies (Bank for International Settlements 2023).

There have been many digital government initiatives in many countries: the New America think tank has a useful tracker. Increasingly, policy debates speak of this stack as digital public infrastructure (DPI), strongly advocated in the developing country context by the Gates Foundation and praised by institutions like the World Bank and G20 (World Bank 2022). One of the Gates documents describes it in this way: "DPI is a digital network that enables countries to safely and efficiently deliver economic opportunities and social services to all residents. DPI can be compared to roads, which form a physical network that connects people and provides access to a huge range of goods and services" (Hong 2023). The DPI is conceived as a trio of digital identity, data exchange, and digital payment mechanism (Figure 6.5). The interoperable, universal combination of these three is touted as having

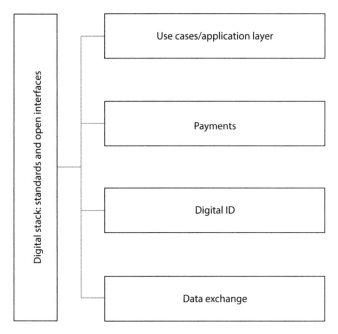

FIGURE 6.5. The digital stack. *Source:* Adapted from
World Bank (2022).

marvellous economic effects, unleashing entrepreneurship and reducing transactions costs.

A specific version of this is known as India Stack,[2] with the country's
Aadhaar digital identity at its core, using biometrics to identify each
resident. Its website states: "Although the name of this project bears the
word India, the vision of India Stack is not limited to one country; it can
be adopted by any nation, be it a developed one or an emerging one.
Having said that, this project was conceptualized and first implemented
in India, where its rapid adoption by billions of individuals and businesses has helped promote financial and social inclusion and positioned
the country for the Internet Age." The country's ambition is stated in
plain sight here: my PhD student Sumedha Deshmukh has traced the
development of this version of digital public infrastructure as an Indian
industrial and export policy, building on India's already leading role as

2. https://indiastack.org/

an IT services exporter (beaten only by Ireland). India has signed several agreements with other countries to provide a version of DPI using its technologies and companies' services. Globally, its main competitor is Estonia's X-Road, also exported to other governments.

The DPI debate is active in the context of development practice, which means there are an awful lot of hype-strewn documents along with the more analytical approaches. But there is little academic literature, although a large and rapidly growing "grey" literature exists. It is even stranger that economists, even those focusing on the digital economy, have paid little attention to the process of digitising government activities. (The exception is the research hyperactivity around central bank digital currencies, not an issue I know much about.) This seems a substantial omission. Economies comprise both private and public sectors, in a mutually dependent relationship. Digital technologies have changed the opportunities to deliver some basic state functions, including identity and payments. It is bad enough that there is scant useful data on digitally enabled commercial activity, but even worse that there is virtual silence about what global production networks, digital services trade, or cross-border data flows in the cloud imply for public infrastructure largely provided by the nation-state. I think the DPI construct is useful, and that countries like the United Kingdom and United States, which have been incrementally digitising their governments, could learn from India's or Estonia's initiatives. A handful of companies have become so powerful that only the systematic use of state power can ensure they share the value that they create, and the value that they extract in monopoly rents, with workers and consumers.

To achieve this, governments will need to ensure they operate a technology stack that gives them points of control over powerful companies. While the concept of digital public infrastructure is mainly prominent in the context of economic development, it has the potential to be considered as a far broader concept, a digital scaffolding to deliver the public good. This will require a change of mindset; digital public infrastructure is commonly seen as a means of delivering government services to individuals. It could be the locus of interaction between the government, businesses, and people. Firms as well as individuals can have a digital identity, and their transactions in any jurisdiction will run through the payments system. The digital infrastructure needs to be put in place to implement policies or collect taxes—such as Paul Romer's proposed tax on digital advertising or even a tax on the number of parcels Amazon sends out to cover the local government costs of waste collection and recycling. A successful market economy has to be a partnership between government and businesses; businesses need a social licence to operate. They may manage their own affairs subject to paying taxes, to operating policies such as collecting employee tax or monitoring immigration status, and to obeying regulations. Too many big businesses are in breach of this implicit contract. They minimize the tax they pay and break laws such as observing copyright. They are no longer even serving their customers well. It is time to put the institutional mechanisms in place that force the sharing of value built on the efforts of many but captured by the few.

This chapter has described a range of aspects of international trade—global production networks, digital services, e-commerce, data, and digital infrastructure—where the data available gives an incomplete picture. The IMF/OECD/WTO handbook on digital trade contains Figure 6.6, which in light of this discussion makes the startling claim that "digital trade" is for the most part included in conventional trade statistics—the dotted boxes in the upper-left sections (DIP stands for "digitally intermediated platforms"). It categorises the transactions of interest in a way that seems to bear no relation to reality. The only aspect it portrays as excluded is non-monetary data, a category that floats by itself, seemingly not linked to any of the economic actors or any of the products, although it is integral to digital trade. I disagree with this bizarre construction and am instead with experts on global production networks like Richard Baldwin and my colleague Vasco Carvalho in observing the inadequacy of the data needed to understand these significant economic phenomena. Current data are constructed around economic relationships and conceptual frameworks that are decades out of date. The statistics needed to understand the global economy are not only better trade figures, especially on services, but also a mapping of the infrastructure involved across the whole stack.

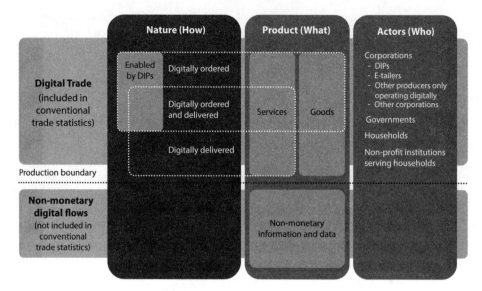

FIGURE 6.6. A conceptual framework for digital trade. *Source:* IMF, OECD, UNCTAD, and WTO (2023). *Note:* DIPs refer to "digitally intermediated platforms."

Conclusion

This chapter has been about another set of features of the economy that are invisible in standard statistics, those that cross borders. For the most part, the phenomena such as global production networks, digital services trade, and cross-border e-commerce are somewhat familiar, understood to be extensive in scale and scope, and have generated substantial or at least reasonable research literatures. But there are also some omissions in what economists have been analysing in the digital-ised globalised world of production and consumption, and such silences are revealing. Data flows across borders are not measured at all. Mainstream economics has generally paid little attention to the digital stack although it is fundamentally important to the digital economy, perhaps because India is middle income, Estonia is small and ex-USSR. I am inclined to think that ignoring the infrastructure aspects of global digitalisation is of a piece with economists' lack of interest in the role of infrastructure in general (save for deep but narrow interest in some aspects, such as the operation of electricity markets).

It is surely also apparent to readers, six chapters in, that the invisibility of the economy as it is now in the statistics available is extraordinary. The final chapter of this book will return to the broad "hard-to-measure" issue: what might be an appropriate framework for better understanding and measuring an economy whose value added is increasingly intangible due to digital technologies, and thus hard to confine within boundaries—either geographic or sectoral—and with characteristics that contrast with physical goods (non-rival rather than rival, increasing rather than constant returns to scale, and therefore featuring many externalities). This chapter and the preceding ones have illustrated some specific gaps: statistics on time use, digital adoption, new modes of work, cloud computing, cross-border digital transactions, data on data, and so on. In short, the surveys on which so many official statistics are based need revising—quickly and frequently—to track observed new types of activity, and new methods of data collection will likely be needed. This will require statistical agencies to invest in innovation, and probably to spend less on traditional statistics given the state of their budgets.

First, the next two chapters broaden the discussion, turning from descriptions of what is not being measured well currently to the fundamental question of why better measurement is important. They are concerned with economic welfare—or in other words, progress. Economic statistics are partly descriptive but also partly prescriptive and normative. Growth in real terms GDP is widely taken as a measure of economic progress, and indeed it is highly correlated over time with things we would sensibly value, such as life expectancy or well-being. But it is an imperfect measure of welfare and, for reasons I have discussed elsewhere, a decreasingly good measure (Coyle 2014). So the next chapter will look at price indices to offer one perspective on why changes in economic welfare are currently not well measured because qualitative change is not well accounted for, and the following chapter introduces the economy's balance sheet, including natural resources, as fundamental for evaluating sustainability and thus the scope for progress into the future.

7

Value

DURING THE HIGH INFLATION YEARS of the mid- to late 1970s, I was an impressionable teenager and observed how my working mother worried about feeding the family as the price of staples such as tea, flour, and vegetables shot up. She had been newly married with very young children during the years of postwar rationing (and sometimes reminisced about going without meals herself, fuelled only by sweet tea). These memories of going short in the 1950s turned her into a commodities stockpiler, on a modest scale, two decades later. We had a cupboard piled with sugar and flour and tea bought when they were available on offer. It obviously stuck with me as I now have a cupboard at home we call our air raid shelter, similarly stocked up—and very useful it was during the more recent post-Brexit and post-lockdown shortages. This personal experience has made me wary about inflation, knowing how it played havoc with working-class families in the seventies; it is no surprise that the recent surge has been so unpopular politically. It also meant that until relatively recently in my career as an economist, I had not thought much about how inflation is measured. *Of course* we want to adjust nominal values by a price index to understand how high inflation is and how much GDP, and people's incomes, are changing in real terms.

But starting a decade ago when writing my book about GDP (Coyle 2014), the process of deflation started to seem more puzzling. A comment I found in a chapter by Thomas Schelling crystallised the puzzle: "What we call 'real' magnitudes are not completely real; only the money

IMAGE 7.1. Postwar. © Diane Coyle.

magnitudes are real. The 'real' ones are hypothetical" (Schelling 1958). This chapter is about what he meant, and how to start thinking about "real" value created in the economy. GDP is described as a value added measure as if this is a technical, definitional matter yet it embeds a normative concept of value, which is precisely what the Beyond GDP movement challenges.

The question of value goes to the heart of Zvi's "hard-to-measure" conundrum. Our intuition is to think of nominal amounts as divisible into price times quantity: a car manufacturer sells a million cars at $12,000 each, or a restaurant eighty meals at an average of $100 each. So nominal GDP divided by a price index combining the prices of all goods and services is then real or volume-terms GDP. But this entity has no natural units; there is no metric combining cars, meals, management consultancy, smartphones, and everything else. Real GDP is either an index number or expressed in terms of the dollar amount for an arbitrarily chosen base year. There is a further problem in that the composition of products in the economy changes constantly. Consumers are no longer

TABLE 7.1. Hard to Measure: Revenue, Quantity, and Quality

	Price observed	Price not observed
Quantity & quality observed	Some market goods Some market services	Barter transactions
Quantity observed, quality not	Other market goods Other market services	Imputed transactions (owner-occupied housing, FISIM, advertising); public services; household production
Quantity & quality not observed	New delivery models (online platforms)	Free digital services, cryptocurrencies

Source: Author's own.

riding penny-farthing bicycles or taking photos with 35mm cameras, but they are using electric scooters and smartphones. How should disappearing goods and new goods be factored into the price and quantity calculations, and when in fact do they count as new—when is a smartphone a better phone or instead a new kind of device altogether?

Introducing quality change as well makes it yet more complicated. Here too Zvi was a pioneer, recognising that a 1950 car and a 1970 car were not equivalent quantities given all the technological improvements involved. So even if the ticket price of the vehicle had gone up, one would want to adjust it down to account for the improved quality (Griliches 1961, 1994). He introduced the idea of hedonic adjustment for quality improvements, discussed further in this chapter. This technique assumes quality change can be measured as a combination of observable characteristics, for example the speed, memory, disk space, and other features of a laptop. But what if the price charged is the only observable measure of quality, such as the price of a fancy Covent Garden haircut versus the local salon or of a white-shoe law firm compared with the main-street attorney? Table 7.1 provides another way of thinking about the scope of the hard-to-measure problem: most of the economy falls outside the top left-hand box. What is a volume unit of accountancy or nursing or online search? How should their changing quality be taken into account?

What Is a Price Index?

The guru of price indices and author of the 2004 handbook on their statistical construction is Erwin Diewert. He writes at the start of the handbook, "Economics is the study of choice under constraints. Thus the economic approach to index number theory applied to households generally involves the assumption of cost minimising or utility maximising behavior on the part of consumers subject to one or more constraints" (p2). He immediately goes on to accept that this is unrealistic, but useful. This introduction immediately highlights the fact that consumer price indices (CPIs) are based on the microeconomics of utility maximisation. This implies that the deflators applied to two-thirds of GDP, the consumption component, aim to estimate how much of the increase in the nominal GDP amount between two periods is a "real" utility increase and how much is to be designated as inflation. If we are in the world of utility maximisation, this makes real-terms GDP an economic welfare construct. National accountants resist this claim, in part by pointing out that producer price deflators are also used to deflate the revenues in nominal GDP; but the consumption part dominates.

Index number theory is complicated, and the vast technical literature is well captured in the handbook. For my purposes here, it is enough to think about the classic Laspeyres and Paasche index formulae. The Laspeyres calculates the change cost of a basket of goods since a base period:

$$\text{Laspeyres} = \sum_i p_{it} q_{i0} / \sum_i p_{i0} q_{i0} \qquad (7.1)$$

where p_i is the price of good i and q_i its quantity, t is the current period, and 0 is the base period. Equivalently,

$$\text{Laspeyres} = \sum_i s_{i0} * p_{it}/p_{i0} \qquad (7.2)$$

where the s_{i0} are the initial period expenditure shares for each commodity in the basket. Thus, the Laspeyres price index is a weighted average of the price changes for every good and service purchased, and the weights are the expenditure share of each good in the *initial period*. A Laspeyres index tells you what *out of the goods available yesterday* you could buy with today's money. An alternative price index is the Paasche index, which uses *current-period* weights.

$$\text{Paasche} = \sum_i p_{it} q_{it} / \sum_i p_{i0} q_{it} \sum_i s_{it} * p_{it} / p_{i0} \qquad (7.3)$$

The Laspeyres index therefore calculates what has happened today to the cost of *yesterday's* basket of goods, while the Paasche index calculates how the cost of *today's* basket of goods has changed since yesterday. There is always journalistic excitement in the United Kingdom in February each year when the ONS announces which items are being dropped from the CPI basket and which added, reflecting changing spending patterns. For instance, in March 2023, out of an initial 743 items, 16 were dropped and 23 added; e-bikes and surveillance cameras were in, digital compact cameras and "spirit-based drinks" out.

Many official price indices are variants of the Laspeyres. The US Bureau of Economic Analysis uses a Fisher index to deflate GDP that combines the Laspeyres and Paasche indices by taking their geometric mean.

$$\text{Fisher} = \sqrt{\left[\frac{\sum_i p_{it} q_{i0}}{\sum_i p_{i0} q_{i0}}\right] * \left[\frac{\sum_i p_{it} q_{it}}{\sum_i p_{i0} q_{it}}\right]} \qquad (7.4)$$

So if the Laspeyres inflation rate is 12 per cent and the Paasche inflation rate is 8 per cent, the Fisher inflation rate would be $\sqrt{(1.12)*(1.08)} - 1 = 9.98$ per cent. The Fisher is a "superlative" index, whose merit—if the consumption baskets are the same in each period—is that it will allow calculation of how much a consumer will need compared with the previous period to keep their utility constant.

Problems with Consumer Price Indices

The formulae will be familiar from economic textbooks, although the statistical practice is naturally more complicated. A blog post by Brad DeLong in 1998 first opened my eyes to the philosophical conundrum. The question he posed was the same as mine: "How fast is modern economic growth?" The post was prompted by mid-1990s claims that official inflation measures were greatly overstating inflation and therefore understating what could be considered as real economic growth because they failed to account for technological progress and quality change. The blog post points out that this must be correct because the price indices do not account for changes in the availability of goods and services at different times. The Laspeyres is measuring increases in the price of goods available in the past, so so-called real income calculated using it tells us how much better off we are now than then if confined to buying only products available then, and conversely with the Paasche. Superlative indices have their nice constant utility properties when the component items are the same in both periods. However, new products are without question the source of tremendous increases in utility, whether amazing medical discoveries that prolong healthy lives or everyday innovations such as a new flavour of breakfast cereal (Hausman 1996).

In consumer theory the concept of the Hicksian reservation price is the price at which the demand for a good would be zero—it is where the demand curve hits the vertical axis of the price-quantity diagram. The reservation prices for obsolete products will be lower than the price of new products, especially when those new products deliver a lot of utility: How much would you have paid for an antibiotic if suffering from a serious infection in the late nineteenth century (Landes 1998)? A (supposedly) constant-utility deflator will overstate inflation and understate real growth if it omits or underplays the product churn, and indeed price indices for goods with rapid technology progress are likely to be biased upward (Diewert et al. 2018).

There is another problem, less often remarked. It is the assumption in the underlying theory that consumers can substitute readily between different products. The index number formulae used in practice also assume homotheticity, which means the ratios of quantities demanded for different products depend only on their relative prices, not on either the quantity consumed or on the consumer's level of income. As Erwin Diewert drily observes, "This assumption is not strictly justified from the viewpoint of actual economic behavior, but . . . it leads to economic price indexes that do not depend on the consumer's standard of living" (p8). "Not strictly justified" is a nice understatement. It is abundantly clear that the composition of people's expenditure shifts substantially when their incomes increase or fall; people on low incomes spend a much larger share of their money on food, energy, and accommodation.

The amount they spend on going out for meals or taking holidays does not depend on the relative price of these leisure goods to food. The same is true within categories: there is even the concept of a Giffen good, whose consumption increases when its price rises because the higher price reduces their spending power; inferior staple foods are the standard example. The choice between own-brand pasta and Wagyu beef does not depend only on their relative prices.

This issue has come to the fore given the recent surge in inflation. Campaigners on poverty specifically attacked the way inflation is measured. In the United Kingdom the ONS (2023b) responded by restarting publication of distinct consumer price indices for different income levels (based on the same dataset of price observations but different baskets for each group), and committed to collecting a much broader range of price data:

> If one variety of apple goes up in price while another falls, do some people switch varieties to avoid a price rise? And given that people of different means undoubtedly buy different varieties of products, what happens to the price of own brand versus branded baked beans? We are currently developing radical new plans to increase the number of price points dramatically each month from 180,000 to hundreds of millions, using prices sent to us directly from supermarket checkouts. This will mean we won't just include one apple in a shop—picked to be representative based on shelf space and market intelligence—but how much every apple costs, and how many of each type were purchased, in many more shops in every area of the country.

In the United States the BLS has similarly experimented with calculating indices for households at different income levels based on differing expenditure shares (but again using the same underlying price data) (Klick and Stockburger 2021). The differences in inflation rates can be considerable, as Figure 7.1 illustrates. Similarly, one can think of constructing different indices for different populations, such as older people with fixed savings or pensions, or working-class families with four kids like mine in the 1970s, or urban professionals. There is growing interest in "democratic" price indices in particular in the research literature (Aitken and Weale 2020, Martin 2022).

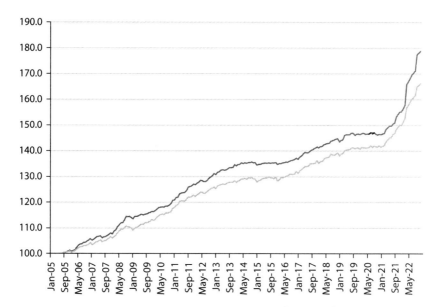

FIGURE 7.1. Consumer price index for poorest (light line) and richest (dark line) tenths of the UK population. September 2005 = 100. *Source:* ONS.

Inflation statistics are a good example of the use of the authority of expertly constructed numbers to claim objectivity (Porter 1995). They are among the most politically fraught official statistics. When pension payments or debt interest payments on government bonds are linked to a particular price index, any technical change to the index will create groups of losers; so the Boskin Report in the United States was controversial in its view that inflation was lower than measured (Gordon 1999), while in the United Kingdom the ONS's valid technical objections to the use of the Retail Price Index (RPI) was controversial for years because many of those receiving income on their holdings of gilts, or seeing benefits normally uprated by RPI, which generally grew faster than the CPI, would lose out (Giles 2017). Even when there are no contractual issues, there have been political debates about the "true" cost of living. In his superb history of the calculation of price indices in the United States, Thomas Stapleford (2009) illustrates the normative and intrinsically political character of price statistics through an account of the policy debates throughout the twentieth century, such as debates about food prices and the cost of living in the 1930s and 1940s, or the indexing of social security payments in the 1990s: "A full specification of the proper methods for a statistical calculation requires a full speci- fication of its objectives down to a high level of detail, which means that judgments with political valences extend all the way through the calcu- lation process" (p9). Times of high inflation, as experienced recently, often translate debates about economic distribution to the technical arena of price indices.

The conceptual issue with the standard price indices when it comes to these political and distributional points of contention is that there are in practice limited possibilities for substitution between products, whereas index number theory assumes continuous substitutability. It just isn't so, particularly when it comes to questions of distributional fairness. As food prices rise, incomes will need to rise by more for a low-income than for a high-income household to maintain constant utility, given that cheaper toys or laptops are not good substitutes for food. Additionally, low-income consumers may be income constrained and unable to substitute as they would prefer: a price increase may lead to an increasing expenditure share out of necessity. For example, sup- pose that the price of a small car rose and a family became unable to afford it, instead having to use public transport. The family would be likely to perceive it as a significant decline in their standard of living, with the substitution to public transport not affording the same level of utility as before. The assumption that any standard chain-linked price indices reflect the ability of households to minimise their cost of attain- ing a given level of welfare is unlikely to be correct (see Box 7.1).

The implications of non-homothetic utility are normally considered in the context of necessities whose price is rising, such as food. How- ever, they apply also to necessities whose price is declining, such as mobile phones. In the case of some technology goods, though, there may not be a decline in price but rather an improvement in quality such that there are significant quality-adjusted price declines. In the United Kingdom very few goods prices are hedonically adjusted—the practice varies a lot between countries—but the argument is often made that more quality adjustment is needed to calculate "true" price indices; and

Box 7.1 Consumer utility when goods are not perfectly substitutable

The implications of lack of substitutability can be illustrated using a Stone-Geary utility function, often used to represent "needs" or a subsistence level of consumption (this could be taken as social necessities rather than literal survival needs). The utility function takes the following form:

$$U(x_i) = \sum_{i=1}^{n} \ln(x_i - a_i)^{\alpha_i} \qquad (7.5)$$

- Consumption goods x_i, $i = 1, \ldots, n$
- Subsistence levels of consumption of each good a_i
- Parameters a_i

The consumers maximises $U(x_i)$ subject to the budget constraint:

$$y = \sum_{i=1}^{n} x_i p_i \qquad (7.6)$$

where p_i is the price of good i.

It can be shown that the demand functions for each good are given by the linear expenditure system (LES):

$$x_i = a_i + (\alpha_i / p_i)\left(y - \sum_{j=1}^{n} a_j p_j\right) \qquad (7.7)$$

This is a convenient form for empirical estimation of the demand for goods. However, an implication of the Stone-Geary utility function is that if any x_i is below its required subsistence level a_i then $U(\cdot)$ is undefined. This implies that the standard cost-of-living index, defined as the ratio of the expenditure functions, is also undefined. Hence if a consumer is priced out of something which is (socially or physically) essential, then the usual assumption of smooth substitution between goods does not apply. Indeed, the observed shifts in expenditure shares in many contexts are bigger than those consistent with the LES here. And the inflation statistics are uninformative about the consumer's experienced loss of utility.

thus that "true" inflation is overstated by failure to quality adjust. Low-income consumers might not want to purchase the improved quality, but as there is no choice, it is for them an effective increase in price.

There is a considerable research literature on the distributional consequences of relative price changes. One pioneering contribution was from Muellbauer (1974), who divided goods into luxuries and necessities according to their estimated demand elasticities and constructed constant-utility cost-of-living indices for different household types. Weichenrieder and Gürer (2018) documented higher inflation in the consumption bundles of low-income households in Europe for 2001–2015. For the United States, Argente and Lee (2020) constructed price indices for different income groups and decomposed the changes in these indices for 2004–2016 into four components: product price changes, product substitution, outlet substitution, and new goods bias. Crawford and Oldfield (2002) calculated fixed-weight price indices for different households based on UK expenditure data for 1975–1999. Typically, the literature uses an "ideal" price index, but all these approaches assume that consumers are always able to substitute between purchases to achieve a given level of utility at minimum cost, and that the marginal rates of substitution are determined by relative prices. But low-income households may in effect be rationed in their ability to purchase certain goods, and their inflation rate as measured by conventional price indices is thus understated (Geary 1950). So the research literature has not ignored the issue. But statistical agencies have neither the time nor capacity to do demanding econometric exercises to calculate monthly price indices that have to be published in a timely manner.

Established Methods for Accounting for New Goods and Quality Change

Now, the statisticians who calculate price indices are more aware than anybody of the challenges involved in trying to take account of new goods, more choice, and disappearing goods, and they have various fixes (I discuss these in detail in Coyle 2024b). The main method in practice is *matched models*: when a new washing machine model appears on the market, the price change of the old model will, if available, be used to calculate the price change for the new model. If not available, the statisticians will impute a price using the price of similar items (Groshen et al. 2017). To give a simple example, if the price of the old good at time t is P_t^O and its price is observed for periods t and $t+1$, while the price of the new good P^N is observed only at $t+1$ and $t+2$, then an overlap ratio P_{t+1}^N / P_{t+1}^O will be used to give an implicitly quality-adjusted price of the new good for the base period, P_t^N. Another similar method of implicit quality adjustment is *class mean imputation*, which applies price changes in continuing items judged to be a close substitute as a proxy for the new item whose price is missing. Such approaches have the merit of practicality and are widely used by statistical agencies.

The approach more prominent in the academic literature is hedonic price adjustment. This method requires data on quantifiable characteristics of quality—such as memory and processing speed for computers. The hedonic regression estimates an implicit price for each characteristic. The price differential due to quality change can be used to adjust the index. For example, if a hedonic regression estimates that additional memory and a faster microprocessor increase the prices of laptops by $500, then this amount would be deducted from the difference between the price of the new computer model with the extra memory and faster chip and the price of the old model that it replaced. The characteristics included in the model depend on what indicators are available in practice even though other unobserved characteristics may be important (Erickson and Pakes 2011). The items hedonically adjusted by statistical agencies vary a lot between countries. In the United Kingdom adjustment involves very few consumer electronic items, such as smartphones; in the United States the Bureau of Labor Statistics (BLS) adjusts for a much wider range, including washers, refrigerators, and microwaves. Some countries adjust for quality changes in clothing or in used cars. None as far as I am aware apply the method to services prices. So although it appeals in terms of its clear link to utility theory, hedonic adjustment is arbitrarily applied in practice.

The other conventional methods available for tackling new and improved products involve econometric estimation, so they are too resource intensive and slow to be useful for constructing regular economic statistics. Many researchers have estimated Hicksian reservation prices or demand functions. One widely used approach due to Feenstra (1994) adjusts the matched-model price index previously described, which includes only the continuing varieties, by using the market shares of the continuing varieties (their share of total spending) in the periods being compared and the estimated elasticity of substitution between varieties. If the expenditure share of the new varieties in the final period exceeds the expenditure share of the disappearing varieties in the initial period, this suggests that consumers like the new varieties more, and the magnitude of the welfare gain (and hence downward adjustment to price) depends on the extent of substitution between varieties: Is the substitution a new variety of orange juice or a brand-new mixed-citrus variety with added kombucha? The availability of scanner data has made this approach popular in the literature. It tends to find that inflation measures should be adjusted downwards.

Do the Problems with Deflators Matter?

How much does the challenge posed by new goods and varieties matter for understanding real-terms output growth, or economic progress? In the United States a series of authoritative reports have estimated the extent to which consumer price inflation has been overstated because the effects of new goods and technological quality improvements have been omitted. The Stigler Commission (1961) first concluded that CPI inflation in the 1950s was overstated due to the failure to account for quality change. The Boskin Commission (1996) calculated that published US inflation was overstated by an average of 1.1 percentage points a year, of which 0.6 percentage points a year were due to quality change and new product bias. These are not insignificant numbers in the context of a published inflation rate that was not high in each case. But a recent defence of US statistical practice (Groshen et al. 2017) argues that current methods mitigate some of the biases these reports had identified, so the degree of overstatement of CPI inflation is likely to be considerably lower now than in the 1990s. The paper specifically considers digital phenomena such as free consumer goods and claims they do not imply price mismeasurement: "All told, we believe that concerns about a downward bias on output are overstated because for most cases mentioned, either the value of these products is outside the scope of GDP or is embedded in other measured market activity." Moulton (2018) updated the Boskin approach and found the US CPI bias had fallen to 0.85 per cent a year, somewhat lower than the earlier finding. An IMF/OECD study (Reinsdorf and Schreyer 2020) also considered digital economy implications for prices, aiming to put an upper limit on the impact on measured inflation of different phenomena from free digital goods to quality change to substitution of digital for physical products. They conclude the overall impact on the GDP deflator is a reduction of about 0.5 percentage points: "A correction in the order of over half a percentage point to annual real consumption growth would be significant. Nonetheless more than half of the gap between the post-slowdown and pre-slowdown rates of productivity growth would remain even without considering the corrections for sources of mismeasurement in the pre-lowdown era" (p341).

A different view is taken by other researchers. For example, Goolsbee and Klenow (2018) investigated online prices compared with offline and estimated that if substitution to online goods were better accounted for, CPI inflation in the United States would be a whole two percentage points lower than implied by the best (matching-models) method used by the BLS. Byrne and Corrado (2020) estimate the decline in price for what they term "consumer digital access services," that is, internet access, mobile, streaming services, and cable TV. The official prices for these increased slightly from 1988 to 2018, whereas an alternative price index based on spending on each category divided by volume of use declined substantially and by a faster amount each decade, an annual minus 19 per cent from 2008 to 2018. So the bias in this part of the CPI has been increasing, they argue.

There seem to be some deep challenges that in part account for the divergent views about the extent of inflation mismeasurement (overstatement for digital goods, understatement for the kind of products low-income people purchase). Think about the hedonic adjustment often considered to be the best method for accounting for quality change. Its aim is to estimate the supposedly true cost of living in utility terms. One issue is that the greater the hedonic adjustment, the bigger the gap between the actual price paid and the estimated price. It might not be possible to buy the older model, yet consumers will need to be able to pay the actual price for the new model whether they want the new features or not—or can afford them or not. For example, if my ten-year-old washing machine breaks down, I will need to pay £100 more than its original price to replace it, even if the new one has improved features such as greater energy efficiency or more programmes.

Another issue arises from the way price indices are used to estimate real output growth rates. Applying a hedonically adjusted index introduces abstract utility considerations into reality with some paradoxical implications. Think about an electronic product like a mobile phone whose quality improvements have consisted of packing more and more features into ever-smaller and lighter physical space—one of the manifestations of increasing weightlessness. A hedonic index will imply much faster growth in mobile phone handset output than an index that does not take account of characteristics such as the chip set, camera quality, processing power, and so on. Imagine that we reach a point where all the technology in the handset could be captured in one chip implanted in your hand. The "real" output of mobile handsets would have increased enormously when there is almost no physical output and consumers are paying for smart tattoos. The "real" output or genuine economic value in this case is—as Schelling observed—all imaginary, the ideas. There is something odd about the exercise of calculating an inflation rate for ideas. (Milton Gilbert, one of the architects of the current SNA, had this debate with Zvi Griliches in the early days of hedonics, using the example of swimsuits: hedonic adjustment would show increasing real-terms output thanks to improvements in fabrics and methods of construction, even as the volume of fabric decreased between voluminous nineteenth-century outfits and twentieth-century trunks or bikinis.)

The issue is the constant utility construct for measuring inflation. Philip Trammell (2023) makes a powerful case against the idea that consumer welfare can be captured by a unidimensional measure over consumption. More consumption of existing products is treated as equivalent to the consumption of new products. He argues that this greatly understates the welfare benefits of at least some new products. In a vivid example, he compares the utility of a modern-day middle-class Westerner with that of a member of the thirteenth-century Golden Horde that swept across middle Europe. We have no trouble accepting that the former has much higher economic welfare than the latter, even though they have far fewer horses, because they have modern medicines, indoor plumbing, iPhones, and so on. Trammell thinks this makes a focus on price measurement to get at any utility metric a hopeless task: "No adjustments to price indices can allow for welfare-relevant unidimensional consumption comparisons across periods following the introduction of new products." He advocates instead understanding the welfare effects of long-term growth by thinking in terms of multidimensional utility functions which depend on the number of products, a number that can change. Trammell argues, I think convincingly, that the attempt to construct a cost-of-living index that will enable construction of a supposedly real-income and consumption aggregate is not well defined whenever the question is one of defining later-period outcomes in terms of earlier-period products—which is exactly the perspective of the Laspeyres index and similar ones, widely used in constructing inflation statistics for reasons of data availability, timeliness, and practicality. Even a Paasche-style index is problematic because of the large welfare increments created by some new goods.

For short periods these issues are not too serious. For purposes such as monetary policy, it is entirely reasonable to use any of the standard deflator types, as even if an amazing new product is introduced, it will take time to be used and account for a sizeable share of expenditure. But over any length of time—as few as five years with some digital services given their speed of diffusion—the exercise is close to meaningless. Is there any hope for comparing standards of living in different eras? Keynes (1930, p97) wrote: "If we want to compile a Consumption Index-Number for the value of gold or silver over the past 3000 years, I doubt we can do better than to base on composite on the price of

TABLE 7.2. Prices and Hours in 1990 and 2019, Selected Goods

	1990	Hours at median 1990 wage (£8.97)	2019 closest match	Hours at median 2019 wage (£14.31)
Small car	£8,000.00	891 hrs 52 mins	£15,000.00	1048 hrs 13 mins
Large white loaf	£0.51	3.4 mins	£1.10	4.6 mins
Fridge/freezer	£279.95	31 hrs 13 mins	£229.99	16 hrs 4 mins
Bottom-of-range adult bike	£84.99	9 hrs 28 mins	£179.99	12 hrs 35 mins
Branded women's jeans	£24.99	2 hrs 47 mins	£139.95	9 hrs 47 mins
Basic vacuum cleaner	£109.99	12 hrs 16 mins	£59.99	4 hrs 12 mins
Men's trainers	£14.99	1 hr 40 mins	£90.00	6 hrs 17 mins
Beef mince per kg	£1.52	10 mins	£6.29	26 mins
Electric cooker	£299.99	33 hrs 27 mins	£319.00	22 hrs 18 mins
Washing machine	£269.99	30 hrs 6 mins	£279.99	19 hrs 34 mins
Takeaway coffee	£0.40	3 mins	£2.55	11 mins
Draught bitter (per pint)	£0.98	7 mins	£3.10	13 mins
Domestic cleaner hourly rate	£2.50	17 mins	£12.50	52 mins
Women's hairdressing cut and blowdry	£8.50	57 mins	£34.00	2 hrs 23 mins
Standard adult evening cinema ticket	£2.50	17 mins	£11.95	50 mins
Men's suit	£79.95	8 hrs 55 mins	£79.00	5 hrs 31 mins
Child's coat	£22.99	2 hrs 34 mins	£28.00	1 hr 57 mins

Source: Author's own based on ONS data (2017, 2023).

wheat and the price of a day's labour throughout that period. We cannot hope to find a ratio of equivalent satisfaction for gladiators against cinemas." Brad DeLong's 1998 blog post, mentioned earlier, compared the number of hours a median earner would need to work to buy certain standard goods from the Montgomery Ward catalogue in 1895 and in 1995. He concluded that the average American worker in 1995 needed to work one-sixth as many hours as their 1895 counterpart to pay for a representative selection of consumer goods available in both periods. Table 7.2 shows a similar comparison for a selection of products in the United Kingdom in 1900 and 2019.

For many of these items, there has been a substantial increase in the hours of work needed to purchase similar items, although the modern versions will generally be higher quality. Looking at the longer list of items, hospitality items such as takeaway drinks and services such as repairs and cleaning, hairdressing, and cinema tickets all consistently require longer hours of work now to purchase them than in 1990. Among foods, meat requires more labour hours but fresh fruit and vegetables fewer. On the other hand, many items of clothing and household appliances are generally cheaper in terms of labour hours. More hours had to be worked in 2019 to pay for a small car or an adult's bike. The price of basic versions has risen over time even though the quality has also improved a lot—compare basic trainers or a car in 1990 to one now. But people still have to pay the actual price for the item. In a blog post about a book coauthored with Arjun Jayadev, J. W. Mason sets out the problem clearly:

> Human productive activity is not in itself describable in terms of aggregate quantities. Obviously particular physical quantities, like the materials in this building, do exist. But there is no way to make a quantitative comparison between these heterogeneous things except on the basis of money prices—prices are not measuring any preexisting value. Prices within an exchange community are objective, from the point of view of those within the community. But there is no logically consistent procedure for comparing "real" output once you leave boundaries of a given exchange community, whether across time or between countries. (Mason 2024)

Producer Prices

So far this chapter has focused on consumer prices, but there are equally thorny issues concerning producer prices. For physical products purchased by one firm from another, there are similar questions about quality adjustment. There may have been even more substantial technological progress in some of these than others. For intermediate services the question is again how to distinguish price and quantity: What is the unit delivering economic value? Producer prices also affect the GDP deflator; therefore, they matter for diagnosing the productivity puzzle.

Computers are a good example of the former. Businesses buy much of the same computer equipment that consumers do, such as laptops and routers, but some also buy servers or alternatively computation services from cloud providers who themselves buy servers or—more likely in the case of the hyperscalers—the components to build their own servers. Some of these will be imported, for example, the chips from Taiwan or South Korea; other components will come from elsewhere in Asia. How should a producer price index be constructed? As noted in Chapter 3, business purchases of cloud services are not yet capitalised in company and therefore in the national accounts. It is possible, however, to construct an imperfect price of a cloud computing index (imperfect because no quantity data is available to weight the prices of different services and because there is an expanding product range). Byrne, Corrado, and Sichel (2018) and Coyle and Nguyen (2019, updated by Coyle and Hampton 2023) take slightly different approaches, using web-scraped data from AWS for the United States and United Kingdom, respectively. Both approaches find modest price declines up to 2014, then rapid declines for a while (as Microsoft and Google entered the market) and then more modest declines again. Figure 7.2 shows the pattern for the United Kingdom. The decline in the cost of these intermediate services is not yet taken into account in official economic statistics.

Another lens on the cost to businesses of carrying out computation is to take an engineering-inspired approach to the cost of the fundamental underlying services. David Byrne and coauthors (2023) count transistors per chip coming out of factories (in the five countries that manufacture chips, China, Japan, South Korea, Taiwan, and the United States) as a volume measure to divide into revenues for a price index. They argue this gives a direct quality adjustment, one that is more reliable than a hedonic approach using other product characteristics such as clock speed. My coauthor Lucy Hampton and I were inspired by a classic Nordhaus (2007) paper looking at the cost of carrying out computation over centuries using different technologies, from the abacus through mid-twentieth-century mainframes to modern computers, in terms of the number of instructions per second. In our paper we calculated the cost in terms of several metrics of computation (floating point [FP] and integer [INT] computing, which

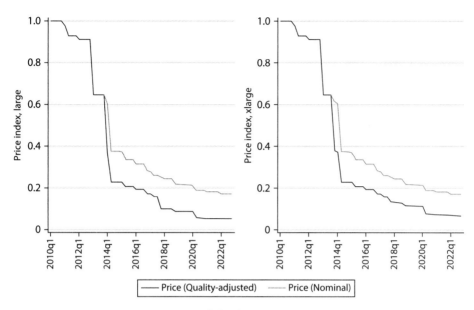

FIGURE 7.2. Price of cloud services, UK, 2010–2022.
Source: Coyle and Hampton (2023).

are further divided into scores for *speed* [time to complete a single task] and *rate* [throughput, or tasks completed in a time]). We patched in the newer types of chip (graphics processing units, or GPUs) to traditional central processing units (CPUs), making assumptions about the pace at which users are transitioning to their use. Both engineering-based approaches find price declines substantially greater than the official producer price index for semiconductors. (Nor did the speed of computation price decline or diverge much before 2015 from the path implied by Moore's Law—and even then not by much, thanks to innovations like GPUs and Tensor Processing Units [TPUs]—in contrast to the widespread assumption noted in Chapter 2 that Moore's Law has slowed.)

The same story of price declines being underestimated in official statistics is true for software as well. Martin Fleming (2023) estimates that the published price index has underestimated software price declines by 6.5 percentage points between 2015 and 2020 (the same index is used in the United States and the United Kingdom). The official index includes only prepackaged software prices and the wages rates of computer programmers and systems analysts creating own-account software. Fleming points out that businesses face a wide range of options in determining how to acquire the software services they need to produce: internal own-produced code, cloud services, other purchased software and services, open-source software. AI will only add to the options available. Some of these will enter into an existing price index; for others like cloud services, one can perhaps envisage a separate price index. But the question of interest to economists is not having a price index for its own sake but rather to understand the economic value due to software creation. For this, the measure we need is a shadow price, "the marginal profit contribution of the functional activity, considering alternative capital allocation in capturing the opportunity cost in choosing one alternative over another" (p2). The shadow price in his paper is calculated as the weighted average of the changes in input prices and wage rates adjusted for productivity change. The conceptual shift the paper proposes is to incorporate the change in the prices of *all* the resources used to create software (adjusted for their productivity changes), weighted by the share of each in total costs.

Yet another example is the case of telecommunications services. My work on this came about because telecoms engineers at the Institute of Engineering and Technology (IET) in the United Kingdom, their professional body, approached ONS to query the official producer price index, which had been flat for years. The engineers objected that this did not seem to reflect reality, neither the post-2007 surge in the use of data services thanks to 5G, Wi-Fi, and smartphones, nor what they as engineers knew about the technological improvements over that period, such as improved compression and reduced latency. We held some workshops that began with learning each other's languages and tussled with the question of what exactly was meant by "quantity" and "price" of these services. For the engineers, only physical metrics made sense; for the economists, the issue is economic value, which can and does diverge from physical quantities such as bytes transmitted. Telecoms companies charge a different price per byte even for similar services; for example, the cost per byte of an SMS message is higher than that per byte of a WhatsApp message. Consumers are steadily switching to the

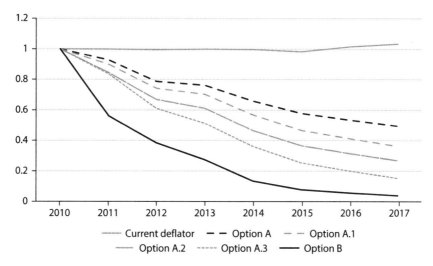

FIGURE 7.3. Price of UK telecommunications services, 2010–2017.
Source: Abdirahman et al. (2020). Note: 2010 = 1.

low-price alternatives, but this process has not been instantaneous. Calculating a price index is further complicated by the existence of a fixed access charge for fixed-line services and the fact that many consumers purchase bundles of data and services for wireless services. In time, working with ONS and IET coauthors, we constructed several alternative telecoms services price indices, shown in Figure 7.3 (Abdirahman et al. 2020, 2022). The original official index is the flat line at the top. A unit value index, telecoms industry revenues divided by bytes of data transmitted over their networks, is shown by the line at the bottom (labelled Option B), which showed a 90 per cent decline. In between are a range depending on things like the allocation of standing charges but fundamentally on the weights used on the different services such as voice calls, SMS, and data services. A unit value index uses pure volume weights: How many bytes of data are used? The line showing the least dramatic decline (Option A, although still a steeper fall than the previous official index) uses revenue weights: What is the share of telco revenues that comes from each service?

The ONS subsequently adopted Option A as the official index, which mainly increased the real output of the telecoms industry but also added to estimated GDP growth in real terms over the period of the revisions, with the change implemented when ONS was also introducing double deflation (of inputs and outputs separately) into the national accounts (ONS 2021).

Which is the correct deflator to use? Revenue weights or volume weights? It is not at all obvious. The choice indicates where we are attributing the creation of economic value. From this perspective, all bytes of data are certainly not equal, and although the telecoms networks have been transmitting vastly greater volumes of data, their contribution to our eventual utility as owners of wires and network equipment to the services we enjoy is surely small. So this implies that pure volume weights would be the wrong choice. On the other hand, using revenue weights seems wrong too: although the telcos are able to charge a higher price for some of their services, this is changing, and in any case the economic value attributable to a message via SMS is the same (or perhaps lower because not encrypted) as exactly the same message via a messenger service. As Shane Greenstein underlined when he commented on our work at a conference, the problem is that most of the valuable innovation has been taking place in downstream sectors whose content is carried on the networks, but the quality improvements on the often unpriced-to-user services are not captured in any price index anywhere: "The GDP accounts were organised for a prior era and do not fit with modern usage," he concluded. We are trying to calculate a price index for an industry which has indeed innovated itself, but the bigger gains to user experience stem from even more dramatic innovations in complementary sectors. These complementary sectors include data centres and cloud computing upstream from use of the communications service, and e-commerce, gaming, streaming services, and search downstream. There are some challenging and as yet unanswered questions raised by the highly technical issues of constructing price indices in this context:

- How should quality improvement in the complementary services be measured?
- Do we need price indices for (mainly) unpriced internet services?

- How do we value a byte or bit of data the same over time? Does its value diminish over time as volume increases?
- What kind of price index is helpful for markets that are linked as complements, particularly in an era of innovation, when price index theory assumes that products are always perfect substitutes?
- Would data on time use be helpful in thinking about prices in this context?

I would add to these questions, emerging from the discussion with Shane, that some of the same issues arise with other forms of infrastructure. These have not yet seen the same pace of innovation, but energy generation might with the transition to net-zero generation. The problem is that demand for any form of infrastructure is derived demand, as picked up in the next chapter.

Prices as Quality Signals

There seems to be an absence of thinking about how to measure inflation when higher prices are the main signal of better quality, which is a feature of many physical goods and many services. Approaches like hedonic regression or demand estimation can tackle the quality-of-goods question, albeit not entirely satisfactorily. With services, it is much harder to do so because quality is often unobservable until after the service has been delivered (if then—think about a new software system) and may lack any easily measurable characteristics in contrast to something like memory size or processing speed for a computer. Consider a haircut. Costs will obviously play a role, so the fancy city centre salon will have to cover higher rents. It might pay higher wages, but this will be partly because it is hiring stylists with a better reputation. Customers will expect a better haircut than if they paid a fraction of the price at the local barbershop, and they will generally be right because otherwise the fancy salon would soon close. If incomes rise and more people choose the expensive haircut, is this simply inflation? Another example: management consultancy. A company like Bain or McKinsey will charge more per billable hour than a less-well-known outfit. Is this because they are actually delivering a better-quality service, or is it that they have managed to establish a brand value? And suppose a statistician wanted to split their revenues into quality-adjusted price and quantity of service; how could they do this when there is no obvious unit of output but only the unit of input (is it billable hours)? Hedonic approaches would not help with this. With services accounting for around four-fifths of US and UK GDP, this is not a minor issue.

As the Eurostat/OECD 2014 handbook on constructing services price indices puts it: "Service output may be hard to identify on purely theoretical grounds, and even more difficult to measure reliably. For example, services may be unique and have to be treated like new products (e.g. various consultancy services) or they can be tailored or bundled in different ways for different users. All this implies complexity and high costs for price measurement" (p13). Given this, it recommends unit value indices for some services, estimation of margins in financial services, and prices based on labour time spent for others such as engineering services. So there are practical means for statisticians to construct deflators. But economists should still ask what these mean in terms of economic value. If the observed contracts in the management consultancy sector reveal an increase in price per billable hour and more hours being contracted, does this mean improved quality (implying demand has risen), reduced efficiency (effective supply has fallen), or something else such as increasing market power and profits?

Conclusion

The measurement of deflators is a subject that quickly becomes highly technical and detailed. The aim of this chapter has been to step back and ask what the purpose is of measuring inflation and thus trying to identify separate price and "real" components. For, as Schelling observed, there is nothing real about this "real" concept. It also introduces some confusion. It is news to a few people that the components of the national accounts do not add up in real terms, only in nominal terms, as different deflators are applied to the different components. Now that the national accounts statistics use chained indices—using each year's

expenditure weights rather than updating the base year periodically—
interpreting the statistics is less intuitive in any case. The weights used
to construct the index change annually, and as this creates two different
levels for the index, they are linked by rescaling one to the other for an
overlap year (ONS 2020a). Again, the real-terms aggregates do not equal
the sum of their real-terms components, with the difference being larger
the larger the change in relative prices, as in recent times with ICT
goods. This is somewhat paradoxical as the reason chain-linking was
introduced was because updates to base years were previously too infre-
quent to cope with the substitutions towards technology goods with
rapidly declining relative prices. Chain-linked data still have a base year
when nominal and real GDP are equal in dollar terms, but it is chosen
arbitrarily. Chained aggregates will grow more slowly than their fixed-
weight counterparts after the selected base year, and faster prior to that
year. In the twenty years since Karl Whelan (2002) wrote his crystal-
clear explainer, mistaken calculations continue to crop up in commentary. Any calculations such as separating out the growth of a particular
sector or shares of one component in GDP or contributions to aggregate
growth made using simple addition or subtraction will be misleading.
(There are of course alternative, correct ways to do such calculations.)

The broader point is that most users of the statistics, including economists, want to use them to answer questions that are either directly
normative—what has been happening to people's standard of living—
or indirectly so—how much a certain sector has contributed to real-
terms growth and productivity. Deflators are at the heart of how economic welfare in the aggregate is understood, by construction, even
though national statisticians often resist the idea. The normative character is exactly why there is a clamour for distributional price indices at
times of high inflation. Real-terms data are a flawed tool for understanding change in economic welfare. The next chapter expands on the need
for a broader economic welfare framework, including the issue of determining shadow prices that reflect social value, rather than the prices
observed in transactions. If the aim is to track economic progress (rather
than something more tightly defined such as to manage the business
cycle), then the observed market prices or exchange values used in

current national accounts statistics are too narrow a lens, not only for currently excluded components of economic activity such as natural capital services but also for the many non-market products, goods, and services produced in non-competitive markets, or those produced subject to increasing returns to scale. The digital revolution and, alongside it, the environmental crisis have led and are leading to such rapid changes in activity and relative prices that they have catalysed the need for a different approach to understanding economic welfare in the aggregate.

8

Wealth

WE ARE ALL MUCH POORER than we think.

We have been using nature for free, and at an accelerating rate since the 1950s. The bill has come due. Awareness of the damage now being caused by climate change has grown, now that parts of the world that are reported in global media (the West Coast of the United States, eastern Australia) are visibly burning because of drought and high winds. More and more of us are becoming aware of the threat to food supplies and human health caused by loss of biodiversity and human encroachment on habitats, thanks to crop failures or zoonotic diseases like Ebola and COVID-19. In the years and decades ahead, there will be reduced potential growth, higher prices, and more disasters like destructive wildfires, hurricanes, floods, and epidemics.

In the rich countries the relative share of economic value that is non-material has been rising (as described in Chapter 1), but the world is increasing its demand on natural resources in absolute terms. Ed Conway's *Material World* (2023) highlights the growth in the human planetary footprint: "In 2019, the latest year of data at the time of writing, we mined, dug and blasted more materials from the earth's surface than the sum total of everything we extracted from the dawn of humanity all the way through to 1950" (p15). The fastest growth is in extraction of minerals—mainly construction materials like sand and rock—which has soared since the mid-twentieth century. Put starkly, we are progressively deforesting and concreting the earth. Figure 8.1 shows the startling journey of global material use from extraction to emissions and

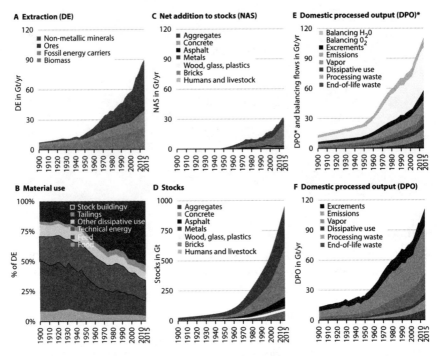

FIGURE 8.1. Global material footprint, 1900–2015.
Source: Krausmann et al. (2018).

waste. Energy use is continuing to grow even though the energy intensity of that growth is declining: data centres in Ireland used almost a fifth of the electricity the country generated in 2022, up from 5 per cent in 2015[1]; China is opening new coal-fired power stations to keep pace with demand, reportedly granting permits for two new stations each week.

There is a similarly alarming story regarding living resources and biodiversity. The latest *Global Assessment Report on Biodiversity and Ecosystem Services* found that fourteen of the eighteen categories of ecosystem assessed had been rapidly deteriorating (IPBES 2019). My revered colleague at Cambridge, Professor Sir Partha Dasgupta, became so famous for his 610-page *Economics of Biodiversity* review (2021) for the UK Treasury that Hollywood actor Alexander Skarsgard made a video

1. https://www.cso.ie/en/releasesandpublications/ep/pdcmec/datacentresmeteredelectri cityconsumption2022/keyfindings/

about him.[2] The review explains the consequences of the economy using nature freely: paying nothing for important inputs into production has enabled faster GDP and income growth to date than would otherwise have been possible, but at some point depleting renewable resources below the level at which they can renew themselves will enforce lower growth in future. Substitutions and technical innovations can postpone that moment. People can eat another type of fish if the population of one type collapses. Improvements in farming methods can increase yields and reduce the incentive to encroach on forests. But some resources will reach irreversible tipping points; it looks like we are there with climate. And as Conway (2023) points out, some non-renewable resource uses are highly specific and their supplies seem constrained; not all sand is the same, and substitutions are not in sight. Technological innovation will in many cases get us a long way and buy some time to change economic behaviour. But the unsustainability is summed up simply:

$$\text{Impact } I = N \times y/a \qquad (8.1)$$

Impact of economic activity on biosphere =
Total population $\times$ per capita GDP $\div$ a

where a is a technology parameter, "a numerical measure of the efficiency with which we are able to convert the biosphere's goods and services into the final products we produce and consume" (Dasgupta 2021). We do not know how big a is; how much of a bet do we want to place on its being big enough not to worry?

Sustainability is generally thought about in terms of the environment. The unsustainable is never sustained, and the fact that unsustainability is upon us is becoming clearer when it comes to nature. But sustainability is a broader concept. Robert Solow's (1991) definition was "that we leave to the future the option or the capacity to be as well off as we are" (p181). What will it take for my grandchildren to have at least as good a standard of living as I do?

2. https://www.youtube.com/watch?v=Ggo07G1XB6A

IMAGE 8.1. The future. © Diane Coyle.

Think about this question in terms of the production function construct introduced early in this book. Successive generations will need to be able to use enough economic inputs to produce at least the same level of output as now for the foreseeable future. The input and output measures are flows, such as labour hours, capital services from machines, goods and services consumed, per unit of time. The production function framework (Figure 8.2) relates flows of capital, labour, energy, and materials services a month (or quarter or year) to flows of output: the

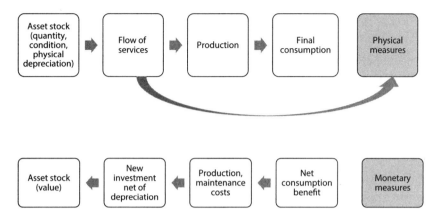

FIGURE 8.2. The economy's production function. *Source:* Author's own.

upper panel shows these in physical terms, such as the use of machine tools and buildings, hours of work, megawatts of power, crop of wheat needed to produce a hundred loaves and the resulting nutrition, and so on. For the output flow per time period to be constant or grow, the flows of input services and hence the asset stocks need to be sufficient (taking account of technological progress that reduces the amount of input needed, and maintenance and depreciation or depletion). The lower panel then shows the flow of monetary value from the payment for final consumption, with deductions for maintenance and depreciation, to the value of the physical assets.

For the most part, economic analysis focuses on the flows rather than on the stock of assets—analogous to thinking about a company's health in terms of its profit and loss rather than its balance sheet. Physical capital is generally readily understood to be fundamental to output and productivity: the number of machines or warehouses, or in the case of infrastructure the generating capacity of power stations or kilometers of rail networks; but productivity calculations involve the flow of capital services, such as hours of machine operation in a factory. Economists do think of the source of labour services in terms of human capital, following Schultz (1961), Becker (1962), and Mincer (1958) in conceiving of people's decisions to learn skills as an investment, with the skills acquired over time subsequently delivering an ongoing flow of labor hours and incomes (Jorgenson and Fraumeni 1989). Businesses will also often claim something like "people are our greatest asset," although one can be cynical about their sincerity. The other inputs—especially those from nature—needed to produce output are more often overlooked in thinking about the economy's health. Although there is a massive amount of research on environmental economics and on developing the relevant environmental statistics, these are not yet mainstreamed into the measurement of productivity, or into the press releases on GDP growth that are the focus for politicians and the media. Moreover, we are completely habituated to working with the flows that are measured in the standard SNA statistics, yet sustainable progress requires measuring the quantity and quality of the assets that generate the required flows of services, too. In effect, the economy needs a comprehensive balance sheet. Without it, it is impossible to evaluate the sustainability of economic activity. Why so, and what are the other assets? To answer this, a framework incorporating and linking the different kinds of asset or capital is needed, usually referred to as the comprehensive wealth approach.

Comprehensive Wealth

If an economy's total stock of wealth—appropriately defined and measured—rises, economic welfare will increase. Given that caveat, this is a statement of logic, straightforwardly demonstrated, as summarised in Box 8.1 (Arrow et al. [2012] and Dasgupta and Maler [2000] give general proofs). A long literature (Hicks 1940, Samuelson 1961, Mirrlees 1969, Sen 1976) has established the normative equivalence between real national income and social well-being, provided the weights being used on goods and services to estimate real national income are shadow prices (sometimes unintuitively referred to as accounting prices), *not* market prices. Weitzman (1998) first set this out in a dynamic context, using the Ramsey (1928) formula to discount the welfare of all future generations. Dasgupta and Maler (2000) assumed that welfare is a non-linear function of consumption and generalised the result that in a dynamic economy, changes in the stock of total wealth, rather than higher income or output flows, correspond to changes in well-being across the

Box 8.1 Comprehensive wealth and economic welfare

A simple version of the result that a change in comprehensive wealth corresponds to a change in welfare is as follows. There are M capital assets, labelled by i. Let $K_i(t)$ be the stock of asset i at time t and $P_i(t)$ be its shadow price. $W(t)$ is the economy's wealth at t and is the sum of the assets over all i, up to M:

$$W(t) = \sum_{i=1}^{M} \left[P_i(t) K_i(t) \right] \tag{8.2}$$

Intergenerational well-being increases from time t if and only if wealth per capita at constant shadow prices increases over that same period. Let $V(t)$ denote intergenerational well-being at t. Then equation (8.2) and the proposition about well-being imply

$$dV(t) = \sum_{i=1}^{M} \left[P_i(t) . dK_i(t) \right] \tag{8.3}$$

If dt is a short interval starting at time t, then

$$dK_i(t) = \sum_{i=1}^{M} \left[dK_i(t) / dt \right] dt$$

which, substituted into (8.3), yields

$$dV(t) = \sum_{i=1}^{M} \left[P_i(t) . dK_i(t) / dt \right] dt \tag{8.4}$$

The right-hand side of equation (8.4) is net investment during the interval dt. That implies that intergenerational well-being increases over the interval if and only if net investment in total wealth is positive in that same period such that its stock increases.

generations. Again, in defining and measuring wealth, the weights that are to be attached to capital assets (including natural capital) are shadow prices, not exchange prices. More on this important qualification later, but this assumption accommodates multiple distortions and externalities; no optimality assumption is needed for the equivalence of an increase in wealth and an increase in welfare.

This is a powerful result because it is straightforward. If we do not measure what is generally called comprehensive (or sometimes inclusive) wealth, and only have statistics on past and current flows such as GDP or income, we are performing an autopsy on the economy looking back rather than providing a diagnosis useful for steering human action and state policy going forward (Agarwala et al. 2024). As the purpose of statistics is to enable the state to govern well, wealth statistics are essential. But this raises the difficult question of what the correct definition of wealth is—which assets should be included? And what about the "appropriate" measurement of its components, particularly the shadow prices that make (8.3) a meaningful economic welfare statement?

Classifying the Components of Comprehensive Wealth

There are different ways of classifying the assets that are required to enable sustainable economic production and consumption. The World Bank's research program on comprehensive wealth categorises the national balance sheet into produced (or physical), natural, human capitals, and net financial capital (World Bank 2021). My research team has used the "Six Capitals" approach that is now becoming increasingly popular in business: physical or produced capital and human, natural, social, institutional, and knowledge/intangible capital. These are a mix of the material (physical, natural, human) and non-material (the rest). Partha Dasgupta (2011) describes these three latter non-material assets as "enabling" assets, arguing that in practice they cannot be distinguished from his a or the technology parameter A of a standard production function. In other words, they are aspects of social organisation and the use of knowledge that shift the production function rather than entering it as factors of production. This distinction is not identifiable empirically. In any case, it is important to think about measuring the non-material assets because the size of the *a* matters.

It is worth appreciating the magnitude of the broader set of assets that are generally not counted in official statistics, compared with the ones that are. Figure 8.3 sets out the relationships—not to scale but giving some indication of relative importance. Some parts of natural and intangible capital (shaded in the figure) are already classified in official statistics as lying within the asset boundary of the economy in the national accounts and so inside the production boundary for the associated flows, but these are almost certainly small proportions of the total. Human capital estimates are published in many countries but not as part of the national accounts; these include skills and education, but not yet health. Work in incorporating health into human capital is nascent (e.g., O'Mahony and Samek 2021, Gu 2024). Both World Bank and national estimates nevertheless show that human capital is far larger than produced capital, although their published figures are also probably underestimates.

Similarly, the natural capital estimate is smaller than the true total, as the available figures cover only a part of nature. Collecting these statistics is in its infancy. The United Kingdom's ONS has been a pioneer and is continuing to expand its statistics on comprehensive wealth (Taylor et al. 2024), as has Statistics Netherlands, whereas the United States started on official natural capital statistics only in 2023, and many countries do not yet collect much of the relevant data. Some produced capital is also uncounted in practice in the national accounts, although it is in theory; for example, historic buildings, collections, and unique assets such as the Crown Jewels are not included (see Bakhshi et al. 2023), although they produce cultural capital services that may act as an intangible input into the creative industries sector, tourism for example. Data on infrastructure (private and public) and public capital (or parts of soft infrastructure, such as schools and hospital buildings) is generally patchy. Organisational and social capital are concepts that, empirically,

are positively correlated with economic outcomes and perhaps ame-
nable to policy action. In much of the economic literature, social capital
is either measured as "trust" from survey data or referred to as "institutions," considered as fundamentally important for economic development (e.g., Acemoglu and Robinson 2012) and perhaps measured by
some composite indicator. It is an indicator of how effectively a society
can collectively organise the allocation of resources, so concerns the
relationships between people, and is multidimensional. Organisational
capital is a similar concept at the level of economic entities such as businesses and is sometimes considered a component of a firm's intangible
capital. Some businesses are run better than others, with more efficient
processes, better management, and strong brands, characteristics that
do not depend on the skills of particular individuals. There is no settled
way to classify these different types of asset, all discussed later in this
chapter, and in any case most of them are not well measured. Yet we
would have no economy without them.

Figure 8.3 thus sets out a schematic of the comprehensive balance
sheet, giving the UK 2020 estimates in figures where available but using
the size of the rectangle to roughly indicate true relative scale (although
as noted earlier, my colleague Partha would put intangibles in the same
enabling category as social and organisational capital, while Mordecai
Kurz [2023] argues that they are entirely indicators of monopoly rents;
these are included in the figure given that official statistics on them are
increasingly being collected and reported). As these are official statistics, the monetary figures use exchange values—either a market price
or equivalent, or a cost of investment—because this is what the SNA
requires. Sometimes in the literature the distinction is made that *comprehensive wealth* uses exchange values to value the assets, and *inclusive
wealth* uses shadow prices that reflect social values; but this is not a firm
descriptive convention (I use *comprehensive wealth* as the term in this
book). The hatched square in the centre of the figure is what is formally
on the nation's balance sheet; there are some small overlaps, as part of
natural and intangible capital are already in the SNA. But what is formally counted now is a small part of the assets needed to support current living standards and future sustainable growth. The figure is set out

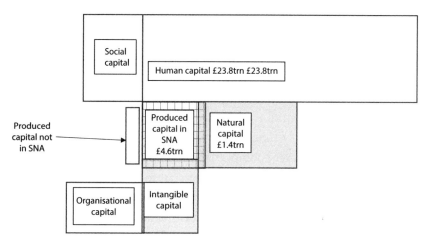

FIGURE 8.3. Comprehensive wealth. *Source:* Author's own based on
ONS data for 2022.

to illustrate overlaps and likely correlations: for example, nature has an
impact on human health and well-being, and individual human capital
will be related to collective social capital.

Official statistics are on this measurement journey. The current standard, SNA08, defines an asset as "a store of value representing a benefit
or series of benefits accruing to the economic owner by holding or using
the entity over a period of time. It is a means of carrying forward value
from one accounting period to another." The 2025 revision of the SNA
will incorporate more intangible assets and will start to integrate natural
capital measures on the SEEA basis (that is, valued at exchange values)
into the statistics. It remains to be seen whether the reporting by statistical agencies will change after 2025—will they continue to headline
short-term changes in GDP, or will they net off the decline in natural
capital during the reporting period? The agencies are also working on
human capital measures that account for health status, given impetus
by the experience of the pandemic and the subsequent increase in long-
term illness or withdrawal from the labour market. These various assets
and corresponding flows will be valued at exchange values, so will not
lead to immediate economic welfare conclusions. At the same time,
many of the components of comprehensive wealth will not be

incorporated in the SNA because they do not meet the criteria of being produced assets (rather than naturally occurring, non-produced assets) with an economic owner. Many economically important natural capital assets are not owned. But this means the accounts will continue to omit important sources of economic growth and welfare—such as Earth's oceans or a healthy workforce.

The remainder of this chapter will give some necessarily brief summaries of the different components of comprehensive wealth (each has its own large research literature). First, it focuses on what can turn the accounting into an economic welfare exercise. Given quantities of the material assets, these can be valued either at something like market prices or at shadow prices; what can be said about estimating shadow prices? Then I address the deep concerns many people have about bringing an economic lens to bear on certain assets at all. What is the ethical status of thinking about human progress in terms of assets and wealth?

Shadow Prices

For understandable reasons, economists like to use prices based on people's actual behaviour, namely revealed preference. Ideally, this would be prices observed in actual transactions, market prices. Failing that, a market-based or exchange value such as the costs of production, or a unit value index based on observed revenues and quantities, would be preferred. This is partly because the presumption is that actual behaviour must reflect people's true preferences, and partly because according to the fundamental welfare theorems, market outcomes are optimal (subject to a set of assumptions that are rarely valid in practice). In any case, economists consider this approach to be better than the available alternatives, in particular better than any form of stated preference values: what people *do* seems more solid than what people *say*. Unfortunately, some assets or economic goods have no price, ranging from online search to the survival of an ecosystem. In other cases, even where there is an observable price, the externalities, or the public good characteristics of the product in question, make the market price an egregiously bad gauge of economic welfare—think of prevailing prices in carbon markets, generally lower than the social cost of carbon, or the (zero) price of a visit to the Library of Congress. This matters for businesses as well as national accountants; as one recent paper (Cairns and Davis 2024) on the value of non-marketed capital observes, "While non-marketed assets do not have market prices, they are essential components of a firm or project's value."

The range of alternative approaches to estimating shadow prices is limited, and it urgently needs further thought and research, including empirical applications. There are two broad avenues to follow. One is to refine and make systematic use of stated preference methods. These are widely used for individual studies in the fields of environmental and cultural economics. The extensive use of contingent valuation methods, in particular for environmental values, was boosted by the report of the expert commission led by Kenneth Arrow (Arrow et al. 1993) in the wake of the 1989 Exxon Valdez disaster (to better inform the subsequent lawsuits), which set out the prevailing understanding of best practice in contingent valuation exercises. However, sentiment in the economics profession toward the method of surveying people to ask how much they would be willing to accept (WTA) to lose an amenity or willing to pay (WTP) to gain it is well exemplified by a pair of articles by Jerry Hausman. In the first (Diamond and Hausman 1994) he concluded that the method left much to be desired but "some number is better than no number." In the second (2012) he reversed, saying the numbers uncovered by the method are "hopeless." On the other hand, the profession has not provided much alternative (Blinder 1991). Moreover, the stated preference methodology has progressed substantially (see McFadden and Train 2017 for a relatively recent survey and critique), in particular in implementing incentive compatibility to reduce survey biases or using discrete choice approaches to enforce consistency in what people state. There are some pioneering approaches to using stated preference and survey methods at scale to create aggregate economic statistics for digital products (Brynjolfsson et al. 2019a, 2019b, 2020, Coyle and Nguyen 2023). More economists are also interested in using surveys in general to generate relevant data that would not otherwise be available (Stantcheva 2023, Almås et al. 2023). With well-designed surveys or experiments, what people say may be sufficiently reliable.

A significant limitation, however, is that the method is well suited to economic products that people understand, but not to those more distant from everyday life, whether that is biodiversity or the Apache open-source software that underpins the internet. Similarly, some things people actively dislike—like wasps—may be vital to ecosystem health. Yet given the absence of data for so many of the most important economic issues, whether the environment or the digital economy, there is no excuse for dismissing such approaches to estimating values, although much work still needs to be done on improving and scaling them. I think it is not often fully realised that many existing, conventional economic statistics rely on statistical agencies sending surveys to millions of businesses and households in any case; they are asking for data points rather than opinions, but they are nevertheless survey based and there is without question considerable reporting error. Once, when I did a public talk about GDP, an audience member revealed that his job used to be filling out the ONS survey for his employer, a giant corporation. As it was a hassle, he said he used to just add a plausible increase to the previous survey responses. After more than a decade of development, there is now a standard digital format for company reporting, the eXtensible Business Reporting Language (XBRL) open-data format for tagging components of company financial reports. UK and many US companies are now legally required to use it, and it is used in about sixty countries.[3] Digitalisation will perhaps improve the accuracy of such statistics, but the survey has been effectively pushed from corporate bureaucrats to their accountants.

There is also another set of possibilities for estimating shadow prices using revealed preference methods even where there is no readily observable market price or cost. Again, the basic approaches such as hedonic regressions and estimates of defensive expenditure are well known and used in the environmental economics literature. Fenichel

3. In the United States, domestic and foreign companies subject to standard accounting rules have been required to report using XBRL since 2009, https://www.fasb.org/page/PageContent?pageId=/staticpages/what-is-xbrl.html&isstaticpage=true; while in the United Kingdom companies have had to send their tax returns using iXBRL since 2010: https://www.gov.uk/government/publications/xbrl-guide-for-uk-businesses/xbrl-guide-for-uk-businesses

and Abbott (2014), for instance, demonstrate an empirical approach to estimating environmental shadow prices rooted in both standard capital theory and in biological science, where the price is equal to the marginal service flow from the natural asset. They estimate a range of empirical values for Gulf of Mexico fish stocks as an application. Their method requires assumptions and approximations, but then so do many existing economic statistics. The method involves incorporating not only an assumed discount-rate level (contentious in this literature) but also the behavioural and institutional feedbacks to changes in the asset's stock over time. They write: "Our framework concretely illustrates the necessity of incorporating the two-way feedbacks between natural systems and human behaviour under nonidealised economic programs when valuing natural capital. Valuation without incorporating feedbacks is incomplete" (p23). It is theoretically robust but unrealistically complicated for everyday statistical production. But, as they observe, empirical efforts are essential if natural capital is to move from the realm of metaphor to being a useful statistic guiding human behaviour.

This is an important research agenda for economists and statisticians. It matters for comprehensive wealth accounting and applies to a wide range of assets that support the use of resources in creating economic value. This includes natural capital, digital assets such as data, other intangibles, infrastructure including both digital infrastructure and physical assets, public goods, and cultural and heritage assets. Many economic transactions do not occur in a market, and even if they do, it is likely not a competitive market. Using market prices only is to wear blinkers, while facing backwards, in understanding the state of the economy and its future prospects.

Sustainability and the Ethics of Growth

Economists aim to understand societal progress in economic terms. Many people find this discomforting or even abhorrent. Advocates of "degrowth" challenge the ethics of further growth of any kind, sustainable or not. Theirs is a minority (albeit vocal) cause, but economics must engage with both this extreme view and the wider debate about the perceived economisation of public life and the damage it causes. Books like Michael Sandel's (2012) *What Money Can't Buy* or Kate Raworth's (2017) *Doughnut Economics* are bestsellers. In the academic literature, Eli Cook's (2017) *The Pricing of Progress*, Elizabeth Anderson's (1995) *Value in Ethics and Economics*, and Debra Satz's (2010) *Why Some Things Should Not Be for Sale* articulate important arguments for limits not only on the role of markets but also on attaching numerical estimates to things of intrinsic value. This resistance extends to the idea of denoting some things as "assets"; the very term causes an allergic reaction in some quarters. For example, in a volume titled *Assetization* (Birch and Muniesa 2020), the contributors argue that conceptualising everything in terms of investments and returns on the one hand does impose a longer-term focus—sustained economic rents replace short-term market gains—but on the other hand commodifies and financialises things that ought not be included in the economic domain. Some people seem to think the idea of comprehensive wealth is a device to assign property rights over all of nature. Others see it as an extension of a self-interested elite political project to control the economy.

As Cook points out in his interesting history, statistics are products of their societies and how they are governed. So the development of the idea in the nineteenth century that prosperity can be measured in monetary terms required a monetised market economy. As discussed in Chapter 1, statistics do have a dual character: as the outcome of the prevailing power structures and as reflections of the created reality. Economists focus on the latter, but we need to appreciate the former to understand why at times of political polarisation, the philosophy of the statistics—rather than just the numbers—becomes contested.

Ironically, the absence of economic growth and the scant income growth for the majority of the OECD's populations during the post-crisis era may have done much to ignite the broader questioning of the economic framework and its measurement. We are already in a no-growth or slow-growth era. There are many counterarguments to the degrowth agenda, including its misunderstandings of what GDP statistics actually measure, and its sheer political implausibility given the way recessions (short spells of degrowth) cost politicians re-election. This is not the place to get into an extensive discussion. But the key ethical point is that economic growth in its broader sense of living standards getting progressively better, of hope for a better future for children and grandchildren, is what people want; and it is essential for healthy democracy, as well as global justice. Ben Friedman puts this concisely: "Countries where living standards improve over sustained periods of time are more likely to seek and preserve an open, tolerant society and to broaden and strengthen their democratic institutions. But where most citizens sense they are getting ahead, society instead becomes rigid and democracy weakens" (2006, p399). He cites Tocqueville's *Democracy in America*: "A slow and gradual rise of wages is one of the general laws of democratic communities." The West may be in the middle of a sort of natural experiment testing this hypothesis, after approaching twenty years of little growth in median incomes and evidence on the ebbing of support for democracy, particularly among younger age groups (Foa et al. 2020, 2022).

It would be useful to have another term in place of "assets," or indeed "growth," that did not prompt an allergic reaction among either the many who are sceptical that the economy (and economics) is working for them or among those making philosophical cases against economic thinking. The usefulness of the concept of wealth or assets is that it is future facing and has connotations of stewardship for the future. In any case, the contested nature of economic statistics underlines the importance for economists of contributing to the measurement debate. In particular, we *must* be able to deliver a better measurement framework for understanding changes in economic welfare.

With that plea, the rest of this chapter will briefly discuss the state of play in the less-well-measured components of comprehensive wealth—beginning with the most well-developed in practice, natural capital.

Natural Capital Accounting

Official national natural capital accounting is about a decade old, and a formal UN standard exists for collecting the statistics. The System of Environmental-Economic Accounting (SEEA) Central Framework was adopted in 2012 (UN 2012), followed by SEEA Ecosystem Accounting in 2021. A growing number of countries collect some (although incomplete) natural capital data; eighty-nine countries reported implementing the SEEA Central Framework in 2020, and thirty-six reported SEEA Ecosystem Accounting, and there is rapid progress. However, gaps often include, for example, blue natural capital (marine and freshwater), ecosystems, soil quality, and biodiversity. These are much harder to define and measure. Although the SEEA conforms to national accounting by requiring the use of exchange values, it includes important natural assets that are ignored by the SNA because they have no owner—such as the air and oceans.

Natural capital accounting also uses the production function framework: assets produce services that are inputs (with other factors) to economic goods (Figure 8.4).

For global figures, the World Bank has the most comprehensive data. Its most recent report estimates that natural capital (or rather, the parts for which there are figures) makes up about 6 per cent of comprehensive wealth on average across countries, but considerably more for low-income countries, which tend to be rich in natural resources but to have invested less over time than rich countries in human capital. The value of the natural capital stock has been declining over time. Intuitively, this estimate of the share of natural capital in total wealth seems low, which is no doubt partly due to omissions and data gaps, but it also reflects the fact that market prices are used. These will generally be lower than shadow prices that incorporate the large negative externalities. In addition, they are not risk adjusted as capital theory would require, so the impact of potential natural tipping points is not incorporated.

Apart from telling us that we are depleting nature unsustainably, the availability of natural capital accounts is finding some policy uses. For example, in 2021 the World Bank for the Rwandan Government estimated that US$3.9 billion needed to be invested in environmental assets to ensure nature-based tourism could return to pre-pandemic levels and continue to grow, while also providing ecosystem services like carbon sequestration and soil retention; the estimate informed requests for development assistance (Benitez et al. 2021). Countries like Rwanda stand to have their future growth badly affected by climate change impacts.

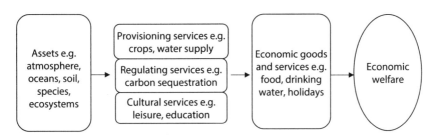

FIGURE 8.4. Natural capital. *Source:* Author's own.

Natural capital accounts can also inform governments' decisions about the speed and scale of climate mitigation and adaptation investments, as they directly link emissions or pollution to economic data like GDP growth and so improve integrated economic and environmental modelling. For example, Indonesian government modelling in 2021 estimated that selecting low-carbon policies would raise annual GDP growth from about 4 per cent in the no-change base case to 6 per cent by 2045—a big difference, implying incomes doubling about every ten to eleven years rather than every seventeen to eighteen years (Bappenas 2021). There are also many empirical studies concerning elements of natural capital services such as air quality, or urban cooling by trees, or flood mitigation by planting. Such studies—and more importantly, better natural capital statistics at a range of spatial scales—could help inform private and public investment decisions: Why build costly concrete urban flood defences if trees planted upstream and a safeguarded wetland downstream could provide similar flood protection and also deliver other services from biodiversity to leisure amenities (United Nations 2012)? Why allow air pollution to continue to cost so many lives, as well as imposing costs through the need for more treatment of respiratory diseases such as childhood asthma or COVID-19? Natural capital data can also be important at a very local scale. The ONS (2019b) has estimated that being 100 meters from an urban green space added over 1 per cent to home prices compared with dwellings 500 meters away; it provides popular interactive tools that people can use to explore their neighborhood's natural capital.

Investment and resource allocation decisions will be inefficient if they ignore some of the assets in the national portfolio. Even imperfect numbers—as they will always be for natural capital—are better than a zero that is definitely wrong. Businesses increasingly recognise this and are starting to venture into company-level natural capital accounting (Natural Capital Coalition 2021), while thanks to the new focus on natural capital, awareness is dawning in the financial markets that credit ratings and risk assessments need to incorporate nature-related risks; to the extent that a business is using natural capital services—as all are—investors need to incorporate the appropriately risk-adjusted returns to that business in assessing their portfolios, as do investors contemplating investing in sovereign bonds at a national scale (Agarwala and Zenghelis 2021, Agarwala et al. 2024).

There is no conceptual dissent from the idea that nature is fundamental to the economy. The economic theory is solid and widely accepted. However, it is not mainstreamed. To the extent that students are taught about national accounting, natural capital does not feature, nor does it always appear in textbooks as a fundamental factor of production, whereas human capital has a central place across the literature. The top five academic journals that determine who gets hired and promoted in top departments have published vanishingly few papers on environmental issues. Data gaps are possibly part of the reason that all economics is not yet environmental economics. There are several data challenges, from definitions and classification (how to define biodiversity? How does it relate to pollination services?), to the daunting task of data collection at appropriate geographic scales, to the need for statisticians to work with ecologists or soil scientists as well as the familiar economists and accountants. Nevertheless, progress is rapid, and the SNA25 revision will weave natural capital more tightly into the standard official economic statistics.

Human Capital Accounting

It is possibly even more uncomfortable to think about human beings as economic assets than it is nature. After all, slave societies literally count humans as assets, and US slave owners' record-keeping contributed to the early spread of accountancy (Rosenthal 2018). At least early in the literature on the role of human capital in labor markets and growth, economists were well aware of the historical shadow and were careful to contextualise the concept as used in economics. For example, Theodore Schultz, in his American Economic Association Presidential Address, was explicit about this: "To treat human beings as wealth that can be augmented by investment runs counter to deeply held values. It seems to reduce man [*sic*] once again to a mere material component, to something akin to property. And for man to look upon himself as a capital good, even if it did not impair his freedom, may seem to debase him" (1961, p2). He underlined the centrality of the idea that people are investing in themselves (or their children) to enlarge the opportunities open to them by acquiring skills, generating a future return in higher incomes. Since then, economists (and the world beyond the profession) have internalised the idea as normal. It is a concept fundamental in labor economics, and also in development and growth economics, where—conditional on similar economic institutions—investment in human capital is an important contributor to countries' catch-up growth.

The World Bank's (2021) estimates of comprehensive wealth show human capital to be the largest component, making up more than 60 per cent of the total on average across all countries. Human capital is nevertheless excluded from the national accounts—and spending on education is classed as consumption rather than investment. The rationale for this is that human capital is inappropriable—you cannot sell your mind and experience to another person—and is non-physical (which sounds bizarre but suggests that it is thought of as a component of mind, in a Cartesian dualist manner). However, OECD economies construct satellite accounts. There are three main approaches to valuing an economy's human capital: educational attainment, the cost of gaining skills, and lifetime earnings.

The latter is a forward-looking construct, consistent with capital theory (Jorgenson and Fraumeni 1992) and preferable in the context of comprehensive wealth accounting. But it assumes people are paid their marginal product. It also requires an assumed discount rate and retirement age, and also data on skills and earnings, and survival rates at different ages. The United Kingdom's ONS uses this approach, as does Statistics Canada. Several categories of educational attainment are used, and people are classified by age and gender.

This approach has some obvious limitations as well as assuming that the labour market is competitive. It omits other types of earnings, such as returns to entrepreneurship, and also skills other than those leading to formal academic qualifications, such as experience and formal on-the-job training. It omits non-market labour, such as care in the home or voluntary work. For all that, it is a large number.

However, the main omission is health, although Becker (2007) among others has argued for its inclusion. Health can affect human capital estimates either by changing the quantity of labor—sending employees into economic inactivity or early retirement—or its quality—affecting effort or productivity on the job. One estimate for the United Kingdom (O'Mahony and Samek 2021) using the same Jorgenson-Fraumeni approach, with some approximations, calculates a productive human capital stock by indexing equation (9.2) by health status also. It requires estimating a health index for each age/skill group. Health status affects retirement at given age probabilities, mortality/survival rates, and wage rates also. Their productive human capital stock estimate is 12 per cent lower than the non-health-adjusted "potential" human capital stock. Long-term illnesses, led by orthopedic problems (back pain) and mental ill-health, but also others such as respiratory disease and diabetes, account for almost all the gap. Poor health long term is concentrated among those with low educational qualifications, highlighting the nexus between education, health, and economic opportunity (Case and Deaton 2020). A similar study for Canada estimated that net investment in health represented 4 per cent to 5 per cent of total net investment in human capital from 1980 to 2010. Several statistical agencies and the World Bank are working on better incorporating health into human capital measures.

Even though education expenditure obviously has a large investment component, as does health expenditure, there are no plans to reclassify any parts of these from consumption to investment in the SNA revisions for 2025. Nor will human capital be moved inside the asset

Box 8.2 Estimating the stock of human capital

A simple version of the ONS formula for estimating human capital is:

$$LI = emp_{q,a} * inc_{q,a}$$
$$+ \left[\left(\sum_q LI_{q+1,a} * prob_{q,a} \right) * (1 - mort_a) * (1+r)/(1+\delta) \right] \quad (9.1)$$

where q indexes skill level, a indexes age group. LI is lifetime earnings, emp the employment rate for individuals at a given age and skill level, inc the current average income for the same, $mort_a$ the mortality rate at age a, r the labour productivity growth rate, and δ the discount rate. The income term LI is defined for each age group and qualification level. $Prob_{q,a}$ is the probability that the individual at a given age and educational attainment level will change to a different educational attainment level in a year. The second term captures how much more people will earn if they upskill by next year, given the probability of this occurring. Empirically, this is implemented by backward recursion. The national human capital stock is then calculated as:

$$HC = \Sigma_q \Sigma_a LI_{q,a} * POP_{q,a} \quad (9.2)$$

where POP is the number of people of each age group and qualification level. As with all official statistics, the implementation involves additional practical complexity.

boundary. Still, the economic importance of both forms of expenditure is recognised in the fact that many OECD countries have a satellite human capital account. (In the United States the BLS produces research estimates but not yet a satellite account.) Just as nature has intrinsic value, so do education and health. So the point of estimating human capital in intricate calculations requiring much data and many assumptions is to ensure that nations do prioritise intrinsically valuable investments in their people.

The Enabling Capitals: Intangibles, Organisation, and Trust

I have clustered together the three enabling capitals—intangibles, organisation, and trust—as there are similarities in the conceptual and measurement challenges, given that they are all intangible. Definitional boundaries are difficult to draw precisely (although there are also arbitrary boundaries for physical capital too, such as the one-year dividing line between an intermediate purchase and a capital investment). And while some intangibles have crossed the production boundary and entered into statistical production, most of the assets in all these categories have not.

The conceptual framework for categorising intangibles is due to Corrado, Hulten, and Sichel (2005, 2009) and summarised by Corrado et al. (2022) (Table 8.1).

Intangibles currently measured as assets or activities within the SNA are shaded in the table. This includes, for example, the value of patented medications, movies, software, and proven mineral reserves. The criteria for inclusion are that assets are produced and have an economic owner. The new SNA25 definitions will expand the number of data assets recorded from the currently measured purchased databases to include own-account database assets. This will take a sum-of-costs approach, given the absence of any consensus alternative to data valuation (Coyle and Manley 2024). The hatched category, marketing and brands, has been under consideration for inclusion too.

What is the scale of intangible investment? Figure 8.5 shows the fixed investment and investment in national accounts intangibles and non-national accounts intangibles in the United Kingdom, the United States, and Germany as a share of GDP (current price measures). Figure 8.6 shows ONS estimates of UK annual investment in intangibles in current pounds for 2020, for both categories, inside and outside GDP; for comparison, total fixed investment was about £360 million. (ONS provides an especially detailed breakdown.)

The case for considering intangibles as substantive economic assets is well summarised in Corrado et al. (2022) as the "large widening gap

TABLE 8.1. Classification of Intangible Assets

Digitised information	Software
	Databases
Innovative property	R&D
	Mineral exploration
	Artistic, entertainment, & literary originals
	Attributed (industrial) designs
	Financial product development
Economic competencies	Market research & brands
	Operating models, platforms, supply
	chains, & distribution networks
	Employer-provided training

Source: Corrado et al. (2022). *Note:* Table 8.1. is expanded.

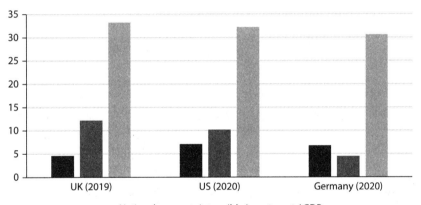

■ National accounts intangible investment / GDP

■ Non-national accounts intangible investment / GDP

▨ Total fixed investment / GDP

FIGURE 8.5. Fixed and intangibles investment, share of GDP (current prices).
Source: Bontadini et al. (2023).

between market valuation of firms based on equity markets and accounting valuations of firms based on the physical plant, property, and
equipment" (p5). As they note, the accountancy and management literature has long pointed to intangible assets as key drivers of firms'
performance (Lev 2000), while economic research during the 1990s

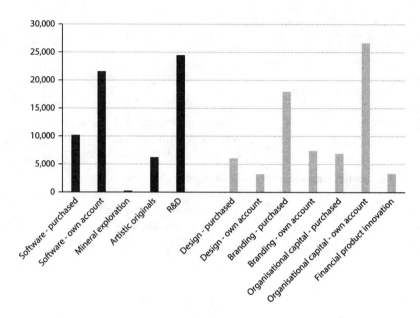

FIGURE 8.6. UK intangible investment, 000s current £, 2020.
Source: ONS (2022b).

dot-com-related productivity boom identified investment in organisational intangibles as the means by which firms could turn investments in physical ICT equipment into productivity gains (Brynjolfsson and Hitt 2000, Brynjolfsson et al. 2002). Kurz (2023) argues that all intangibles—like the gap between market capitalisation and physical capital value—represent monopoly rent. This may be an overstatement, but it certainly largely represents distinctive capabilities of firms that enable them to grow. As noted in Chapter 2, the productivity performance of firms is diverging, and the literature has attributed that to the organisational capacity to use digital tools or data.

Corrado et al. (2022) argue that the importance of intangibles investment is implicit in endogenous growth theory, which stresses the non-rival nature of ideas. The value of intangibles as capitalised assets, however, is that they can be partly appropriated by their owners. These ownership rights may be created and enforced by legal means (as with IP products, brands, or mining rights) and/or technical means (as with databases), or through tacit knowledge inside the firm. This latter category, falling under "economic competencies" in Table 8.1, seems different in character—more difficult both to create and to appropriate. For example, business models can be imitated relatively easily, but supply chain networks are harder to mimic, as is engineering know-how to make processes flow more smoothly. These intangibles are sometimes described as organisational capital, although this can also be a more expansive definition including, for example, tacit knowledge shared between employees (learned by "sitting with Nellie," as the phrase had it in the old Lancashire cotton industry) and organisational culture or institutional memory. Organisational capital might also incorporate management quality or improvements in the production process—recall the importance of process innovation for productivity growth.

Organisational capital is in effect a form of social capital that operates within organisations. Social capital per se operates at a community or societal level. It is not included in comprehensive wealth in the World Bank's approach, but as the bank noted in its latest report, tracking social capital is nevertheless important for understanding economic potential:

> Social capital exhibits wealth-like characteristics: it underpins future flows of benefits, people can invest in it, it can be degraded and depleted over time, and it contributes to production without necessarily being consumed in the process. However, . . . as a latent construct, it has no standard unit of measurement, it is less straightforward to think of growth rates and stock dynamics for social capital than for other components of wealth, and it is particularly difficult to disentangle from human capital and other intangible assets. Nonetheless, social capital is clearly important to understanding changes in the capacity of individuals, firms, and nations to generate welfare into the future. (Agarwala and Zenghelis 2021, p400)

There are many definitions and categorisations of social capital, all relating to the way in which an individual acts in relation to other individuals or a network in which they sit. In one survey, Adler and Kwon (2002) suggest that definitions of social capital can be broadly divided based on the focus of the main actor. If the focus is on the relationship of the main actor with other individuals, they label this as an "internal" definition. If the focus is on the relationship of multiple actors with their community, they label them as "external" definitions. Their own definition of social capital is "the goodwill available to individuals or groups. Its source lies in the structure and content of the actor's social relations. Its effects flow from the information, influence, and solidarity it makes available to the actor." This sounds both ill-defined and hard to measure. However, whether measured as a survey variable such as generalised trust or as an indicator of the effectiveness of an economy's institutional arrangements, there is persuasive empirical evidence of the importance of social capital (at least some aspects) for economic development and growth at different spatial scales. The link is theorised in several ways, such as the link between trust and transactions costs (Dasgupta 2005, 2011). Bjørnskov (2022) summarises the wide range of evidence linking social capital and growth, using a growth-accounting framework on a large cross-country panel to argue that social capital measured by trust affects TFP growth.

There are different classifications of types of social capital: bonding, bridging, and linking is a common distinction. Other approaches define social capital in terms of networks. Measures of social capital are survey based and elicit responses about a range of indicators covering trust, social norms, reciprocity of behaviour, and so on. The ONS's social capital measurement covers four domains: personal relationships, social network support, civic engagement, and trust and cooperative norms. A range of indicators address these domains (ONS 2020c). On trust, for example, it is a standard, "On a scale of 0-10, where 0 is not at all, and 10 is completely, in general how much do you trust most people?" For social network support it is, "To what extent do you agree or disagree with the statement 'I can rely on the people in my life if I have a serious problem'?"

There is a considerable amount of data on generalised trust responses over time and across and within countries. The challenges of identification in macroeconomic evidence mean there is an older body of work on the trust-growth correlation but not much recently, even though recent events in terms of declining trust in many societies mean there is new variation in the survey data. More recent measurement approaches involve methods of reducing the dimensionality of survey data. One is to use principal components analysis, which neatly delivers two main components, one broadly speaking outward-facing trust in society or social norms, and one inward-facing reliance on personal relationships (Bjørnskov 2006). While the former has a positive relationship with economic outcomes, strong personal networks can have negative collective effects—for instance, a criminal gang will have strong internal social capital. Another dimensionality-reduction approach is to apply a suitable ML algorithm to data descriptive of local labor market networks and identify the indicators most strongly linked to the network (e.g., Asquith et al. 2017). The research agenda is now moving on to the links between trust, well-being, and productivity or growth.

Well-Being Measurement

As noted, the argument made for developing better measures of comprehensive wealth, a broad national balance sheet, is that increases in wealth (appropriately measured) correspond to increases in economic welfare. Why go to all the bother? This task, sometimes referred to as the "missing capitals" agenda, involves a lot of raw data gathering, a lot of extra work for statisticians, and anyway requires some theoretical and conceptual advances, particularly to be able to estimate the appropriate shadow prices. The alternative some economists favour is some form of direct measurement of well-being. It has influential advocates and popular appeal. Many of those who are keen on the Beyond GDP agenda often cite policy approaches such as New Zealand's Living Standards Framework or even Bhutan's Gross National Happiness Index.

Well-being measures are, just like GDP and its component statistics, backward looking. Using them to guide policy is still steering through the rearview mirror. Only assets valued at shadow prices directly embed societal sustainability, as they are forward looking. Beyond that, there is a sense in which well-being measurement has exactly the same aim as any other approach to economic measurement, which is to assess whether things are getting better or not. Whereas economics generally uses preference satisfaction as the criterion, or objective measures as is more typical in capability approaches, subjective well-being (SWB) measurement focuses on mental states and how people evaluate their own lives. It has the merit of enabling construction of an aggregated number, which improves communication and has impact; one of the reasons for the long reign of GDP growth as the principal economic metric is the "power of a single number" (Lepenies 2016). However, as with any other approach, well-being measurement is more complex than it might seem—and certainly more so than the reductionist version sometimes used to urge policy change.

The first issue is the straightforward question: How is well-being to be measured? As well-being is a multidimensional concept (e.g., Stiglitz et al. 2009, Anderson 1995), any direct measurement will be seeking to reduce that dimensionality. There are three main measurement approaches to SWB in social science, in all of which individuals self-report: evaluation (life satisfaction), experience (momentary mood), and eudaemonia (purpose) (see Dolan and Metcalfe 2012 and Fabian 2022b for surveys). Many (national and international) surveys ask about life satisfaction, and this metric has generated a large empirical literature correlating the measure with a range of variables such as income, unemployment, marriage, religious participation, education, and health. The metric is a scalar, such as the Likert scale, or Cantril's ladder of life, which asks respondents to evaluate their current life on a scale from 0 (worst possible life) to 10 (best possible life). An alternative is to survey people about their experiences, such as the Day Reconstruction Method (Kahneman et al. 2004). This asks people to write a diary of the main episodes of the previous day and recall the type and intensity of feelings experienced during each event. Eudaemonic measures ask people to evaluate how much meaning their lives have (Huppert 2009). Life satisfaction or happiness is the most widely used measure in economics for empirical and policy applications for obvious pragmatic reasons. Some statistical agencies publish regular survey results, such as the ONS, which uses the ONS4, now widely adopted as standard SWB questions (shown in Table 8.2) (ONS 2018). It is worth noting that different metrics are used in the psychology literature, such as the WHO5, a diagnostic

TABLE 8.2. The ONS Four Measures of Personal Well-Being

Next I would like to ask you four questions about your feelings on aspects of your life. There are no right or wrong answers. For each of these questions I'd like you to give an answer on a scale of 0 to 10, where 0 is "not at all" and 10 is "completely."	
Measure	Question
Life Satisfaction	Overall, how satisfied are you with your life nowadays?
Worthwhile	Overall, to what extent do you feel that the things you do in your life are worthwhile?
Happiness	Overall, how happy did you feel yesterday?
Anxiety	On a scale where 0 is "not at all anxious" and 10 is "completely anxious," overall, how anxious did you feel yesterday?

Source: ONS.

tool from the World Health Organization. These are positively correlated with SWB metrics in social science (Disabato et al. 2016), but the differences point to the lack of a settled conceptualisation of well-being constructs. Any single measurement of what is happening in people's mental states should be used with caution.

Advocates argue that using people's own evaluations is democratic and correlates well with outcomes most people would agree are good, such as health. There now exists a large evidence base on the empirical regularities, and policymakers are increasingly using SWB measures (Clark et al. 2018, Graham et al. 2018, Layard and De Neve 2023). Survey results can even be converted into a policy-relevant metric, the WELLBY. A WELLBY is defined as one point of life satisfaction on a zero-to-ten scale for one individual for one year (Frijters and Krekel 2021). It thus has two components, well-being in life and length of life. Growth in the national WELLBY total is a figure equivalent to growth in GDP. The UK Treasury permits WELLBYs to be used in cost-benefit evaluation, having calculated the central value at £13,000 (HM Treasury 2021).

Well-being frameworks, adopted in different formats by a range of countries and subnational governments, generally include many indicators that contribute to SWB, such as income, health, education, environment,

and sometimes governance, as well as summary indicators such as life satisfaction. They bear a close relationship to earlier alternative approaches
to assessing progress, such as the Human Development Index (Cooper
et al. 2023). So, although derived from the SWB conceptualisation of social
welfare, these often end up drawing in practice on the objective welfare/
capabilities tradition, which lists factors generally considered to be determinants of well-being. The New Zealand Living Standards Framework
(New Zealand Treasury 2021) is a bit of an exception in that it draws explicitly on the theory of wealth accounting, including human, natural, and
social capital, in order to monitor sustainability. Well-being approaches
thus generally expand from the pleasing simplicity of a single number to
the use of a dashboard to capture the multidimensional nature of progress.
There is, in the end, no getting away from the paradox pointed out by Anderson (1995), who argues strongly—and persuasively—that "evidence
from our actual practice and failures to construct plausible global measures
of value suggests there is no single measure of value valid for all contexts"
(p63). Yet, having pointed out that economic welfare is multidimensional
and its components are incommensurable, Anderson also implicitly accepts that decisions (by individuals or policymakers) must be made as if
there is a best course of action.

There are enthusiasts for direct well-being measurement who see it
as an escape route from the unwelcome economisation of life, as discussed. The Easterlin paradox (see Easterlin and O'Connor 2022 for a
review) has a firm hold among some. This is the observation that at any
moment in cross-section data, life satisfaction is always strongly correlated with incomes, but over the long run in time series data, it is
highly correlated with GDP per capita only up to a certain point, after
which the correlation tails off rapidly; there seem to be diminishing
marginal happiness returns to higher income above a threshold. Easterlin's account is that the cross-section correlation reflects social comparisons
and positional effects, whereas over time well-being and incomes are
not linked: "Economic growth does not in itself increase happiness in
the long-term" (p19). It has been pointed out that the time series result
is an artefact of trying to correlate a stationary (life satisfaction) with a
non-stationary (income) time series; just as height does increase with

incomes up to a point but then the correlation diminishes, so with the well-being measures that are bounded by construction from 1 to 10. The variance of a stationary time series is constant, while that of a non-stationary series like GDP is increasing over time; the theoretical correlation coefficient between them will therefore decline over time and is in general meaningless. There is some evidence that the correlation of life satisfaction with GDP *growth* (a stationary time series) remains positive over time (Stevenson and Wolfers 2013, Deaton 2008), although this is disputed (Easterlin and O'Connor 2022). However, some people are unpersuaded by statistical and empirical challenges to the paradox, insisting that the Easterlin results demonstrate that economic growth does not contribute to happiness.

There are other tricky measurement issues in the well-being literature. One is the well-known "hedonic adaptation" phenomenon, whereby people evaluate their SWB response in relation to reference points or norms: people return to an apparent set point in their responses after a positive or negative life event. A less widely appreciated phenomenon is scale norming (Fabian 2022a), whereby respondents use qualitatively different scales to reply to the same question across different waves of a survey. They can reply with, say, a 7 on the Likert scale in successive surveys, while also believing they are better off than they were a year ago. This is similar to adaptation but occurs when people reconceptualise the scale or ladder—for example, if they migrate to another country, or if a disaster like a wildfire has struck.

As noted earlier, another striking issue is the way economics has settled on a set of questions and surveys that differ from the evaluations of well-being in the psychology literature. For example, the widely used WHO5 (Topp et al. 2015) is a short self-reported survey scaling responses from 0 ("at no time") to 5 ("all of the time"), whose questions (Table 8.3) do not overlap with the ONS4.

Another example is the Warwick-Edinburgh Mental Wellbeing Scale, which has either seven or fourteen questions on a five-point scale. Questions include, for example, "I've been feeling close to other people," "I've been feeling useful," "I've been interested in new things." The empirical economics literature, however, rarely uses the surveys emerging from

CHAPTER EIGHT

TABLE 8.3. The WHO Five Measures of Personal Well-Being

Over the last two weeks	All the time	Most of the time	More than half the time	Less than half the time	Some of the time	At no time
I have felt cheerful and in good spirits	5	4	3	2	1	0
I have felt calm and relaxed	5	4	3	2	1	0
I have felt active and vigorous	5	4	3	2	1	0
I woke up feeling fresh and rested	5	4	3	2	1	0
My daily life has been filled with things that interest me	5	4	3	2	1	0

Source: Topp et al. (2015).

medical practice. I suspect the reason may be data availability, with long-time series and cross-sections available from a wide variety of life satisfaction surveys globally.

If the aim of measuring what is happening in the economy is to help steer policy and private decisions toward making things better for people, the well-being measurement agenda is an important one. While there are certainly significant questions the research must address, there is an active research agenda on the conceptualisation and measurement issues. And as an alternative to conventional economic statistics, it has considerable momentum in the Beyond GDP policy debates and practice. However, given the gap between social science and psychology, there is a real need for a more solid theoretical grounding for well-being; the empirical economics of well-being consists of reduced-form estimation that does not validate strong policy recommendations (Fabian et al. 2023). Another reservation about it is the leap by SWB advocates to policy conclusions with the same technocratic confidence about the answers as economists have long had using conventional statistics. Much of the policy advocacy based on SWB empirics is just as technocratic and top down as ever, missing the opportunity to take advantage of the democratic nature of SWB measurement (Fabian et al. 2023). Indeed, there is something High Victorian about the claim by an economist to be able to maximise people's happiness for them, a more paternalistic-sounding aim than maximising either GDP growth or comprehensive wealth.

Conclusion

The previous chapters have pointed out that the usual measures of how the economy is doing—real-terms GDP and associated statistics—are highly imperfect measures of progress. Much of the focus in this book has been the structural transformation brought about by digital technologies and AI, which make the fog obscuring our understanding of what is happening even denser than usual. Chapter 7 introduced an even more significant wedge between what we measure and what we would like to know by looking at the construction of deflators used to calculate real-terms growth or productivity. This chapter has expanded the discussion of measuring economic welfare by introducing the theoretically well-grounded comprehensive wealth framework and discussing what additional measurement requirements this would introduce. It does not discard all the information in the present national accounts; it does link the current approach to a more systematic (rather than almost accidental) consideration of economic welfare. The final chapter turns more explicitly to the framework needed for measuring economic progress.

9

A New Framework?

AT THE HEART OF THIS BOOK is a question addressed by many people in recent decades, the question of how to measure economic progress for society as a whole. The economic and social phenomena so clear in everyday experience, whether extreme wildfires or floods as manifestations of the environmental changes underway or almost everyone's dependence on Big Tech 24/7, are invisible in the standard national accounts and GDP statistics. Long-standing questions about how to account for the human economy's dependence on nature on the one hand or for innovation and social change on the other hand have grown in salience because of the unmissable changes around us. Answering fundamental questions such as these requires a view about what should be counted as creating value. The current concept of valued added used to construct GDP numbers does not correspond to the views many people hold about societal value. This disconnect has given momentum to the Beyond GDP movement and to those similarly challenging the metrics of shareholder value that determine how businesses act. The digitalisation of the economy, in shifting the ways economic value can be created, amplifies the case for revisiting the existing economic statistics.

Without good statistics, states cannot function. In my work focusing on both the digital economy and the natural economy, I have worked closely with official statisticians in the ONS, BEA, OECD, INSEE, and elsewhere for many years now. Official statisticians are committed public servants, generally underresourced for what they are expected to do.

However, it is not helpful for public trust in official statistics to have the statisticians producing the numbers supposed to capture economic progress claiming that the definitions just need a few tweaks. For without question there has been a widespread loss of belief in conventional statistics even among knowledgeable commentators, as the vigorous Beyond GDP agenda testifies. Yet nothing amid the proliferation of alternatives has gained a critical mass of support. This is partly a matter of the co-ordination needed to move from one statistical standard to another (Coyle 2017a) and the institutional inertia of the embedded machinery of official statistics; but part of the reason is the absence of a consistent and persuasive alternative analytical framework. There is no alternative consensus about what to switch to. This, unfortunately, means that inertia won out in the SNA25 revision. There will be some welcome improvements in measuring the environment, work inside the household, and the digital economy, but these are far from adding up to providing a clear lens on the economy or addressing the various gaps in knowledge set out in previous chapters. SNA25 does not provide a conceptual framework for understanding and measuring progress.

The ambitious aim of this chapter is to sketch what such a framework might involve, drawing together the threads from earlier chapters. It is inevitably preliminary and partial. But I want to start by briefly setting out why some commonly proposed measurement suggestions will not fit the bill.

Why Not Well-Being?

As discussed in the previous chapter, an alternative metric of social welfare that many people find appealing is the direct measurement of well-being. Economists who focus on well-being have differing views on exactly how to measure it, but the balance of opinion has tilted toward life satisfaction measured on a fixed scale (such as the Cantril ladder). Public policy for well-being has made some headway in the United Kingdom, New Zealand, and a few other places, using the headline metrics and a body of reduced-form evidence linking average life satisfaction survey scores to various drivers (such as unemployment, age, or marriage status). Using well-being as a measure to inform policy has some impressive advocates (Layard and De Neve 2023).

Although people's well-being is the ultimate aim of collective action, using it as a measurement is problematic in several ways. One is the set of measurement issues highlighted in research by Mark Fabian, one of my coauthors, and described in the previous chapter. These include scale norming, whereby when people state their life satisfaction as, say, a 7 on a scale of 1 to 10 at different time periods, they are doing so by reference to the scale rather than events in their life (Fabian 2022a, Cooper et al. 2023). One of the more firmly established behavioural facts is the idea of an individual set point, whereby individuals generally revert to an initial level of well-being after experiencing events that send it up or down, but this is hardly a reason for concluding that nothing can improve in their lives. Another issue is that the empirical literature is atheoretical, providing a weak basis for policy intervention in people's lives. Our conclusion from our research project on well-being was that while national policy could certainly be informed by top-down life satisfaction survey statistics, at smaller scales people's well-being will depend on the context and on who is affected; the definition and measurement of well-being should be tailored appropriately, and it is not a very useful metric for policy at an aggregate level (Alexandrova et al. 2021).

Why Not an Alternative Index?

Over the years, several single indices as alternatives to GDP have been proposed. However, indices internalise the trade-offs to present a single number that advocates hope will dethrone conventional measures. Some of these are explicit about the social welfare framework they involve. GDP itself uses price theory, weighting together its components using their relative prices. Another example is provided by Jones and Klenow (2016), who include consumption, leisure, inequality, and mortality in social welfare. They convert the other indicators into "consumption-equivalent welfare," which has a long tradition in economics (Lucas 1987). In their paper, they observe that France has much lower consumption per capita than the United States—it is only at 60 per cent of the US level—but less inequality, greater life expectancy at birth, and longer leisure hours. Their adjustment puts France at 92 per cent of the consumption-equivalent level of the United States. An older alternative including similar indicators, albeit in a less formal theoretical framework, was Nordhaus and Tobin's (1972) well-known "measure of economic welfare." This index netted off capital depreciation (but only of physical capital), reclassifying health and education spending as investment rather than consumption, deducting some "regrettable" government expenditures (police services, sanitation services, road maintenance) as intermediate rather than final goods, and adding some imputations for leisure and non-market production. The spirit of the exercise was to stay with the broad SNA framework.

A well-established alternative index is the Human Development Index (HDI), inspired by Amartya Sen's capabilities approach (more on this later). In his account of the flaws of GDP, Ehsan Masood (2016) recounts that when approached by the founder of the HDI, Mahbub ul-Haq, Sen was reluctant to develop an indicator on the basis of the theory for exactly the reason that the capabilities approach conceives of human welfare as being multidimensional and context-specific. However, he agreed, so the HDI and accompanying report have become firmly established in the development policy world. The index does, though, demonstrate the dangers of combining a number of indicators, each one measuring something relevant, without having a conceptual structure for the trade-offs and how the components should be weighted together. The late Martin Ravallion of the World Bank advocated for a multidimensional set of indicators, with the aggregation necessary to get to these being informed by talking to poor people about their priorities (Ravallion 2011). For he argued that not only is the selection of indicators for an index arbitrary—and generally determined by experts outside the context of measurement—but also that the weights applied imply trade-offs between components that are rarely discussed: "The literature has also been close to silent about the tradeoffs between attainments" (p242). Yet they imply "relative prices" between different components, such as health and income, that will differ among countries. For example, equal weights on both components will value the improved health in a low-income country as being worth less than the same improvement in a high-income country. The implicit trade-offs should be explicitly considered. And does one really want to consider at all a trade-off between, say, infant mortality and internet access? Ravallion's conclusion identifies the key issue:

> The role played by prices lies at the heart of the matter. It is widely agreed that prices can be missing for some goods and deceptive for others. There are continuing challenges facing applied economists in addressing these problems. However, it is one thing to recognize that markets and prices are missing or imperfect, and quite another to ignore them in welfare and poverty measurement. There is a peculiar inconsistency in the literature on multidimensional indices of poverty whereby prices are regarded as an unreliable guide to the tradeoffs, and are largely ignored, while the actual weights being assumed in lieu of prices are not made explicit in the same space as prices. We have no basis for believing that the weights being used are any better than market price. (p247)

These indices I have highlighted here omit adjustment for environmental resource use and damage, although Nordhaus and Tobin discuss it, as do many editions of the *Human Development Report*. There are several indices that do include it, such as the Genuine Progress Indicator and the Index of Sustainable Economic Welfare. Not only do these raise the same question about the selection of weights, but they also subtract "bads" from GDP without adding "goods," such as life-improving innovations. So any single index disguises the need to worry about how to internalise trade-offs in aggregation. This points to the importance of shadow prices (sometimes known as accounting prices)—more on this to follow.

Why Not a Dashboard?

One frequent proposal, which certainly has intuitive appeal, is replacing the political and policy focus on GDP growth and related macroeconomic statistics with a broader dashboard. This was the recommendation of the influential Stiglitz-Sen-Fitoussi 2009 report on economic measurement that gave such momentum to the Beyond GDP movement. But there are three big challenges related to what to display on the dashboard. One, which indicators? A proliferation of alternatives has focused on what their advocates think is important rather than being shaped by either theory or broad consensus. So potential users face an array of possibilities and can select what interests them. Second, there are trade-offs and dependencies between indicators, and although dashboards could be designed to display these clearly, often they do not. Consequently, the third challenge is how to weight or display the various component indicators for decision purposes.

The selection of indicators is at best only loosely informed by theory, so there are many alternatives consisting of many indicators and only modest overlap between them. These range from the seventeen Sustainable Development Goals (SDGs) beneath which sit 231 indicators (United Nations n.d.) to the 57 indicators in the ONS Well-being Dashboard (2023a) to the 60 indicators combined into a single Social Progress Index (latest average world score 63.44).[1] The New Zealand Treasury (2021) uses a more theory-driven Living Standards Framework (LSF), and its multiple indicators are presented against the concepts in the framework. Another dashboard approach with firmer foundations is the SAGE framework (Lima de Miranda and Snower 2020). Table 9.1 lists the headline categories for four frequently cited dashboards, showing how little they overlap. The selection of indicators to represent an underlying concept is evidently arbitrary, in the sense that the lists do not have a clear theoretical basis, and the selection of indicators is generally determined by what data are available or even by political negotiation. For instance, I was told by someone closely involved in the process that the debate within the UN about the SDGs included a discussion about the definition of a tree; depending on the height specified in the definition, coffee bushes might or might not be included, which for some countries would affect their measure of deforestation. Practicality and arbitrary decisions certainly affect mainstream economic statistics too, but these result from decades of debate and practice among the

---

1. https://www.socialprogress.org/social-progress-index

TABLE 9.1. Comparison of Dashboards

Social Progress Index	ONS Well-being Indicators	UN SDGs	New Zealand LSF
	Personal well-being		Subjective well-being
	Relationships		
	Satisfaction with time use		Leisure and play
	Personal finance	Poverty	Income, consumption, and wealth
Nutrition & medical care		Hunger & nutrition	
Health	Health	Health & well-being	Health
Education	Education and skills	Quality education	Human capital Knowledge and skills Families & households Family and friends
Advanced education			
ICT			
Water/sanitation		Water/sanitation	
		Clean energy	
		Employment/growth	Firms & markets
		Industry/infrastructure	Physical & financial capital International connections
		Reduced inequalities	
Housing	Where we live	Sustainable cities	Housing
Environmental quality	Environment	Responsible consumption	Natural environment Environmental amenity
		Climate action Aquatic health	
		Health of land	
Rights & voice	Governance	Institutions	Central & local government Engagement & voice
Inclusive society			Social cohesion Work, care, and volunteering
Freedom & choice			Civil society
Safety			Safety
		Partnerships	Cultural capability & belonging Maori connection to marae

Source: Author's own.

community of relevant experts informed by a theoretical basis. We are not there yet with dashboards.

Still, there are many things people care about in life, even if one confines the question to their economic well-being. Indeed, one of the criticisms that I pointed out in Chapter 7 of using growth of real GDP (deflated by a utility-constant price index) as a guide was the flawed assumption that utility can be collapsed to a single dimension. So in this sense dashboards are desirable. In any case, there are many other statistics behind the GDP figure that is the focus of news and policy debate, so the difference between current practice and a dashboard can be overstated. There is an imperative to think more carefully about the presentation of dashboards in terms of the psychology of processing information and presenting it; I am surprised there appears to be little work on this, given the evidence on the "power of a single number" in influencing behaviour (Lepenies 2016).

Comprehensive Wealth

So if not well-being directly measured, nor (yet) a dashboard, nor a single index number alternative to GDP, what are the options? It will already be clear from the previous chapter that I favour the comprehensive wealth, or capitals, framework, and it would help answer the conundrum about selecting indicators for a dashboard by grounding the choice in economic theory. The comprehensive wealth framework has other merits.

First, it embeds sustainability because of its focus on assets. Adding in effect a balance sheet recording stocks—or equivalently a full account of the flow of services provided by the assets—immediately highlights the key trade-off between present and future consumption. One measurement challenge is to identify the economically relevant assets and collect the underlying data. Focusing on assets revives an old debate in economics during the 1950s and early 1960s between the "two Cambridges"— Cambridge, Massachusetts, home to MIT and Harvard (where I did my PhD), and Cambridge, England (where I now work). That debate was about whether it made any sense to think of (physical) capital as a single aggregate when this would inevitably be a mash-up of many different types of physical buildings and equipment. The American Cambridge (led by Paul Samuelson and Robert Solow) said yes, and the concept has become the "K" of production functions and growth accounting. The British Cambridge (particularly Piero Sraffa and Joan Robinson) disputed this, arguing for example that different vintages of capital would embed different generations of technology, so even a straightforward machine tool to stamp out components could not be aggregated with a twenty-year-old equivalent. Even the review articles discussing the debate (Cohen and Harcourt 2003, Stiglitz 1974) take sides, but the mainstream profession has given total victory to the US single-aggregate version. While a comprehensive wealth approach—indeed any statistical framework—requires some degree of aggregation, it will also require the measurement of different categories of asset, including within the neoclassical K. Most physical infrastructure assets are poorly measured, including their depreciation and maintenance, despite their fundamental importance to the economy. Different types of buildings have limitations on their functions and involve different bundles of assets: consider an e-commerce warehouse packed with logistics robotics and a hospital with beds and MRI scanners. The notion of infrastructure is expanding in policy debates to embrace social and cultural infrastructure (Kelsey and Kenny 2021) and digital public infrastructure (Eaves et al. 2024), so an appreciation of the importance of assets is in the air. Chapter 3 discussed the growing as-a-service phenomenon in the digital economy, making the identification of flows of services provided by assets important in that context. There is also, as discussed earlier, a strong case for improved measurement of intangible capital assets, as they are becoming increasingly important in creating additional economic value.

This leads to the second point in favour of a comprehensive wealth approach, which is that investment for future consumption always involves different types of assets in combination. This means it will be important to consider not just the stocks of different assets—whether machines, patents, or urban trees (which cool the ambient temperature)—but also the extent to which the services they provide are substitutes or complements for each other: What is the correlation matrix? A patent for a new gadget will require investment in specific machines to put it into production and may benefit from tree planting if the production process heats the factory; the trees may substitute for an air-conditioning plant and also for concrete flood defences downstream if their roots absorb enough rain. A recent paper (Cairns and Davis 2024) highlights the importance of understanding the complementarities: "So long as a particular irreversible capital good remains with its project, in many cases until it is scrapped, its contribution comes not solely on its own account but as a result of complementarity with other capital goods. The project's income is not composed of distinct contributions from individual assets" (p8). They underline that non-marketed capital, such as a firm's organisation or internal knowledge, is another essential complement in thinking about assets in a comprehensive way. This argument supports the case for incorporating social capital or organisational capital in a comprehensive wealth framework—although as explained in the last chapter, views differ about this. Cairns and Davis write: "Non-marketed capital also includes [as well as standard intangibles such as intellectual property] organization, entrepreneurship, reputation, some tangible environmental goods without property rights, etc., that are not mediated in markets because they are qualitative and do not have natural units of measurement." With no natural units, non-market assets do not have a well-defined marginal price, and in any case when a bundle of complementary assets are needed together, it is not meaningful to try to distinguish separately the returns (or capital services) they provide. Concrete plus wetland planting plus pumping equipment *together* provide flood defence services.

A balance-sheet approach also helps integrate the role of debt into consideration of progress. Debt is how consumption occurs now at the expense of consumption in future. In addition to financial debt, whether issued by governments or businesses or owed by individuals, there is a large and unmeasured burden of debt to nature. In a range of natural capital assets, including a stable climate, past and current consumption is reducing future opportunities.

In summary, to track sustainable economic welfare, a comprehensive wealth approach is desirable, identifying separately the types of assets that contribute capital services to economic actors. Some of them have no natural volume units. (You can count the number of isotope ratio mass spectrometers, but how do you count the accumulated know-how of a top law firm?) Many will not have a market price at all, and if they do, it is likely not to be the shadow price relevant to social welfare, so the monetary valuation needed to aggregate individual assets (by putting them into a common unit of account) is problematic (Hicks 1974). And the complementarities and substitutability across categories need to be better understood, including non-market assets such as organisational capabilities. (The development economics literature talks about this in terms of institutions or social capital; Singapore had few physical assets and little manufacturing industry to speak of in 1946, so it clearly relied on other assets to become one of the world's highest per capita income countries.)

This is a challenging measurement agenda to say the least, but it is an obvious path for statistical development. Some readers will find the sustainability argument the most persuasive. There are two other supporting rationales, though. One is that a significant body of economic theory (appealing to both neoclassical and heterodox economists) supports it (Dasgupta and Maler 2000, Weitzman 1976): an increase in comprehensive wealth, at appropriately measured shadow prices, corresponds to an increase in social well-being. The other is that the statistical community has already started heading down this path with the agreement of UN statistical standards for measuring (some) natural capital and the services it provides. The 2025 SNA revision will include a little more detail about how official statisticians should be implementing this. It is a giant step forward, conceptually and practically—although it does not go far enough in that it insists on the use of valuations as close as possible to market prices, when the main issue in accounting for the environment is that markets grotesquely misprice resource use.

Capabilities

Comprehensive wealth involves a kind of dashboard approach, one whose selected indicators are informed by economic theory and shaped by a production function concept. On the supply side of the economy, the set of assets involved in economic production is conceptualised as providing capital services as inputs into economically valuable activities. This includes labour, with labour services seen as a flow deriving from the stock of human capital—and this makes many expenditures on health and education a form of investment rather than consumption.

On the consumption side, the comprehensive wealth framework has generally used the standard utility-maximisation approach, over an infinite horizon with a (much-debated) Ramsey social discount rate. However, it can also accommodate the capabilities perspective, with assets interpreted as a capabilities set. This does not lead to an immediate measure of aggregate social welfare, which will depend on individual "conversion factors," but it does provide an informationally rich environment for this evaluation. One of the objections to wider adoption of the capabilities approach in economics (where it is largely confined to development economics) has been the apparent difficulty of applying it in practical empirical contexts—as noted, even Amartya Sen was hesitant on this front. However, recent research (e.g., Comim 2008, Wdowin 2024) has demonstrated that some standard survey data lends itself to an empirical application of the capabilities approach. In any case, the availability of a broad set of assets, from which people may be able to derive a flow of services enabling them to undertake the activities they want, maps cleanly to Sen's concept of "our capability to lead the kind of lives we have reason to value" (Sen 1999, p285). The further development of comprehensive wealth measurement may open the way to further development of an approach to social welfare that could finally dethrone the grip of philosophically naïve utilitarianism on economic science. Economic students are rapidly socialised into the machinery of utility theory, which is deeply internalised among economic researchers, but it is a Heath-Robinson theoretical construct with a weak empirical basis in human psychology.

Shadow Prices

There are many obstacles to developing a measure of aggregate economic progress, not least the impossibility theorems of social choice theory. These restate formally the problem of selecting weights to combine separate metrics into an aggregate, as previously discussed: aggregation involves normative judgments, the identification of some outcomes (or people) as mattering more than others. But any decision made in the collective context of public policy—for which statistics are developed—will require a choice to be made. Presenting a set of measures as in the comprehensive wealth approach, instead of a single measure, makes this more explicit. Given that there will always be some degree of aggregation involved in any measurement framework, though, thinking about weights becomes a central issue.

The merit of the existing national accounts statistics is that market prices, or exchange values, are used as the weights to aggregate individual activities. This is conceptually clear. But it has created an illusion of objectivity, as prices seem to be measures in the real world that can be observed and collected, more or less accurately. Considerable effort has gone into getting ever more granular and speedy data on prices, such as scanner data direct from stores or online prices, to improve the accuracy and timeliness of price statistics. But while the observational data is what it is, there is no value-free construction of price indices and the use of prices to determine a "real" aggregate outcome (as discussed in Chapter 7). Constructing deflators is a normative, as well as a positive, exercise.

Moreover, any economist accepts that market prices allocate resources inefficiently from the social welfare perspective in many contexts. This includes not only obvious environmental externalities, such as depletion of common-pool resources or harmful emissions, but also prices in any markets where there is imperfect competition or significant increasing returns to scale. Given that pretty much no existing economy even remotely conforms to the perfect-information, flat world of the welfare theorems, market prices are clearly inadequate measures. Their sole advantage is transparency. However, the SNA cleaves tightly to using market prices or exchange values, as does its SEEA extension. There is huge resistance among statisticians to devising alternatives, which I think is again driven by the absence of a consensus about what would be better. In theory, it is clear that estimates of shadow prices are needed, but there is no settled practice about how to estimate them. The trouble is that this means all externalities are priced at zero in the national accounts, which is even more wrong than an estimated shadow price would be. As Partha Dasgupta set out so clearly in his landmark *The Economics of Biodiversity* (2021), the zero price for nature as the economy has grown since the 1950s has led to existentially threatening overuse of natural resources. In this domain if nowhere else, it is imperative to develop statistics that involve estimates of shadow prices. But it is not just environmental contexts that are at stake. Cultural and heritage assets, social assets, digital assets that appear to be free including data, and newer common-pool resources such as those used for training generative AI all require the use of shadow price estimates.

The environmental and cultural economics literatures already offer several approaches to estimating shadow prices, and newer digital methods are offering some novel possibilities. These generally involve a specific context and are one-offs. Much work would be needed to develop methods that can systematically be used for statistical production, and there are certainly some daunting conceptual hurdles as well. This is a strand of research I currently have underway with my colleagues, including those at ONS.

So to measure progress—to count what really matters—the comprehensive wealth approach offers a framework that embraces a wide range of the indicators many dashboards would regard as desirable, it embeds considerations of sustainability, and it has a fairly solid grounding in both conventional economic theory and in the capabilities approach. What it does not provide is an accounting framework—although, as pointed out earlier, neither does the existing SNA when its components are measured in real rather than current price terms. Can it be combined, as a supply side framework, with an accounting framework that will incorporate the demand side of the economy? I think so. But first, two other issues are worth mentioning briefly, classifications and geographic granularity.

Classification

One measurement challenge this book has only lightly touched on is that of classifying economic activities. Some of the familiar definitional distinctions have never been as crisp as they seem, and the boundaries are becoming more blurred, as this book has discussed. For instance, distinguishing intermediate purchases from capital investment by companies is one instance of boundary hopping as companies switch to cloud computing. Large-scale leasing already made this a problematic distinction. Some FGP firms that do not manufacture may be classified as manufacturers or they may be classified as wholesalers. The statistical agencies are starting to move the latter businesses into the manufacturing category, but this is not obviously correct either. Another example is the production-boundary blurring brought about by do-it-yourself digital activities, including open-source production. The erosion of conceptual boundaries is a sure sign of an analytical framework ceasing to be useful as the world changes.

Even more pressing, perhaps, are the standard ways of classifying both sectors or industries and occupation. The original frameworks for these date from the 1940s and still include far more detail on manufacturing than on services. There is no question about the need to continue increasing the detail in services classification. As Chapter 3 described, the manufacturing-services distinction is decreasingly useful as all manufacturing involves service activities, which are often the parts that add the most value. Similarly, occupational classifications have not kept up with current changes in the labour market as AI and other digital tools spread. The framework of tasks is more helpful, and researchers use the US O*NET classification of tasks. But the evolution of tasks is also moving faster than this classification. Much research now is applying newer data collection techniques such as web scraping or online job listings and clustering activities according to the patterns that emerge from the data.

Unfortunately, there is no appetite in the world of official statistics for revisiting the official classifications, beyond expanding the existing categories to include more detail, not least because it would imply the loss of backward compatibility in data series over time. But unless there are new official classifications, according to which firms classify themselves in all the basic data collection done by statistics offices, it will not be possible to have a more representative picture of how the economy is evolving. Increasingly frequent studies that use techniques such as web crawling to determine business classifications may make the official statistics decreasingly useful.

Place

Chapter 6 on measurement issues around trade has already highlighted some challenges in measurement when this is framed around national economies in a world of globalised production. A separate issue of scale is the collection of data at subnational scale. Current availability varies greatly between countries depending on how decentralised their governance is; in the highly centralised UK polity it has been poor, although improving. However, the growing economic geography literature has highlighted the gaps that can occur between administrative boundaries and actual economic activity. The "natural" economic geography of different locations—major cities and their hinterlands, coastal communities, rural areas, unconnected small towns—will not align with political and administrative boundaries, although the latter are of vital interest for linking data to policy choices. Economies happen in specific places, and the shifting structure of the economy has led to polarised outcomes between growing urban conglomerations with a rising share of well-paid professional jobs and "left behind" places, whether smaller towns, rural areas, or coastal communities. What's more, the pattern of economic transactions will shift if transport and communications networks change.

Conventional methods of collecting economic statistics quickly become expensive when greater spatial granularity is required. For example, surveys may need to be much larger to ensure each cell of data collected has enough observations to be statistically robust. There are some excellent spatial datasets, such as the United Kingdom's Ordnance Survey, which has geographically located data at a fine spatial scale for many amenities, including libraries, shops, train stations, and hospitals; we used this to explore the differences between English towns, documenting huge variability and making the case for a policy commitment to a Universal Basic Infrastructure for every place (Coyle, Erker, and Westwood 2023). This includes both traditional physical infrastructure (an important element of the economy's physical capital) and social infrastructure, whose importance is increasingly being acknowledged in academic research.

Some newer data sources are also promising, such as satellite images, transactions data from financial service providers or supermarkets, and mobility data from telecoms companies. However, these are not used much in statistical production yet and so not systematically available to statisticians, policymakers, or researchers. This is likely to change as political and economic geographies evolve. Official statistics will, as always, ultimately respond to the needs of the state. A changing economic structure implies a changing economic geography.

A Time-Use Accounting Framework

There is an alternative possible accounting framework, time use. It is a different meaning of accounting—not the standard national accounts meaning of a double-entry (or in fact quadruple-entry) system expressed in a common monetary numeraire, but rather in the sense of accounting for the allocation of a fixed amount of a resource, time (Land and Juster 1981). As discussed in earlier chapters (2 and 4), time offers a useful lens on both production and consumption as the digital economy changes the structure of both. Productivity advances involve saving time, both the process innovations discussed in those earlier chapters and the many product innovations used in business, from the photocopier to (potentially) generative AI. Higher output per hour is the same as fewer hours per unit of output. On the consumption and household production side, both product and process innovations have often been time-savers (washing machines, nylon tights, smartphone apps) or have enhanced the value people get from how they spend their time. This value could be in the form of more hours of high-quality nursing care, or it could be enjoyable streaming videos or mobile games. Leonard Nakamura and I (2022) proposed an expanded approach to consumption based on time use. The welfare outcome would be individual "full incomes," or the sum of utilities (measured in terms of a monetary numeraire) over time, taking into account paid work, household work, and leisure, and measuring the well-being derived from each activity.

Outside the Beckerian tradition, economists have paid surprisingly little attention to time in this respect, despite its being the ultimate scarce resource (although there is a vast literature on savings and interest rates, which are also fundamentally about allocation at the time margin). There is a non-neoclassical tradition of focusing on economic processes occurring through time (e.g., Georgescu-Roegen 1971, Shackle 1967, and Robinson 1980). The heterodox journal *Oeconomia* published a 2017 special issue on time in economics, but only one article (Nisticò 2017) concerns the question I am interested in. Sociologists and historians have thought more about time. For instance, E. P. Thompson's classic article (1967) on how English workers understood time as the country entered the Industrial Revolution made a big impression on me when I read it as a teenager; earlier internalised notions of how (variably) long it took to fulfil a task were replaced by clock-based, external timekeeping as a means of enforcing work discipline in the mills. Thompson highlights not the new technologies as such but rather the "greater sense of time-thrift among the improving capitalist employers" (p78). (On my wall hangs a poster setting out the rules for workers from one of the cotton mills near my hometown in Lancashire; the first is a schedule of fines for lateness even by as few as five minutes.) Sociologist Elizabeth Cohen has analysed time more broadly as a dimension of political control (2018). Jonathan Gershuny has a long-term pioneering project on time use in the United Kingdom, including looking at the reallocation of time during the COVID pandemic and the time spent on digitally mediated activities (Gershuny et al. 2020, 2022).

Yet digital technology is upending how people spend their time, and also how production occurs through time. Everyone has a time budget constraint, which is an identity, whereas the money budget constraint is a weak inequality (you don't have to spend all your money). Consumption choices involve at least two interacting margins: allocating time and money. As the OECD economies have become increasingly services oriented, how people choose between ways to spend their time is obviously a key economic decision. The time dimension crops up in other ways post-pandemic, too, such as the decision to work from home and forgo commuting. Nick Bloom has found that mid-Wednesday afternoon has experienced the biggest increase in use of US golf clubs compared with pre-pandemic times, as people reorganise how they spend their working time; hybrid working has introduced a new flexibility into one of the margins of choice (Bloom and Finan 2023). Yet Ian Steedman's *Consumption Takes Time* (2001) is the only economics text I have found to take the time margin of choice by consumers seriously, while Chris Freeman and Francisco Louça's 2001 book *As Time Goes By* highlights time taken to produce.

The use of a time-based framework raises many of its own challenges concerning evaluation and aggregation. In particular, a shadow value of time is needed alongside other shadow prices. The standard practices are to use the market wage as in Becker (1965), as it is an opportunity cost of household work or leisure, or alternatively to use the market cost of household work. The ONS in the United Kingdom uses the former; the BEA in the United States uses the latter. However, our alternative would be to incorporate the intrinsic value of different activities, and we are considering both revealed and stated preference approaches to putting this into practice. The absence of a standard methodology is similar to the shadow prices challenge for comprehensive wealth measurement.

Nevertheless, a time-use accounting framework alongside the measurement of comprehensive wealth provides a holistic approach to understanding progress: How efficiently do societies use all the resources available to them to produce and consume activities and products of value? How sustainable is this activity—are we serving our own well-being by depleting the resources or capabilities available to future generations? This is a huge conceptual and practical agenda, but it builds on substantial foundations in the economics literature and in the practices of statistical agencies.

Principles for the Measurement of Economic Welfare

This book has covered a lot of territory, each aspect of which involves many scholars around the world working on matters of detail I have not been able to cover. One of the striking things about this vibrant and growing research community is how recently it has come into being. There have been critics of the conventional statistics including GDP for pretty much as long as they have existed, with a particular surge during the 1970s (Coyle 2014). But previously the critics have not gained this much traction, and the community of professional statisticians had not needed to rethink substantially what they do. This has changed during the past fifteen years or so. The Stiglitz-Sen-Fitoussi report in 2009 was a milestone, not only for its rigour and clarity but also because it had been officially commissioned by then president of France, Nicolas Sarkozy. This helped encourage an official response from bodies like the European Commission and OECD. The other trigger for this recent surge of interest has been the digital revolution, bringing the tech sector and investment analysts into a coalition demanding a fresh approach to measuring the economy. Their pressure for better measurement of digital matters was one of the factors prompting an official UK review into statistics, commonly known as the Bean review, in 2016. Other agencies in the United States, Australia, the Netherlands, and elsewhere have also subsequently forged ahead on the broad agenda of digital measurement as well as the much longer-standing agenda of accounting for environmental change and household work.

This chapter has tried to draw together some threads from all the detail. It offers a personal view on what might be needed to develop a measurement framework more useful to policymakers and researchers who want to evaluate how well their society is doing. Are things getting better, what do we mean by better, and for whom? I do not think we are anywhere near a consensus on what might adjust or replace the SNA, the measurement framework set solidly in place from 1946. It has evolved and become more sophisticated—and complicated—but the core elements are unchanged. The SNA revision in 2025 will be another set of incremental changes rather than any changes of principle. One attractive proposal is to take an approach that involves an expanding series of incremental changes, conceiving of measurement on what the authors (Heys et al. 2019, Bucknall et al. 2021) describe as a "spectrum of opportunity." This spectrum would range from a narrow measure of pure market activities within GDP via GDP proper through a range of alternatives that introduce successively some improvements to GDP to account for intangibles and collective goods, through adjustments for

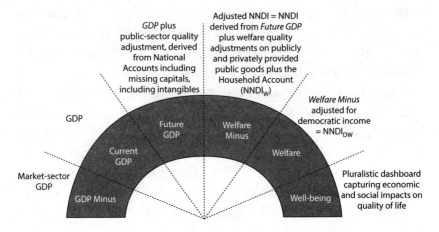

FIGURE 9.1. The spectrum approach. *Source:* Heys et al. (2019).

depreciation and distribution to a full multidimensional welfare evaluation (Figure 9.1).

But the questions of principle will not go away, and I predict the community of researchers will continue to grow and to develop both theoretical and practical advances. If nothing else, the more AI reshapes business and daily life, the more glaring the gap between the actual economy and official economic statistics will be. While there is much work to be done (just as there was in the decades after the Second World War in developing the SNA), some principles are clear:

- The measurement framework must embed sustainability and a balance sheet, and the comprehensive wealth approach is one well-founded way of doing this. Standard statistics could be used to report net product (not GDP) as a first step.
- Time must be spent. Speed of processes in production, and choice over activities in consumption, can provide an accounting framework for economic measurement.
- Any conversion of nominal into real quantities, and any attempt to measure externalities, turns the act of measurement into a social welfare activity. Immediately, we have to ask: Whose welfare?
- Distribution of income and consumption, or access to assets, is therefore required to evaluate economic progress.

- Social welfare is inherently multidimensional, and some things are incommensurable. Yet decisions need to be made, so there will always be explicit or implicit trade-offs. The multiple dimensions will always be reduced to one at the point of decision, and nobody has an alternative suggestion to using money metrics for comparison.
- This means that shadow prices are fundamentally important. Market prices may be observable, but there is nothing objective about them in the normative terrain of aggregate economic measurement.
- Economic measurement is a technical but not a technocratic domain. It is highly value laden.

Economic statistics represent what other social scientists have described as "thick concepts" (e.g., Anderson 2002). These are simultaneously both descriptive and evaluative. Even a definition can be evaluative. In contrast to other social scientists, economists have been resistant to the idea that their work makes value judgments, using terms such as "efficiency" as if it were descriptive of positive reality rather than inherently normative (Coyle 2021). Economics abounds with highly value-laden but seemingly technical concepts, such as discount rates (Deringer 2018, Dasgupta 2008) or price indices (again, see Chapter 7). As my colleagues Anna Alexandrova and Mark Fabian (2022) have put it, "The very definition of a scientific term requires an evaluative standard, often a controversial one. Judgments about moral, political or aesthetic value thus enter into the most technical aspects of research, namely measurement" (p1). There is no getting away from the evaluative aspect of economic measurement.

Existing economic statistics have many compelling features. They form a comprehensive accounting system, are firmly established on theoretical foundations, and provide massive detail on the use of resources in the economy, drawing on decades of expertise. Doing better in terms of a systemic economic welfare measurement framework would be challenging, if possible. But there is no alternative to trying to do better in at least some directions, because the elegant postwar system, updated as it has been several times over, is failing us. It is too narrow a lens on what should be measured to understand the possibilities for economic progress.

Conclusion

Today's official framework for measuring the economy dates from an era when physical capital was scarce and natural resources were seemingly unconstrained. Manufacturing was the leading sector of the economy, and digital technology was in its infancy. The original national accounts were created using a mechanical calculating machine, not on a computer. Digital technologies have transformed the structure of production and consumption, and at a time of such significant structural change the supply side of the economy needs to be taken seriously. Policy decisions taken now will affect people's lives for decades to come because the structure of so many industries is changing significantly. It is no wonder industrial policy is back in fashion among policymakers. The spread of automated decision-making in policy contexts emphasises the urgency of careful construction of the data being used, and reflection about the underlying data-generating processes.

Unfortunately, as earlier chapters set out, there are yawning gaps in our basic statistics. Official statisticians do important work even as many governments have been cutting their budgets—a bizarre and counterproductive decision when the private sector is investing substantially in collecting data. However, the focus of the statistical agencies is on incremental improvement to the existing SNA, which will change for the better but not by much when the new standards are confirmed in 2025. There are huge data collection and analytical gaps in what is needed now, comprehensive wealth and time use, and a huge intellectual agenda when those statistics do become available. Just as the production of the first GDP figures gave birth to theories of economic growth, so sustainable balance sheet and time-use metrics will be generative for economists thinking about how societies progress.

This book has ranged widely over a large body of research into economic statistics, and there is no doubt this area will continue to expand—because it is all too obvious that something new is needed. The critiques of the earlier Beyond GDP movement have given way to a more constructive period of statistical innovation—and I have given some examples of fruitful new methods and types of data. This book will hardly be the last word. However, I think some conclusions are clear. Measures that account for sustainability, natural and societal, are clearly imperative; the comprehensive wealth framework does this, and can potentially provide a broad scaffolding which others can use to tailor dashboards that serve specific purposes. A second conclusion is that while ideas have always driven innovation and progress, their role in adding value is even more central as the share of intangible value in the economy increases.

Finally, economic value added cannot be defined and measured without an underlying conception of value. This normative conception varies greatly between societies and over time, not least because of profound changes in technology and structure. It is a question of public philosophy as much as economics. Welfare economics has hardly moved on from the heyday of social choice theory in the 1970s, with social welfare defined as the sum of individual utilities; the philosophically rich capabilities approach has made little headway in everyday economics, except perhaps for development economics. It is not yet clear whether the OECD economies will break away from the public philosophy of individualism and markets that has dominated policy for the past half century, despite all the critiques of neoliberalism; but the fact of popular discontent and its political consequences suggest they might. No wonder commentators so often reach for Gramsci's famous *Prison Notebooks* comment, "the old order is dying and the new cannot be born; in this interregnum a great variety of morbid symptoms appear." If a new shared understanding of economic value does emerge from the changes underway now, it will acknowledge the importance of context and variety, beyond averages and "representative consumers"; incorporate collective outcomes as well as individual ones; and recognise the difference between them due to pervasive externalities, spillovers, and scale effects; and it will embed the economy in nature, appreciating the binding resource constraints on future growth.

REFERENCES

Abdirahman, M., Coyle, D., Heys, R., and Stewart, W. A. (2020). Comparison of deflators for telecommunications services output. *Economie et Statistique / Economics and Statistics*, 517–519, 103–122. https://doi.org/10.24187/ecostat.2020.517t.2017

Abdirahman, M., Coyle, D., Heys, R., and Stewart, W. A. (2022). Telecoms deflators: A story of volume and revenue weights. *Economie et Statistique / Economics and Statistics*, 530–531, 43–59. https://doi.org/10.24187/ecstat.2022.530.2063

Abramovitz, M. (1956). Resource and output trends in the United States since 1870. *The American Economic Review*, 46(2), 5–23.

Acemoglu, D., and Autor, D. (2011). Skills, tasks and technologies: Implications for employment and earnings. In D. Card and O. Ashenfelter (Eds.), *Handbook of labor economics* (Vol. 4, Part B, pp. 1043–1171). Elsevier.

Acemoglu, D., Makhdoumi, A., Malekian, A., and Ozdaglar, A. (2022). Too much data: Prices and inefficiencies in data markets. *American Economic Journal: Microeconomics*, 14(4), 218–256. https://doi.org/10.1257/mic.20200200

Acemoglu, D., and Robinson, J. A. (2012). *Why nations fail: The origins of power, prosperity, and poverty*. Random House.

Adams-Prassl, A., Adams-Prassl, J., and Coyle, D. (2021). *Uber and beyond: Policy implications for the UK* (Productivity Insights Paper No. 001). The Productivity Institute. https://www.productivity.ac.uk/research/uber-and-beyond-policy-implications-for-the-uk-2/

Adams-Prassl, A., Boneva, T., Golin, M., and Rauh, C. (2022). Work that can be done from home: Evidence on variation within and across occupations and industries. *Labour Economics*, 74, 102083. https://doi.org/10.1016/j.labeco.2021.102083

Adler, P. S., and Kwon, S. W. (2002). Social capital: Prospects for a new concept. *Academy of Management Review*, 27(1), 17–40.

Agarwala, M., Burke, M., and Mei, J.-C. (2024). *An inclusive wealth model of productivity 2024*. SSRN. http://dx.doi.org/10.2139/ssrn.4857812

Agarwala, M., Coyle, D., Peñasco, C., and Zenghelis, D. (2024). Measuring for the future, not the past. In N. Z. Muller, E. P. Fenichel, and M. Bohman (Eds.), *Measuring and accounting for environmental public goods: A national accounts perspective*. University of Chicago Press. https://www.nber.org/books-and-chapters/measuring-and-accounting-environmental-public-goods-national-accounts-perspective/measuring-future-not-past

Agarwala, M., and Martin, J. (2022). *Environmentally-adjusted productivity measures for the UK* (Working Paper No. 028). The Productivity Institute. https://www.productivity.ac.uk/wp

-content/uploads/2022/11/WP028-Environmentally-adjusted-productivity-measure
-FINAL-081122.pdf

Agarwala, M., and Zenghelis, D. (2021). Social capital and the changing wealth of nations. In the World Bank (Ed.), *The changing wealth of nations 2021: Managing assets for the future*. The World Bank.

Aghion, P., Bergeaud, A., Boppart, T., Klenow, P. J., and Li, H. (2019). Missing growth from creative destruction. *American Economic Review, 109*(8), 2795–2822. https://doi.org/10.1257/aer.20171745

Ahmad, N., and Schreyer, P. (2016). Are GDP and productivity measures up to the challenges of the digital economy? *International Productivity Monitor, 30*, 4–27. http://www.csls.ca/ipm/30/ahmadandschreyer.pdf

Ahmad, N., Ribarsky, J., and Reinsdorf, M. (2017). *Can potential mismeasurement of the digital economy explain the post-crisis slowdown in GDP and productivity growth?* (OECD Statistics Working Papers No. 2017/09). OECD Publishing, Paris. http://dx.doi.org/10.1787/a8e751b7-en

Ahuja, K., Chandra, V., Lord, V., and Peens, C. (2021, September 22). *Ordering in: The rapid evolution of food delivery*. McKinsey and Company. https://www.mckinsey.com/industries/technology-media-and-telecommunications/our-insights/ordering-in-the-rapid-evolution-of-food-delivery

Aitken, A., and Weale, M. (2020). A democratic measure of household income growth: Theory and application to the United Kingdom. *Economica, 87*(347), 589–610.

Albanesi, S. (2019, March). *Changing business cycles: The role of women's employment* (Working Paper No. 25655). National Bureau of Economic Research. https://doi.org/10.3386/w25655

Albanesi, S., da Silva, A. D., Jimeno, J. F., Lamo, A., and Wabitsch, A. (2023). *New technologies and jobs in Europe* (CEPR Discussion Paper DP18220). Centre for Economic Policy Research, London.

Alchian, A. A. (1958). *Costs and outputs*. RAND Corporation. https://www.rand.org/pubs/papers/P1449.html

Alexandrova, A., Agarwala, M., Coyle, D., Fabian, M., and Felici, M. (2021). *Wellbeing public policy needs more theory* (Bennett Institute Working Paper). Bennett Institute for Public Policy, University of Cambridge. https://www.bennettinstitute.cam.ac.uk/wp-content/uploads/2020/12/WPP_needs_more_theory_working_paper.pdf

Alexandrova, A., and Fabian, M. (2022). Democratising measurement: Or why thick concepts call for coproduction. *European Journal for Philosophy of Science*, https://doi.org/10.1007/s13194-021-00437-7

Allcott, H., Braghieri, L., Eichmeyer, S., and Gentzkow, M. (2020). The welfare effects of social media. *American Economic Review, 110*(3), 629–676.

Almås, I., Attanasio, O., and Jervis, P. (2023). *Economics and measurement: New measures to model decision making* (NBER Working Paper 30839). National Bureau of Economic Research.

Anderson, E. (1995). *Value in ethics and economics*. Harvard University Press.

Anderson, E. (2002). Situated knowledge and the interplay of value judgments and evidence in scientific inquiry. In P. Gärdenfors, J. Woleński, and K. Kijania-Placek (Eds.), *In the scope of logic, methodology and philosophy of science: Vol. two of the 11th International Congress of Logic,*

Methodology and Philosophy of Science, Cracow, August 1999 (pp. 497–517). Springer Science & Business Media.

Antràs, P., and Chor, D. (2022). Global value chains. In G. Gopinath, E. Helpman, and K. Rogoff (Eds.), *Handbook of international economics* (Vol. 5, pp. 297–376). Elsevier.

Araki, S., Bassanini, A., Green, A., Marcolin, L., and Volpin, C. (2023). *Labor market concentration and competition policy across the Atlantic* (IZA Discussion Paper No. 15641). SSRN. http://dx.doi.org/10.2139/ssrn.4254505

Argente, D., and Lee, M. (2020). Cost of living inequality during the Great Recession. *Journal of the European Economic Association, 19*(2), 913–952. https://doi.org/10.1093/jeea/jvaa018

Arrieta-Ibarra, I. A., Goff, L., Hernández, D. J., Lanier, J., and Weyl, G. E. (2018). Should we treat data as labor? Moving beyond "free." *American Economic Association Papers & Proceedings, 1*(1). https://doi.org/10.1257/pandp.20181003

Arrow, K. J. (1969). The organization of economic activity: Issues pertinent to the choice of market versus non-market allocation. Washington, DC: Joint Economic Committee of Congress. (Reprinted in *Microeconomics: Selected readings*, 4th ed., by Edwin Mansfield, Ed., 1982, Norton.) https://api.semanticscholar.org/CorpusID:10214644

Arrow, K. J., Dasgupta, P., Goulder, L. H., Mumford, K. J., and Oleson, K. (2012). Sustainability and the measurement of wealth. *Environment and Development Economics, 17*(3), 317–353.

Arrow, K., Solow, R., Portney, P. R., Leamer, E. E., Radner, R., and Schuman, H. (1993). Report of the NOAA panel on contingent valuation. *Federal Register, 58*(10), 4601–4614.

Asquith, B. J., Hellerstein, J. K., Kutzbach, M. J., and Neumark, D. (2017). *Social capital and labor market networks* (NBER Working Paper No. w23959). National Bureau of Economic Research.

Assa, J., and Kvangraven, I. H. (2021). Imputing away the ladder: Implications of changes in GDP measurement for convergence debates and the political economy of development. *New Political Economy, 26*(6), 985–1014. https://doi.org/10.1080/13563467.2020.1865899

Atkinson, A. B. (2005). *The Atkinson review: Final report. Measurement of government output and productivity for the national accounts.* Palgrave Macmillan, Basingstoke, England.

Autor, D., Dorn, D., Katz, L. F., Patterson, C., and Van Reenen, J. (2020). The fall of the labor share and the rise of superstar firms. *Quarterly Journal of Economics, 135*(2), 645–709. https://doi.org/10.1093/qje/qjaa004

Azhar, K. (2018, October 1). *Dyson transforming Johor's high-value manufacturing ecosystem.* The Edge Malaysia. https://theedgemalaysia.com/article/dyson-transforming-johors-highvalue-manufacturing-ecosystem

Bahia, K., Castells, P., and Pedrós, X. (2019, June 16–19). *The impact of mobile technology on economic growth: Global insights from 2000–2017 developments* [Conference presentation]. 30th European Conference of the International Telecommunications Society (ITS), Helsinki, Finland.

Bajari, P., Chernozhukov, V., Hortaçsu, A., and Suzuki, J. (2019). The impact of big data on firm performance: An empirical investigation. *AEA Papers and Proceedings, 109*, 33–37.

Bakhshi, H., Coyle, D., and Lawton, R. (2023). *Issues in valuing cultural and heritage capital in the national accounts* (ESCoE Discussion Paper No. DP 2023-04). Economic Statistics Centre of Excellence.

Baldwin, R. (2016a). *The great convergence*. Harvard University Press.

Baldwin, R. (2016b). *Globalization's three unbundlings*. Harvard University Press.

Baldwin, R. (2019). *The globotics upheaval: Globalization, robotics, and the future of work*. Oxford University Press.

Baldwin, R. (2022, August). *Globotics and macroeconomics: Globalisation and automation of the service sector* (Working Paper No. 30317). National Bureau of Economic Research.

Baldwin, R., and Freeman, R. (2022). Risks and global supply chains: What we know and what we need to know. *Annual Review of Economics, 14*, 153–180. https://doi.org/10.1146/annurev-economics-051420-113737

Baldwin, R., and Robert-Nicoud, F. (2014). Trade-in-goods and trade-in-tasks: An integrating framework. *Journal of International Economics, 92*(1), 51–62.

Bank for International Settlements. (2023). *Lessons learnt on CBDCs: Report submitted to the G20 Finance Ministers and Central Bank Governors*. https://www.bis.org/publ/othp73.pdf

Bappenas/Ministry of National Development Planning. (2021). *A green economy for a net-zero future: How Indonesia can build back better after COVID-19 with the Low Carbon Development Initiative (LCDI)*. Low Carbon Development Indonesia. https://lcdi-indonesia.id/wp-content/uploads/2021/10/GE-Report-English-8-Oct-lowres.pdf

Barrero, J. M., Bloom, N., and Davies, S. (2023). The evolution of working from home. Stanford Institute for Economic Policy Research. https://wfhresearch.com/wp-content/uploads/2023/07/SIEPR1.pdf

Baumol, W. J. (1967). Macroeconomics of unbalanced growth: The anatomy of urban crisis. *American Economic Review, 57*(3), 415–426. https://www.jstor.org/stable/1812111

Bayard, K., Byrne, D., and Smith, D. (2015). The scope of U.S. "factoryless manufacturing." In S. Houseman and M. Mandel (Eds.), *Measuring globalization: better trade statistics for better policy: Vol. 2. Factoryless manufacturing, global supply chains, and trade in intangibles and data* (pp. 81–120). W. E. Upjohn Institute for Employment Research.

Becker, G. S. (1962). Investment in human capital: A theoretical analysis. *Journal of Political Economy, 70*(5), 9–49. https://www.jstor.org/stable/1829103

Becker, G. S. (1965). A theory of the allocation of time. *Economic Journal, 75*, 493–517.

Becker, G. S. (2007). Health as human capital: Synthesis and extensions. *Oxford Economic Papers, 59*(3), 379–410.

Belanger, A. (2024, February 17). Air Canada has to honor a refund policy its chatbot made up. *Wired*. https://www.wired.com/story/air-canada-chatbot-refund-policy/

Bénabou, R., and Tirole, J. (2006). Incentives and prosocial behavior. *American Economic Review, 96*(5), 1652–1678. https://doi.org/10.1257/aer.96.5.1652

Benitez, P., Blignaut, J., Kalisa, J., Katanisa, P., and Rutebuka, E. (2021). *Nature-smart post-pandemic economic recovery in Rwanda: A Natural Capital Accounting approach with an emphasis on the natural resources sectors*. World Bank. https://elibrary.worldbank.org/doi/abs/10.1596/36756

Bernard, A. B., and Fort, T. C. (2015). Factoryless goods producing firms. *American Economic Review, 105*(5), 518–523.

Bessen, J. (2022). *The new goliaths: How corporations use software to dominate industries, kill innovation, and undermine regulation*. Yale University Press.

Birch, K., and Muniesa, F. (Eds.). (2020). *Assetization: turning things into assets in technoscientific capitalism*. MIT Press.

Bjørnskov, C. (2006). Determinants of generalized trust: A cross-country comparison. *Public Choice, 130*(1), 1–21.

Bjørnskov, C. (2022). Social trust and patterns of growth. *Southern Economic Journal, 89*(1), 216–237.

Blind, K., and Schubert, T. (2023). Estimating the GDP effect of open source software and its complementarities with R & D and patents: Evidence and policy implications. *Journal of Technology Transfer. 49*(2), 466–491. https://doi.org/10.1007/s10961-023-09993-x

Blinder, A. S. (1991). Why are prices sticky? Preliminary results from an interview study. *American Economic Review, 81*(2), 89–100. https://www.jstor.org/stable/2006832

Bloom, N., and Finan, A. (2023). *Golfing from home* [Presentation]. https://nbloom.people .stanford.edu/sites/g/files/sbiybj24291/files/media/file/golfingfromhome.pdf

Bloom, N., Garicano, L., Sadun, R., and Van Reenen, J. (2014). The distinct effects of information technology and communication technology on firm organization. *Management Science, 60*(12), 2859–2885.

Bloom, N., Han, R., and Liang, J. (2023). How working from home works out (NBER Working Paper 30392). National Bureau of Economic Research.

Bloom, N., Jones, C. I., Van Reenen, J., and Webb, M. (2020). Are ideas getting harder to find? *American Economic Review, 110*(4), 1104–1144. https://doi.org/10.1257/aer.20180338

Bontadini, F., Corrado, C., Haskel, J., Iommi, M., and Jona-Lasinio, C. (2023). *EUKLEMS & INTANProd: Industry productivity accounts with intangibles - Sources of growth and productivity trends: Methods and main measurement challenges*. https://euklems-intanprod-llee.luiss.it/

Booth, L. (2023, September 1). *Statistics on access to cash, bank branches and ATMs*. House of Commons Library. https://commonslibrary.parliament.uk/research-briefings/cbp-8570/

Borin, A., and Mancini, M. (2019, April 4). *Measuring what matters in global value chains and value-added trade* (World Bank Policy Research Working Paper No. 8804). SSRN. https:// ssrn.com/abstract=3366657

Boskin Commission. (1996). *Toward a more accurate measure of the cost of living, final report*. Social Security Administration. https://www.ssa.gov/history/reports/boskinrpt.html#cpi5

Bourgeois, A. (2020). Free services from the digital economy: Do we need to measure their value and how? *Economie et Statistique / Economics and Statistics, 517–518–519,* 157–172. https:// doi.org/10.24187/ecostat.2020.517t.2021

Bournakis, I., Coyle, D., McHale, J., and Mei, J. (2024). Recent trends in firm-level total factor productivity in the United Kingdom: New measures, new puzzles. *Economica. 91*(364), 1320–1348. https://doi.org/10.1111/ecca.12541

Bradonjic, P., Franke, N., and Lüthje, C. (2019). Decision-makers' underestimation of user innovation. *Research Policy, 48*(6), 1354–1361. https://doi.org/10.1016/j.respol.2019.01.020

Bridgman, B. (2016). Accounting for household production in the national accounts: An update, 1965–2014. *Survey of Current Business, 96*(2), 1–5.

Brodkin, J. (2023, February 27). *VW wouldn't help locate car with abducted child because GPS subscription expired*. Ars Technica. https://arstechnica.com/tech-policy/2023/02/vw -wouldnt-help-locate-car-with-abducted-child-because-gps-subscription-expired/

Brynjolfsson, E., Collis, A., Diewert, W. E., Eggers, F., and Fox, K. J. (2019a). *GDP-B: Accounting for the value of new and free products in the digital economy* (NBER Working Paper No. 25695). National Bureau of Economic Research. https://doi.org/10.3386/w25695

Brynjolfsson, E., Collis, A., and Eggers, F. (2019b). Using massive online choice experiments to measure changes in well-being. *Proceedings of the National Academies of Science, 116*(15), 7250–7255. https://doi.org/10.1073/pnas.1815663116

Brynjolfsson, E., Collis, A., Erwin Diewert, W., Eggers, F., and Fox, K. J. (2020). Measuring the impact of free products on real household consumption. *AEA Papers and Proceedings, 110*, 25–30. https://doi.org/10.1257/pandp.20201054

Brynjolfsson, E., and Hitt, L. M. (2000). Beyond computation: Information technology, organizational transformation and business performance. *Journal of Economic Perspectives, 14*(4), 23–48.

Brynjolfsson, E., Hitt, L. M., and Yang, S. (2002). Intangible assets: Computers and organizational capital. *Brookings Papers on Economic Activity, 2002*(1), 137–181. https://www.jstor.org/stable/1209176

Brynjolfsson, E., Li, D., and Raymond, L. R. (2023). *Generative AI at work* (NBER Working Paper 31161). National Bureau of Economic Research. https://doi.org/10.3386/w31161

Brynjolfsson, E., and Oh, J. H. (2012). *The attention economy: Measuring the value of free digital services on the internet* [Conference presentation]. 33rd International Conference on Information Systems, Orlando, FL, United States.

Brynjolfsson, E., Rock, D., and Syverson, C. (2021). The Productivity J-curve: How intangibles complement general purpose technologies. *American Economic Journal: Macroeconomics, 13*(1), 333–372. https://doi.org/10.1257/mac.20180386

Bucknall, R., Christie, S., Heys, R., and Taylor, C. (2021, July). *GDP and welfare: Empirical estimates of a spectrum of opportunity* (ESCoE Discussion Paper No. 2021-08). Economic Statistics Centre of Excellence.

Bureau of Economic Analysis. (2024). *GDP by industry.* https://www.bea.gov/data/gdp/gdp-industry

Byrne, D., and Corrado, C. (2019). *Accounting for innovations in consumer digital services: IT still matters* (Finance and Economics Discussion Series No. 2019-049). Board of Governors of the Federal Reserve System. https://doi.org/10.17016/FEDS.2019.049

Byrne, D. M., and Corrado, C. A. (2020). *The increasing deflationary influence of consumer digital access services* (Finance and Economics Discussion Series No. 2020-021). Board of Governors of the Federal Reserve System. https://doi.org/10.17016/FEDS.2020.021

Byrne, D., Corrado, C., and Sichel, D. E. (2018). *The rise of cloud computing: Minding your P's, Q's and K's* (NBER Working Paper No. 25188). National Bureau of Economic Research. https://www.nber.org/papers/w25188

Byrne, D. M., Hamins-Puertolas, A., and Harnish, M. M. (2023). *Transistors all the way down: Viability of direct volume measurement (and price indexes) for semiconductors.* [Conference paper]. National Bureau of Economic Research. https://conference.nber.org/conf_papers/f188293.pdf

Cagé, J., Hervé, N., and Viaud, M.-L. (2020). The Production of information in an online world. *The Review of Economic Studies, 87*(5), 2126–2164.

Cairns, R. D., and Davis, G. A. (2024). Accounting for non-marketed capital. *Review of Income and Wealth, 70*(3), 639–660. https://doi.org/10.1111/roiw.12650

Calderón, J. B. S., Robbins, C., Guci, L., Korkmaz, G., and Kramer, B. L. (2022). *Measuring the cost of open source software innovation on GitHub* (BEA Working Paper series, WP2022–10). Bureau of Economic Analysis. https://www.bea.gov/system/files/papers/BEA-WP2022 -10.pdf

Case, A., and Deaton, A. (2020). *Deaths of despair and the future of capitalism.* Princeton University Press.

Cathles, A., Nayyar, G., and Rückert, D. (2020). *Digital technologies and firm performance: Evidence from Europe* (EIB Working Papers). European Investment Bank.

Cellan-Jones, R. (2021). *Always on: Hope and fear in the social smartphone era.* Bloomsbury Continuum.

Cellan-Jones, R. (2024, May 29). *Ultrasound—the future of Parkinson's care?* Rory's Always on Newsletter. https://rorycellanjones.substack.com/p/ultrasound-the-future-of -parkinsons

Census Bureau (2013). https://www.census.gov/library/visualizations/2013/comm/home _based_workers.html

Christensen, L. R., and Jorgenson, D. W. (1973). Measuring the performance of the private sector of the U.S. economy, 1929-1969. In M. Moss (Ed.), *Measuring economic and social performance* (pp. 233–351). Columbia University Press.

Christophers, B. (2013). *Banking across boundaries: Placing finance in capitalism.* John Wiley & Sons.

Clark, A. E., Flèche, S., Layard, R., Powdthavee, N., and Ward, G. (2018). *The origins of happiness: The science of wellbeing over the life course.* Princeton University Press.

Cloud Security Alliance. (2022, June 30). 中央深改委通过《关于构建数据基础制度更好 发挥数据要素作用的意见》[*Central Comprehensive Reform Commission approves "Opinions on building data infrastructure system to better utilize data elements"*]. https://c-csa.cn /news-detail/i-762.html

Cohen, D. (2018, September 21). The 10 year fight to offer a cheaper drug. BBC. https://www .bbc.co.uk/news/health-45600433

Cohen, E. F. (2018). *The political value of time: Citizenship, duration, and democratic justice.* Cambridge University Press.

Cohen, A. J., and Harcourt, G. C. (2003). Retrospectives: Whatever happened to the Cambridge capital theory controversies? *Journal of Economic Perspectives, 17*(1), 199–214.

Comim, F. (2008). Measuring capabilities. In *The capability approach: Concepts, measures and applications* (pp. 157–200). Cambridge University Press. https://doi.org/10.1017 /CBO9780511492587.007

Conway, E. (2023). *Material world: The six raw materials that shape modern civilization.* W. H. Allen.

Conway, E. (2024, May 14). *The unbearable lightness of productivity.* Material World. https:// edconway.substack.com/p/the-unbearable-lightness-of-productivity

Cook, E. (2017). *The pricing of progress: Economic indicators and the capitalization of American life.* Harvard University Press.

Cooper, K., Fabian, M., and Krekel, C. (2023). New approaches to measuring welfare. *Fiscal Studies*, 44(2), 123–135.

Corrado, C., Haskel, J., Jona-Lasinio, C., and Iommi, M. (2022). Intangible capital and modern economies. *Journal of Economic Perspectives*, 36(3), 3–28.

Corrado, C., Hulten, C. R., and Sichel, D. (2005). Measuring capital and technology: An expanded framework. In C. Corrado, J. Haltiwanger, and D. Sichel (Eds.), *Measuring capital in the new economy* (Studies in Income and Wealth, Vol. 66, pp. 11–46). University of Chicago Press.

Corrado, C., Hulten, C. R., and Sichel, D. (2009). Intangible capital and U.S. economic growth. *Review of Income and Wealth*, 55(3), 661–685.

Corrigan, J. R., Alhabash, S., Rousu, M., and Cash, S. B. (2018). How much is social media worth? Estimating the value of Facebook by paying users to stop using it. *PLoS ONE*, 13(12), e0207101. https://doi.org/10.1371/journal.pone.0207101

Coyle, D. (1997). *The weightless world*. Capstone/MIT Press.

Coyle, D. (2007; 2010). *The soulful science*. Princeton University Press.

Coyle, D. (2014; 2015). *GDP: A brief but affectionate history*. Princeton University Press.

Coyle, D. (2017a). The future of the national accounts: Statistics and the democratic conversation. *Review of Income and Wealth*, 63, S223–S237.

Coyle, D. (2017b). The political economy of national statistics. In K. Hamilton and C. Hepburn (Eds.), *National Wealth*. Oxford University Press.

Coyle, D. (2017c). Precarious and productive work in the digital economy. *National Institute Economic Review*, 240(1), R5–R14.

Coyle, D. (2019). Do-it-yourself digital: The production boundary, the productivity puzzle and economic welfare. *Economica*, 86(344), 750–774. https://doi.org/10.1111/ecca.12289

Coyle, D. (2020). *Markets, state, and people: Economics for public policy*. Princeton University Press.

Coyle, D. (2021). *Cogs and monsters: What economics is and what it should be*. Princeton University Press.

Coyle, D. (2022). Socializing data. *Daedalus*, 151(2), 348–359. https://www.amacad.org/publication/socializing-data

Coyle, D. (2023a). Economic progress and Adam Smith's dilemma. *National Institute Economic Review*, 265, 5–11. https://doi.org/10.1017/nie.2023.21

Coyle, D. (2023b, December). *The unsustainable is not sustained*. The Health Foundation. https://www.health.org.uk/publications/reports/the-unsustainable-is-not-sustained-productivity-future-NHS

Coyle, D. (2024a). Healthcare as social infrastructure: Productivity and the UK National Health Service during and after COVID-19. In S. Grosskopf, V. Valdmanis, and V. Zelenyuk (Eds.), *The Cambridge Handbook of Healthcare: Productivity, Efficiency, Effectiveness*. Cambridge University Press.

Coyle, D. (2024b). Productivity measurement: New goods, variety and quality. In L. Sheiner and M. Reinsdorf (Eds.), *The measure of economies: Measuring productivity in an age of technological change*. University of Chicago Press.

Coyle, D., and Gamberi, L. (2024). A real options approach to data valuation. *Business Economics*. https://doi.org/10.1057/s11369-024-00374-2

Coyle, D., Diepeveen, S., Kay, L., Tennison, J., and Wdowin, J. (2020). *The value of data*. Bennett Institute for Public Policy, University of Cambridge. https://www.bennettinstitute.cam.ac

.uk/wp-content/uploads/2020/12/Value_of_data_Policy_Implications_Report_26_Feb
_ok4noWn.pdf

Coyle, D., Erker, S., and Westwood, A. (2023, December 5). *Townscapes: A universal basic infra-stucture for the UK*. Bennett Institute for Public Policy University of Cambridge. https://www.bennettinstitute.cam.ac.uk/publications/townscapes-a-universal-basic-infrastructure-for-the-uk/

Coyle, D., Fabian, M., Beinhocker, E., Besley, T., and Stevens, M. (2023). Is it time to reboot welfare economics? Overview. *Fiscal Studies, 44*, 109–121. https://doi.org/10.1111/1475-5890.12334

Coyle, D., and Hampton, L. (2023). *Twenty-first century progress in computing. Telecommunications Policy, 48*(1), 102649. https://doi.org/10.1016/j.telpol.2023.102649

Coyle, D., and Li, W. C. Y. (2021). *The data economy: Market size and global trade* (ESCoE Discussion Paper No. 2021-09). Economic Statistics Centre of Excellence.

Coyle, D., Lind, K., Nguyen, D., and Tong, M. (2020). *Are digital-using UK firms more productive?* (ESCoE Discussion Paper No. 2022-06). Economic Statistics Centre of Excellence. https://www.escoe.ac.uk/publications/are-digital-using-uk-firms-more-productive/

Coyle, D., and Manley, A. (2021). *Potential social value from data: An application of discrete choice analysis*. SSRN. https://dx.doi.org/10.2139/ssrn.3973036

Coyle, D., and Manley, A. (2023). What is the value of data? A review of empirical methods. *Journal of Economic Surveys, 38*, 1317–1337. https://doi.org/10.1111/joes.12585

Coyle, D., Mei, J., and Hampton, S. (2023). *Relative price effects and UK labour productivity growth* (Working paper). Bennett Institute for Public Policy, University of Cambridge https://www.bennettinstitute.cam.ac.uk/wp-content/uploads/2023/05/Relative-price-effects-and-UK-labour-productivity-growth_WP.pdf

Coyle, D., and Msulwa, R. (2024). Digital concrete: Productivity in infrastructure construction. In S. Basu, L. Eldridge, J. Haltiwanger, and E. Strassner (Eds.), *Technology, productivity, and economic growth*. NBER/Chicago University Press.

Coyle, D., and Nakamura, L. (2022). Time use, productivity, and household-centric measurement of welfare in the digital economy. *International Productivity Monitor, 42*, 165–186. https://ideas.repec.org/a/sls/ipmsls/v42y20228.html

Coyle, D., and Nguyen, D. (2018). *Cloud computing and national accounting* (ESCoE Discussion Paper No. 2018-19). Economic Statistics Centre of Excellence. https://escoe-website.s3.amazonaws.com/wp-content/uploads/2020/07/13163356/ESCoE-DP-2018-19.pdf

Coyle, D., and Nguyen, D. (2019). Cloud computing, cross-border data flows and new challenges for measurement in economics. *National Institute Economic Review, 249*, R30–R38. doi:10.1177/002795011924900112

Coyle, D., and Nguyen, D. (2022). No plant, no problem? Factoryless manufacturing, economic measurement and national manufacturing policies. *Review of International Political Economy, 29*(1), 23–43. https://doi.org/10.1080/09692290.2020.1778502

Coyle, D., and Nguyen, D. (2023). Free digital products and aggregate economic measurement. *Economie et Statistique / Economics and Statistics, 539*, 27–50. https://doi.org/10.24187/ecostat.2023.539.2096

Coyle, D., and Weller, A. (2020). "Explaining" machine learning reveals policy challenges. *Science, 368*(6498), 1433–1434.

Crawford, I., and Oldfield, Z. (2002). *Distributional aspects of inflation*. IFS. https://ifs.org.uk /publications/distributional-aspects-inflation

Crozet, M., and Milet, E. (2017). Should everybody be in services? The effect of servitization on manufacturing firm performance. *Journal of Economics & Management Strategy, 26*(4), 820–841. https://doi.org/10.1111/jems.12211

Dachs, B., Biege, S., Borowiecki, M., Lay, G., Jäger, A., and Schartinger, D. (2014). Servitisation of European manufacturing: Evidence from a large scale database. *Service Industries Journal, 34*(1), 5–23. https://doi.org/10.1080/02642069.2013.776543

Dasgupta, P. (2005). Economics of social capital. *Economic Record, 81*, S2–S21. https://doi.org /10.1111/j.1475-4932.2005.00245.x

Dasgupta, P. (2008). Discounting climate change. *Journal of Risk and Uncertainty, 7*, 141–169. https://doi.org/10.1007/s11166-008-9049-6

Dasgupta, P. (2011). A matter of trust: Social capital and economic development. In J. Y. Lin and B. Pleskovic (Eds.), *World Bank Conference on Development Economics—global: Lessons from East Asia and the global financial crisis* (pp. 119–155). World Bank.

Dasgupta, P. (2021). *The economics of biodiversity: The Dasgupta review*. HM Treasury.

Dasgupta, P., and Maler, K. G. (2000). Net national product, wealth, and social well-being. *Environment and Development Economics, 5*(1/2), 69–93. https://www.jstor.org/stable/44404296

Daston, L. (2000). Why statistics tend not only to describe the world but to change it. *London Review of Books, 22*(8).

Davenant, C. (1698). *Discourses on the publick revenues, and on the trade of England*. J. Knapton.

Davenport, T. H., and Beck, J. C. (2001). *The attention economy: Understanding the new currency of business*. Harvard Business School Press.

David, P. A. (1990). The dynamo and the computer: An historical perspective on the modern productivity paradox. *American Economic Review, 80*(2), 355–361. https://www.jstor.org /stable/2006600

Deaton, A. (2008). Income, health, and well-being around the world: Evidence from the Gallup World Poll. *Journal of Economic Perspectives, 22*(2), 53–72. https://www.jstor.org/stable /27648241

Dedrick, J., and Kraemer, K. L. (2017). *Intangible assets and value capture in global value chains: The smartphone industry* (Vol. 41). WIPO.

Dell'Acqua, F., Rajendran, S., McFowland, E., III, Krayer, L., Mollick, E., Candelon, F., Lifshitz-Assaf, H., Lakhani, K. R., and Kellogg, K. C. (2024). *Navigating the jagged technological frontier: Field experimental evidence of the effects of AI on knowledge worker productivity and quality* (HBS Working Paper 24-013). Harvard Business School. https://www.iab.cl/wp -content/uploads/2023/11/SSRN-id4573321.pdf

DellaVigna, S., and La Ferrara, E. (2015). Economic and social impacts of the media. In *Handbook of media economics* (Vol. 1, pp. 723–768). Elsevier. https://doi.org/10.1016/B978-0-444 -63685-0.00019-X

De Loecker, J., Eeckhout, J., and Unger, G. (2020). The rise of market power and the macroeconomic implications. *Quarterly Journal of Economics, 135*(2), 561–644.

DeLong, B. (1998, March 2). *Brad DeLong: How fast is modern economic growth?* DeLong: Long Form. Retrieved April 6, 2020, from https://delong.typepad.com/delong_long_form/1998 /03/how-fast-is-modern-economic-growth.html

Department of Justice (2022). https://storage.courtlistener.com/recap/gov.uscourts.ilnd
.415798/gov.uscourts.ilnd.415798.120.0.pdf

Department for Transport. (2022). *National Travel Survey 2021: Household car availability and trends in car trips.* https://www.gov.uk/government/statistics/national-travel-survey-2021/national-travel-survey-2021-household-car-availability-and-trends-in-car-trips

Deringer, W. (2018). *Calculated values: Finance, politics, and the quantitative age.* Harvard University Press.

Desrosières, A (1998). *The politics of large numbers: A history of statistical reasoning.* Harvard University Press.

Diamond, P. A., and Hausman, J. A. (1994). Contingent valuation: Is some number better than no number? *Journal of Economic Perspectives, 8*(4), 45–64. https://www.jstor.org/stable/2138338

Diao, J. A., Wu, G. J., Taylor, H. A., Tucker, J. K., Powe, N. R., Kohane, I. S., and Manrai, A. K. (2021). Clinical implications of removing race from estimates of kidney function. *JAMA, 325*(2), 184–186. doi:10.1001/jama.2020.22124

Diewert, E. (2004). *Consumer price index manual: Theory and practice.* International Monetary Fund.

Diewert, W. E., Fox, K., and Schreyer, P. (2018). *The digital economy, new products and consumer welfare* (ESCoE Discussion Paper 2018-16). Economic Statistics Centre of Excellence.

Disabato, D. J., Goodman, F. R., Kashdan, T. B., Short, J. L., and Jarden, A. (2016). Different types of well-being? A cross-cultural examination of hedonic and eudaimonic well-being. *Psychological Assessment, 28*(5), 471–482. https://doi.org/10.1037/pas0000209

Doctorow, C. (2023, January 23). The "enshittification" of TikTok. *Wired.* https://www.wired.com/story/tiktok-platforms-cory-doctorow/

Doherty, M. (2015). Reflecting factoryless goods production in the U.S. statistical system. In S. N. Houseman and M. Mandel (Eds.), *Measuring globalization: Better trade statistics for better policy: Vol. 2. Factoryless manufacturing, global supply chains, and trade in intangibles and data* (pp. 13–44). W. E. Upjohn Institute for Employment Research.

Dolan, P., and Metcalfe, R. (2012). Measuring subjective wellbeing: Recommendations on measures for use by national governments. *Journal of Social Policy, 41*(2), 409–427.

Donaldson, D. (2018). Railroads of the Raj: Estimating the impact of transportation infrastructure. *American Economic Review, 108*(4–5): 899–934.

Donaldson, D., and Storeygard, A. (2016). The view from above: Applications of satellite data in economics. *Journal of Economic Perspectives, 30*(4): 171–198.

Dube, A., Jacobs, J., Naidu, S., and Suri, S. (2020). Monopsony in online labor markets. *American Economic Review: Insights, 2*(1), 33–46.

Dutz, M. A., Orszag, J. M., and Willig, R. D. (2012). The liftoff of consumer benefits from the broadband revolution. *Review of Network Economics, 11*(4), 2012. https://doi.org/10.1515/1446-9022.1355

Easterlin, R. A., and O'Connor, K. J. (2022). The Easterlin paradox. In K. Zimmerman (Ed.), *Handbook of labor, human resources and population economics* (pp. 1–25). Springer International Publishing.

Eaves, D., Mazzucato, M., and Vasconcellos, B. (2024). *Digital public infrastructure and public value: What is "public" about DPI?* (IIPP Working Paper 2024-05). UCL Institute for

Innovation and Public Purpose. https://www.ucl.ac.uk/bartlett/public-purpose /publications/2024/mar/digital-public-infrastructure-and-public-value-what-public-about -dpi

The Economist. (2023, June 28). *The working from home delusion fades.* https://www.economist .com/finance-and-economics/2023/06/28/the-working-from-home-delusion-fades?

Eeckhout, J. (2021). *The profit paradox: How thriving firms threaten the future of work* (1st ed.). Princeton University Press.

Eloundou, T., Manning, S., Mishkin, P., and Rock, D. (2024). GPTs are GPTs: An early look at the labor market impact potential of large language models. *Science, 384*(6702), 1306–1308. https://doi.org/10.1126/science.adj0998

Erickson, T., and Pakes, A. (2011). An experimental component index for the CPI: From annual computer data to monthly data on other goods. *American Economic Review, 101*(5), 1707– 1738. doi:10.1257/aer.101.5.1707

European Commission Directorate General for Communications Networks, Content and Technology. (2021). *The impact of open source software and hardware on technological independence, competitiveness and innovation in the EU economy: Final study report.* European Commission. https://data.europa.eu/doi/10.2759/430161

Fabian, M. (2022a). Scale norming undermines the use of life satisfaction scale data for welfare analysis. *Journal of Happiness Studies, 23*(4), 1509–1541.

Fabian, M. (2022b). *A theory of subjective wellbeing.* Oxford University Press.

Fabian, M., Alexandrova, A., Coyle, D., Agarwala, M., and Felici, M. (2023). Respecting the subject in wellbeing public policy: Beyond the social planner perspective. *Journal of European Public Policy, 30*(8), 1494–1517.

FDIC. (n.d). Data Explorer. https://banks.data.fdic.gov/explore/historical/?displayFields =STNAME%2CTOTAL%2CBRANCHES%2CNew_Char&selectedEndDate=2023 &selectedReport=CBS&selectedStartDate=1934&selectedStates=0&sortField =YEAR&sortOrder=desc

Federal Trade Commission Office of Technology. (2023, March 21). *An inquiry into cloud computing business practices: The Federal Trade Commission is seeking public comments.* Federal Trade Commission. https://www.ftc.gov/policy/advocacy-research/tech-at-ftc/2023/03 /inquiry-cloud-computing-business-practices-federal-trade-commission-seeking-public -comments

Feenstra, R. (1994). New product varieties and the measurement of international prices. *American Economic Review, 84*(1), 157–177.

Fenichel, E. P., and Abbott, J. K. (2014). Natural capital: From metaphor to measurement. *Journal of the Association of Environmental and Resource Economists, 1*(1/2), 1–27.

Fleming, M. (2023). *Enterprise information and communications technology - software pricing and developer productivity* (Working Paper No. 037). The Productivity Institute.

Foa, R., Klassen, A., Wenger, D., Rand, A., and Slade, M. (2020). Youth and satisfaction with democracy: Reversing the democratic disconnect? Bennett Institute for Public Policy, University of Cambridge. https://www.bennettinstitute.cam.ac.uk/wp-content/uploads/2022 /06/Youth_and_Satisfaction_with_Democracy-lite.pdf

Foa, R. S., Romero-Vidal, X., Klassen, A., Fuenzalida Concha, J., Quednau, M., and Fenner, L. (2022). The great reset: Public opinion, populism, and the pandemic. Bennett Institute for

Public Policy, University of Cambridge. https://www.bennettinstitute.cam.ac.uk/wp-content/uploads/2022/11/The_Great_Reset.pdf

Fort, T. C. (2023). The changing firm and country boundaries of US manufacturers in global value chains. *Journal of Economic Perspectives*, *37*(3), 31–58.

Foster, L., Grim, C., Haltiwanger, J. C., and Wolf, Z. (2021). Innovation, productivity dispersion, and productivity growth. In C. Corrado, J. Haskel, J. Miranda, and D. Sichel (Eds.), *Measuring and accounting for innovation in the twenty-first century* (pp. 103–136). University of Chicago Press.

Fransen, L., Del Bufalo, G., and Reviglio, E. (2018). Boosting investment in social infrastructure in Europe. European Commission Discussion Paper 074. https://economy-finance.ec.europa.eu/publications/boosting-investment-social-infrastructure-europe_en

Freeman, C., and Louçã, F. (2001). *As time goes by: From the industrial revolutions to the information revolution*. Oxford University Press.

Freeman, R. B., Nakamura, A. O., Nakamura, L. I., Prud'homme, M., and Pyman, A. (2011). Wal-Mart innovation and productivity: A viewpoint. *Canadian Journal of Economics/Revue canadienne d'économique*, *44*(2), 486–508. https://www.jstor.org/stable/41336371

Friedman, B. M. (2006). *The moral consequences of economic growth*. Vintage Books.

Frijters, P., and Krekel, C. (2021). *A handbook for wellbeing policy-making*. Oxford University Press.

Frischmann, B. M. (2012). *Infrastructure: The social value of shared resources*. Oxford University Press. https://doi.org/10.1093/acprof:oso/9780199895656.001.0001

Furman, J., Coyle, D., Fletcher, A., McAuley, D., and Marsden, P. (2019). *Unlocking digital competition: Report of the digital competition expert panel*. Government of the United Kingdom. https://assets.publishing.service.gov.uk/government/uploads/system/uploads/attachment_data/file/785547/unlocking_digital_competition_furman_review_web.pdf

Gal, P., et al. (2019). *Digitalisation and productivity: In search of the holy grail—Firm-level empirical evidence from EU countries* (OECD Economics Department Working Paper No. 1533). OECD Publishing. https://doi.org/10.1787/5080f4b6-en

Ganapati, S., and Wong, W. F. (2023). How far goods travel: Global transport and supply chains from 1965–2020. *Journal of Economic Perspectives*, *37*(3), 3–30.

Garicano, L. (2000). Hierarchies and the organization of knowledge in production. *Journal of Political Economy*, *108*(5), 874–904. https://doi.org/10.1086/317671

Gayfield, A., and Laughlin, L. (2023). *Counting the hustle: Platform workers and digital entrepreneurship in federal household surveys* (Working Paper No. WP2023-13). United States Census Bureau. https://www.census.gov/library/working-papers/2023/demo/SEHSD-WP2023-13.html

Geary, R. C. (1950). A note on "a constant-utility index of the cost of living." *Review of Economic Studies*, *18*(1), 65–66.

Georgescu-Roegen, N. (1971). *The entropy law and the economic process*. Harvard University Press.

Gershuny, J., Perez J., Sullivan, O., and Vega-Rapun M. (2022). Time use survey 6-wave sequence across the COVID-19 pandemic, 2016–2021. *Centre for Time Use Research*. https://10.5255/UKDA-SN-8741-4

Gershuny, J., Vega-Rapun, M., and Lamote, J. (2020). *Multinational time use study*. Centre for Time Use Research, Institute of Education, University College London.

Gibbons, S., Heblich, S., and Pinchbeck, T. (2018). *The spatial impacts of a massive rail disinvestment program: The Beeching axe* (CEP Discussion Papers dp1563). Centre for Economic Performance, London School of Economics.

Giles, C. (2017, July 20). The benefits of repairing Britain's broken retail prices index. *Financial Times*. https://www.ft.com/content/b71eabae-6c7f-11e7-bfeb-33fe0c5b7eaa

Goodridge, P., and Haskel, J. (2023). Accounting for the slowdown in UK innovation and productivity. *Economica, 90*(359), 780–812. doi: 10.1111/ecca.12468

Goolsbee, A., and Klenow, P. J. (2006). Valuing consumer products by the time spent using them: An application to the internet. *American Economic Review, 96*(2), 108–113.

Goolsbee, A., and Klenow, P. J. (2018). *Internet rising, prices falling: Measuring inflation in a world of e-commerce* (Becker Friedman Institute for Research in Economics Working Paper No. 2018-35). Becker Friedman Institute. http://dx.doi.org/10.2139/ssrn.3191099

Gordon, R.-J. (1999). The Boskin Commission report and its aftermath. *Monetary and Economic Studies, 17*(3), 41–68. Institute for Monetary and Economic Studies, Bank of Japan. https://www.imes.boj.or.jp/research/papers/english/me17-3-2.pdf

Gordon, R. J. (2016). *The rise and fall of American growth: The U.S. standard of living since the Civil War*. Princeton University Press.

Graboyes, R. (2016, October 19). A hand for innovation—Ivan Owen, Jon Schull and e-NABLE. Inside Sources. https://insidesources.com/a-hand-for-innovation-ivan-owen-jon-schull-and-e-nable/

Graham, C., Laffan, K., and Pinto, S. (2018). Wellbeing in metrics and policy. *Science, 362*(6412), 287–288.

Gramsci, A. (2005 edition). *Selections from the prison notebooks*. Lawrence Wishart.

Greenstein, S., and McDevitt, R. C. (2011). The broadband bonus: Estimating broadband internet's economic value. *Telecommunications Policy, 35*(7), 617–632. https://doi.org/10.1016/j.telpol.2011.05.001

Greenstein, S., and Nagle, F. (2014). Digital dark matter and the economic contribution of Apache. *Research Policy, 43*(4), 623–631. https://doi.org/10.1016/j.respol.2014.01.003

Greenwood, J., Seshadri, A., and Yorukoglu, M. (2005). Engines of liberation. *Review of Economic Studies, 72*(1), 109–133. https://www.jstor.org/stable/3700686

Grice, J. (2016). National accounting for infrastructure. *Oxford Review of Economic Policy, 32*(3), 431–445.

Griliches, Z. (1961). Hedonic price indexes for automobiles: An econometric analysis of quality change. In Report of the Price Statistics Review Committee (Ed.), *The price statistics of the federal government* (General Series no. 73, pp. 173–196). National Bureau of Economic Research.

Griliches, Z. (1994). Productivity, R&D, and the data constraint. *American Economic Review, 84*(1), 1–23.

Griliches, Z., and Mairesse, J. (1995). *Production functions: The search for identification* (NBER Working Paper 5067). National Bureau of Economic Research.

Groshen, E. L., Moyer, B. C., Aizcorbe, A. M., Bradley, R., and Friedman, D. M. (2017). How government statistics adjust for potential biases from quality change and new goods in an age of digital technologies: A view from the trenches. *Journal of Economic Perspectives, 31*(2), 187–210.

Gu, W. (2024). Health, human capital and its contribution to economic growth. In S. Grosskopf, V. Valdmanis, and V. Zelenyuk (Eds.), *The Cambridge handbook of healthcare: Productivity, efficiency, effectiveness.* Cambridge University Press.

Hall, B. H. (1993). The stock market's valuation of R&D investment during the 1980's. *American Economic Association, 83*(2), 259–264.

Harding, S. (2023, March 9). *HP outrages printer users with firmware update suddenly bricking third-party ink.* Ars Technica. https://arstechnica.com/gadgets/2023/03/customers-fume-as-hp-blocks-third-party-ink-from-more-of-its-printers/

Haskel, J., and Westlake, S. (2018). *Capitalism without capital: The rise of the intangible economy.* Princeton University Press.

Hausman, J. A. (1996). Valuation of new goods under perfect and imperfect competition. In T. F. Bresnahan and R. J. Gordon (Eds.), *The economics of new goods* (pp. 207–248). University of Chicago Press. https://www.nber.org/chapters/c6068

Hausman, J. (2012). Contingent valuation: From dubious to hopeless. *Journal of Economic Perspectives, 26*(4): 43–56. https://doi.org/10.1257/jep.26.4.43

Heggeness, M. (2020). Estimating the immediate impact of the COVID-19 shock on parental attachment to the labor market and the double bind of mothers. *Review of Economics of the Household, 18*(4), 1053–1078.

Hennigan, R. (2023). *How to become a digital nomad.* Harvard Business Review. https://hbr.org/2023/02/how-to-become-a-digital-nomad

Heys, R., Martin, J., and Mkandawire, W. (2019). *GDP and welfare: A spectrum of opportunity* (ESCoE Discussion Paper No. 2019-16). Economic Statistics Centre of Excellence.

Hicks, J. R. (1940). The valuation of the social income. *Economica, 7*(26), 105–124. https://doi.org/10.2307/2548691

Hicks, J. (1974). Capital controversies: Ancient and modern. *American Economic Review, 64*(2), 307–316.

Highfill, T., and Surfield, C. (2022). *New and revised statistics of the U.S. digital economy, 2005–2021.* US Bureau of Economic Analysis. https://www.bea.gov/system/files/2022-11/new-and-revised-statistics-of-the-us-digital-economy-2005-2021.pdf

Hinsch, M. E., Stockstrom, C., and Lüthje, C. (2014). User innovation in techniques. *Creativity and Innovation Management, 23*(4), 484–494. https://doi.org/10.1111/caim.12088

Hirschman, D. A. (2016). *Inventing the economy or: How we learned to stop worrying and love the GDP* [University of Michigan, doctoral dissertation]. https://deepblue.lib.umich.edu/handle/2027.42/120713

HM Treasury. (2021). *Wellbeing guidance for appraisal: Supplementary Green Book guidance.* HM Treasury. https://assets.publishing.service.gov.uk/media/60fa9169d3bf7f0448719daf/Wellbeing_guidance_for_appraisal_-_supplementary_Green_Book_guidance.pdf

Hoffmann, M., Nagle, F., and Zhou, Y. (2024, January 1). *The value of open source software* (Harvard Business School Strategy Unit Working Paper No. 24-038). https://dx.doi.org/10.2139/ssrn.4693148

Hong, T. (2023, August 16). *Explainer: What is digital public infrastructure?* Bill & Melinda Gates Foundation. https://www.gatesfoundation.org/ideas/articles/what-is-digital-public-infrastructure

Hulten, C., and Nakamura, L. (2020). Expanded GDP for welfare measurement in the 21st century. In C. Corrado, J. Miranda, J. Haskel, and D. Sichel (Eds.), *Measuring and accounting for innovation in the 21st century* (NBER Studies in Income and Wealth). University of Chicago Press.

Hulten, C., and Nakamura, L. (2022). *Is GDP becoming obsolete? The Beyond GDP debate* (NBER Working Paper No. 30196). National Bureau of Economic Research. https://www.nber.org/papers/w30196

Hummels, D. (2007). Transportation costs and international trade in the second era of globalization. *Journal of Economic Perspectives, 21*(3), 131–154.

Huppert, F.A. (2009). Psychological well-being: Evidence regarding its causes and consequences. *Applied Psychology: Health and wellbeing, 1*(2), 137–164.

IMF et al. (2023). *Handbook on measuring digital trade, second edition.* OECD Publishing, Paris/International Monetary Fund/UNCTAD, Geneva 10/WTO, Geneva. https://doi.org/10.1787/ac99e6d3-en.

Intergovernmental Science-Policy Platform on Biodiversity and Ecosystem Services (IPBES). (2019). *Global assessment report on biodiversity and ecosystem services of the intergovernmental science-policy platform on biodiversity and ecosystem services.* Zenodo. https://doi.org/10.5281/ZENODO.3831673

International Transport Forum. (2019). *What is the value of saving travel time?* ITF. https://www.itf-oecd.org/sites/default/files/docs/value-saving-travel-time.pdf

Jamison, M. A., and Wang, P. (2021). Valuation of digital goods during the coronavirus outbreak in the United States. *Telecommunications Policy, 45*(5), 102–126.

Jennings, F. (2023). *What went so wrong in economics* (MPRA Paper 117699). University Library of Munich, Germany.

Jiang, B. (2023, July 13). People's Daily unit issues first "data certificates" in China to prove data ownership and rights. *South China Morning Post.* https://www.scmp.com/tech/policy/article/3227535/peoples-daily-unit-issues-first-data-certificates-china-prove-data-ownership-and-rights

Johnson, R. C., and Noguera, G. (2012). Accounting for intermediates: Production sharing and trade in value added. *Journal of International Economics, 86*(2), 224–236.

Jones, C. I., and Klenow, P. J. (2016). Beyond GDP? Welfare across countries and time. *American Economic Review, 106*(9), 2426–2457. https://doi.org/10.1257/aer.20110236

Jones, C. I., and Tonetti, C. (2020). Nonrivalry and the economics of data. *American Economic Review, 110*(9), 2819–2858. https://doi.org/10.1257/aer.20191330

Jorgensen, D. W. (2012). The World KLEMS Initiative. *International Productivity Monitor, 24,* 5–19.

Jorgenson, D., and Fraumeni, B. M. (1989). The accumulation of human and nonhuman capital, 1948–84. In R. E. Lipsey and H. S. Tice (Eds.), *The measurement of saving, investment, and wealth* (pp. 227–286). University of Chicago Press. https://www.nber.org/chapters/c8121

Jorgenson, D. W., and Fraumeni, B. M. (1992). The output of the education sector. In Z. Griliches (Ed.), *Output measurement in the service sectors* (pp. 303–341). University of Chicago Press. https://www.nber.org/chapters/c7238

Jorgenson, D. W., Gollop, F. M., and Fraumeni, B. M. (1987). *Productivity and U.S. economic growth.* North-Holland.

Jorgenson, D. W., and Griliches, Z. (1967). The explanation of productivity change. *Review of Economic Studies*, 34(3), 249–283. https://doi.org/10.2307/2296675

Kahneman, D., Krueger, A. B., Schkade, D. A., Schwarz, N., and Stone, A. A. (2004). A survey method for characterizing daily life experience: The day reconstruction method. *Science*, 306(5702), 1776–1780.

Kamal, F., Moulton, B. R., and Ribarsky, J. (2015). Measuring "factoryless" manufacturing: Evidence from U.S. surveys. In S. N. Houseman and M. Mandel (Eds.), *Measuring globalization: Better trade statistics for better policy: Vol. 2. Factoryless manufacturing, global supply chains, and trade in intangibles and data* (pp. 45–80). W. E. Upjohn Institute for Employment Research.

Kane, R. (2012). *Measures and motivations: U.S. national income and product estimates during the Great Depression and World War II* (MPRA Paper No. 44336).

Karabell, Z. (2014). *The leading indicators: A short history of the numbers that rule our world.* Simon & Schuster.

Katz, L. F., and Krueger, A. B. (2019). Understanding trends in alternative work arrangements in the United States. *RSF: The Russell Sage Foundation Journal of the Social Sciences*, 5(5), 132–146. https://doi.org/10.7758/rsf.2019.5.5.07

Kelsey, T., and Kenny, M. (2021). The value of social infrastructure. Bennett Institute for Public Policy, University of Cambridge. https://www.bennettinstitute.cam.ac.uk/wp-content/uploads/2020/12/Townscapes_The_value_of_infrastructure.pdf

Ker, D., and Mazzini, E. (2020). Perspectives on the value of data and data flows (OECD Digital Economy Papers No. 299). OECD Publishing. https://doi.org/10.1787/a2216bc1-en

Keynes, J. M. (1919; 2013). *The economic consequences of the peace.* Macmillan for the Royal Economic Society.

Keynes, J. M. (1930). *Treatise on money.* Macmillan.

Keynes, J. M. (1940; 1989). How to pay for the war. In *Essays in persuasion.* Macmillan for the Royal Economic Society.

Kleinberg, J., Lakkaraju, H., Leskovec, J., Ludwig, J., and Mullainathan, S. (2018). Human decisions and machine predictions. *Quarterly Journal of Economics*, 133(1), 237–293.

Klette, T. J., and Griliches, Z. (1996). The inconsistency of common scale estimators when output prices are unobserved and endogenous. *Journal of Applied Econometrics*, 11(4), 343–361.

Klick, J., and Stockburger, A. (2021). *Experimental CPI for lower and higher income households* (U.S. Bureau of Labor Statistics Working Paper 537). US Department of Labor.

Korkmaz, G., Calderón, J. B. S., Kramer, B. L., Guci, L., Robbins, C. A., (2024). From GitHub to GDP: A framework for measuring open source software innovation. *Research Policy*, 53(3), 104954. https://doi.org/10.1016/j.respol.2024.104954

Krausmann, F., Lauk, C., Haas, W., and Wiedenhofer, D. (2018). From resource extraction to outflows of wastes and emissions: The socioeconomic metabolism of the global economy, 1900–2015. *Global Environmental Change*, 52, 131–140. https://doi.org/10.1016/j.gloenvcha.2018.07.003

Kremer, M., Levin, J., and Snyder, C. M. (2020). Advance market commitments: Insights from theory and experience. *AEA Papers and Proceedings*, 110, 269–273.

Krugman, P. (1990). *The age of diminished expectations: US economic policy in the 1990s.* MIT Press.

Kurz, M. (2023). *The market power of technology: Understanding the second gilded age.* Columbia University Press.

Kuznets, S. (1955, March). Economic growth and income inequality. *American Economic Review, 45,* 1–28.

Kuznets, S. (1973). Concluding remarks. In M. Moss (Ed.), *The measurement of economic and social performance* (pp. 579–592). National Bureau of Economic Research.

Lacey, J. (2011). *Keep from all thoughtful men: How US economists won World War II.* Naval Institute Press.

Lancaster, K. J. (1966). A new approach to consumer theory. *Journal of Political Economy, 74*(2), 132–157.

Land, K. C., and Juster, F. T. (1981). Social accounting systems: An overview. In F. T. Juster and K. C. Land (Eds.), *Social accounting systems* (pp. 1–21). Academic Press.

Landes, D. S. (1998). *The wealth and poverty of nations.* W. W. Norton.

Lane, J. (2023, March 9). *Reimagining labor market information: A national collaborative for local workforce information.* American Enterprise Institute.

Layard, R., and De Neve, J.-E. (2023). *Wellbeing: Science and policy.* Cambridge University Press.

Lehdonvirta, V. (2022). *Cloud empires: How digital platforms are overtaking the state and how we can regain control.* MIT Press.

Lepenies, P. (2016). *The power of a single number: A political history of GDP.* Columbia University Press.

Lev, B. (2000). *Intangibles: Management, measurement, and reporting.* Rowman & Littlefield.

Li, W. C. Y., and Chi, P. J. (2021). *Online platforms' creative "disruption" in organizational capital— the accumulated information of the firm* (Moon Economics Institute Discussion Paper No. 1). Moon Economics Institute.

Li, W. C. Y., and Hall, B. H. (2020). Depreciation of business R & D capital. *Review of Income and Wealth, 66*(1), 161–180. https://doi.org/10.1111/roiw.12380

Likins, G. (2017, October 1). The subscription economy: Did it start with power-by-the-hour? LinkedIn. https://www.linkedin.com/pulse/subscription-economy-did-start-power-by-the -hour-gene-likins

Lima de Miranda, K., and Snower, D. (2020). *Recoupling economic and social prosperity* (CESifo Working Paper No. 8133). https://dx.doi.org/10.2139/ssrn.3548365

Lowry, A. (2021, July 27). The time tax. *The Atlantic.* https://www.theatlantic.com/politics /archive/2021/07/how-government-learned-waste-your-time-tax/619568/

Lucas, R. E. (1987). *Models of business cycles* (Yrjo Jahnsson Lectures Series). Blackwell.

Ludwig, J., and Mullainathan, S. (2021). Fragile algorithms and fallible decision-makers: Lessons from the justice system. *Journal of Economic Perspectives, 35*(4), 71–96.

MacKenzie, D. (2006). *An engine, not a camera.* MIT Press.

Mancini, M., Montalbano, P., Nenci, S., and Vurchio, D. (2024). Positioning in global value chains: World map and indicators, a new dataset available for GVC analyses. *World Bank Economic Review.* https://doi.org/10.1093/wber/lhae005

Martin, R. S. (2022). *Democratic aggregation: Issues and implications for consumer price indexes* (U.S. Bureau of Labor Statistics Working Paper 600). US Department of Labor. https:// www.bls.gov/osmr/research-papers/2022/pdf/ec220150.pdf

Mason, J. W. (2024, 17 June). Taking money seriously. https://jwmason.org/slackwire/taking -money-seriously/

Masood, E. (2016). *The great invention: The story of GDP and the making and unmaking of the modern world*. Simon & Schuster.

Mastrogiacomo, L., Barravecchia, F., and Franceschini, F. (2019). A worldwide survey on manufacturing servitization. *International Journal of Advanced Manufacturing Technology*, *103*(9–12), 3927–3942. https://doi.org/10.1007/s00170-019-03740-z

Maximize Market Research. (2023). Data broker market: Global industry analysis and forecast (2023-2029) (Report No. 55670). MMR. https://www.maximizemarketresearch.com /market-report/global-data-broker-market/55670/

Mayer, C. (2023). *Capitalism and crises: How to fix them*. Oxford University Press.

McFadden, D., & Train, K. (2017). *Contingent valuation of environmental products: A comprehensive critique*. Edward Elgar.

McKinsey & Company. (2002). *How IT enables productivity growth*. https://www.mckinsey.com /~/media/McKinsey/Business%20Functions/McKinsey%20Digital/Our%20Insights /How%20IT%20enables%20productivity%20growth/MGI_How_IT_enables _productivity_report.ashx

McKinsey & Company. (2021). *Ordering in: The rapid evolution of food delivery*. https://www .mckinsey.com/industries/technology-media-and-telecommunications/our-insights /ordering-in-the-rapid-evolution-of-food-delivery

McKinsey & Company. (2022). *Freelance, side hustles, and gigs: Many more Americans have become independent workers*. https://www.mckinsey.com/~/media/mckinsey/featured%20 insights/future%20of%20america/freelance%20side%20hustles%20and%20gigs%20 many%20more%20americans%20have%20become%20independent%20workers /freelance-side-hustles-and-gigs-many-more-americans-have-become-independent -workers-final.pdf

McNerney, J., Savoie, C., Caravelli, F., Carvalho, V. M., and Farmer, J. D. (2022). How production networks amplify economic growth. *Proceedings of the National Academy of Sciences of the United States of America*, *119*(1), e2106031118. https://doi.org/10.1073/pnas.2106031118

Miller, C. (2022). *Chip war: The fight for the world's most critical technology*. Scribner.

Mincer, J. (1958). Investment in human capital and personal income distribution. *Journal of Political Economy*, *66*(4), 281–302. https://www.jstor.org/stable/1827422

Mirrlees, J. A. (1969). The evaluation of national income in an imperfect economy. *Pakistan Development Review*, *9*(1), 1–13. https://www.jstor.org/stable/41257992

Mitchell, T. (1998). Fixing the economy. *Cultural Studies*, *12*(1), 82–101. https://doi.org/10.1080 /095023898335627

Morgenstern, O. (1950). *On the accuracy of economic observations* (1963, 2nd rev. ed.). Princeton University Press.

Morikawa, M. (2016). Factoryless goods producers in Japan. *Japan and the World Economy*, *40*, 9–15.

Moulton, B. (2018, July 25). *The measurement of output, prices, and productivity: What's changed since the Boskin Commission?* The Hutchins Center on Fiscal and Monetary Policy, The Brookings Institution. https://www.brookings.edu/research/the-measurement-of-output -prices-and-productivity/

Muellbauer, J. (1974). Household production theory, quality, and the "hedonic technique." *American Economic Review, 64*(6), 977–994.

Muenchen, R. A. (n.d.). *The popularity of data science software.* r4stats.com. Retrieved December 21, 2023, from https://r4stats.com/articles/popularity/?utm_content=cmp-true

Murgia, M. (2024). *Code dependent: Living in the shadow of AI.* Picador.

Nagle, F. (2018). Learning by contributing: Gaining competitive advantage through contribution to crowdsourced public goods. *Organization Science, 29*(4), 569–587. https://doi.org/10.1287/orsc.2018.1202

Nagle, F. (2019). Open source software and firm productivity. *Management Science, 65*(3), 1191–1215. https://doi.org/10.1287/mnsc.2017.2977

Nakamura, L. (2020). *Evidence of accelerating mismeasurement of growth and inflation in the U.S. in the 21st century* (ESCoE Discussion Paper 2020-15). Economic Statistics Centre of Excellence. https://escoe-website.s3.amazonaws.com/wp-content/uploads/2020/11/06121347/ESCoE-DP-2020-15.pdf

Nakamura, L. I., Samuels, J., and Soloveichik, R. H. (2017, October 23). *Measuring the "free" digital economy within the GDP and productivity accounts* (FRB of Philadelphia Working Paper No. 17-37). SSRN. https://ssrn.com/abstract=3058017

National Academies of Sciences, Engineering, and Medicine. (2017). *Information technology and the U.S. workforce: Where are we and where do we go from here?* The National Academies Press.

National Institute of Statistics and Economic Studies. (2016). *Ethnic based statistics.* INSEE. https://www.insee.fr/en/information/2388586

Natural Capital Coalition. (2021). *Natural capital protocol.* Natural Capital Coalition. https://capitalscoalition.org/wp-content/uploads/2021/01/NCC_Protocol.pdf

Neely, A. D. (2009). Exploring the financial consequences of the servitization of manufacturing. *Operations Management Research, 2*(1), 103–118.

Neely, A., Benedettini, O., and Visnjic, I. (2011). *The servitization of manufacturing: Further evidence* [Paper presentation]. 18th European Operations Management Association Conference, Cambridge, United Kingdom. https://www.researchgate.net/publication/265006912_The_Servitization_of_Manufacturing_Further_Evidence

Newman, J. (2009, October 1). Amazon settles Kindle "1984" lawsuit. *PCWorld.* https://www.pcworld.com/article/519855/amazon_kindle_1984_lawsuit.html

New Zealand Treasury. (2021). *The Living Standards Framework 2021.* https://www.treasury.govt.nz/sites/default/files/2021-10/tp-living-standards-framework-2021.pdf

Nisticò, S. (2017). Consumption choices and time use: History, theory and potential empirical evidence. *Œconomia, 7*(2), 219–238.

Nordhaus, W. D. (2007). Two centuries of productivity growth in computing. *Journal of Economic History, 67*(1), 128–159. https://www.jstor.org/stable/4501136

Nordhaus, W., and Tobin, J. (1972). Is growth obsolete? In *Economic research: Retrospect and prospect, volume 5, economic growth* (pp. 1–80). National Bureau of Economic Research.

Odlyzko, A. (2001). Internet pricing and the history of communications. *Computer Networks, 36*(5–6), 493–517. https://doi.org/10.1016/S1389-1286(01)00188-8

Ofcom. (n.d.). *Monitoring compliance with net neutrality rules.* Ofcom. https://www.ofcom.org
.uk/internet-based-services/network-neutrality/net-neutrality

Ofcom. (2023a). *Cloud services market study.* https://www.ofcom.org.uk/__data/assets/pdf_file
/0029/256457/cloud-services-market-study-interim-report.pdf

Ofcom. (2023b). *Cloud services market study.* https://www.ofcom.org.uk/__data/assets/pdf
_file/0027/269127/Cloud-services-market-study-final-report.pdf

Office for National Statistics. (2005). *UK material flow review.* https://circabc.europa.eu/sd/a
/2e3e7aa5-3826-40dc-a6c8-2da986b30a27/UK%20material%20flows%20review%20
-%20final%20report.pdf

Office for National Statistics. (2016). *Household satellite accounts: 2005 to 2014.* https://www.ons
.gov.uk/economy/nationalaccounts/satelliteaccounts/compendium/householdsatelliteac
counts/2005to2014

Office for National Statistics. (2017). *Consumer price inflation price quotes (1988 to 1996).* https://
www.ons.gov.uk/economy/inflationandpriceindices/adhocs/007392consumerprice
inflationpricequotes1988to1996

Office for National Statistics. (2018). *Personal well-being user guidance.* https://www.ons.gov.uk
/peoplepopulationandcommunity/wellbeing/methodologies/personalwellbeing
surveyuserguide

Office for National Statistics. (2020a). *Chain-linking in business prices.* https://www.ons.gov
.uk/economy/inflationandpriceindices/articles/chainlinkinginbusinessprices/2020
-07-20

Office for National Statistics. (2020b). *International trade in services.* https://www.ons.gov.uk
/businessindustryandtrade/internationaltrade/datasets/internationaltradeinservices
referencetables

Office for National Statistics. (2020c). *Social capital headline indicators.* https://www.ons.gov
.uk/peoplepopulationandcommunity/wellbeing/datasets/socialcapitalheadline
indicators

Office for National Statistics. (2021). *Double deflation methods and deflator improvements to UK
National Accounts: Blue Book 2021.* https://www.ons.gov.uk/economy/nationalaccounts
/uksectoraccounts/methodologies/doubledeflationmethodsanddeflatorimprovements
touknationalaccountsbluebook2021

Office for National Statistics. (2022a). *Inclusive capital stock, UK: 2019 and 2020.* https://www
.ons.gov.uk/economy/economicoutputandproductivity/output/articles/inclusivecapital
stockuk/2019and2020

Office for National Statistics. (2022b). *Investment in intangible assets in the UK: 2020.* https://www
.ons.gov.uk/economy/economicoutputandproductivity/productivitymeasures/articles/e
xperimentalestimatesofinvestmentinintangibleassetsintheuk2015/2020#:~:text=Exclud-
ing%20this%20asset%2C%20in%202020,%C2%A3137bn%20in%20current%20prices

Office for National Statistics. (2023a). *UK measures of national well-being dashboard.* https://
www.ons.gov.uk/peoplepopulationandcommunity/wellbeing/articles/ukmeasuresofnation
alwellbeing/dashboard

Office for National Statistics. (2023b). *How the ONS is transforming UK prices statistics.* https://
blog.ons.gov.uk/2023/11/30/how-the-ons-is-transforming-uk-prices-statistics/

Office for National Statistics. (2024a). *Time use in the public sector, Great Britain: February 2024.* https://www.ons.gov.uk/economy/economicoutputandproductivity/publicservices productivity/bulletins/timeuseinthepublicsectorgreatbritain/february2024

Office for National Statistics. (2024b). *Material flow accounts.* https://www.ons.gov.uk/economy /environmentalaccounts/datasets/ukenvironmentalaccountsmaterialflowsaccountunited kingdom

Office for National Statistics. (2024c). *UK Whole economy: Output per hour worked SA: Index 2019 = 100.* https://www.ons.gov.uk/employmentandlabourmarket/peopleinwork/labour productivity/timeseries/lzvb/prdy

Office of Management and Budget. (2010). *Economic Classification Policy Committee Recommendation for Classification of Outsourcing in North American Industry Classification System (NAICS) revisions for 2012.* https://www.census.gov/eos/www/naics/fr2010/ECPC _Recommendation_for_Classification_of_Outsourcing.pdf

Olson, M. (1996). Distinguished Lecture on Economics in Government: Big bills left on the sidewalk: Why some nations are rich, and others poor. *Journal of Economic Perspectives, 10*(2), 3–24. https://doi.org/10.1257/jep.10.2.3

O'Mahony, M., and Samek, L. (2021). *Incorporating health status into human capital stocks: An analysis for the UK* (ESCoE Discussion Papers 2021-03). Economic Statistics Centre of Excellence.

O'Neil, C. (2016). *Weapons of math destruction: How big data increases inequality and threatens democracy* (1st ed.). Crown.

O'Reilly, T., Strauss, I., and Mazzucato, M. (2023). *Algorithmic attention rents: A theory of digital platform market power* (UCL Institute for Innovation and Public Purpose Working Paper Series, IIPP WP 2023-10). https://www.ucl.ac.uk/bartlett/public-purpose/wp2023-10

Organisation for Economic Co-operation and Development. (n.d.). Trade in value added. https://www.oecd.org/sti/ind/measuring-trade-in-value-added.htm

Ovallath, S., and Sulthana, B. (2017). Levodopa: History and therapeutic applications. *Annals of Indian Academy of Neurology, 20*(3), 185–189. https://doi.org/10.4103/aian.AIAN _241_17

Parekh, S., Reddin, S., Rowshankish, K., Soller, H., and Strandell-Jansson, M. (2022, June 30). *Localization of data privacy regulations creates competitive opportunities.* McKinsey & Company. https://www.mckinsey.com/capabilities/risk-and-resilience/our-insights /localization-of-data-privacy-regulations-creates-competitive-opportunities

Pearce, J., and Qian, J.-Y. (2022). Economic impact of DIY home manufacturing of consumer products with low-cost 3D printing from free and open source designs. *European Journal of Social Impact and Circular Economy, 3*(2), 1–24. https://doi.org/10.13135/2704-9906/6508

Penrose, E. (1959, 1995). *The theory of the growth of the firm.* Oxford University Press.

Philippon, T. (2019). *The great reversal: How America gave up on free markets.* The Belknap Press of Harvard University Press.

Philips. (2015). [Press release]. Signify. https://www.signify.com/global/our-company/news/press -release-archive/2015/20150416-philips-provides-light-as-a-service-to-schiphol-airport

Pichler, A., et al. (2023). Building an alliance to map global supply networks. *Science, 382,* 270– 272. https://doi.org/10.1126/science.adi7521

Pisano, G. P. (2017). Toward a prescriptive theory of dynamic capabilities: Connecting strategic choice, learning, and competition. *Industrial and Corporate Change, 26*(5), 747–762.

Poquiz, J. L. (2023). Measuring the value of free digital goods. Economic Statistics Centre of Excellence Discussion Paper 2023-16. https://escoe-website.s3.amazonaws.com/wp-content/uploads/2023/10/19094909/ESCoE-DP-2023-16-V2.pdf

Porter, M. (1990). *The competitive advantage of nations.* Free Press.

Porter, T. M. (1995). *Trust in numbers: The pursuit of objectivity in science and public life.* Princeton University Press.

Potoroaca, A. (2023, July 11). *Denuvo wants to prove its DRM doesn't affect game performance.* TechSpot. https://www.techspot.com/news/99357-denuvo-wants-prove-drm-doesnt-affect-game-performance.html

Potts, J. (2023, July 10). *von Hippel innovation.* SSRN. http://dx.doi.org/10.2139/ssrn.4574087

Rachel, L. (2024). *Leisure enhancing technical change.* Mimeo.

Ramsey, F. P. (1928). A mathematical theory of saving. *Economic Journal, 38*(4), 543–559.

Ravallion, M. (2011). On multidimensional indices of poverty. *Journal of Economic Inequality, 9*(2), 235–248.

Raworth, K. (2017). *Doughnut economics: Seven ways to think like a 21st-century economist.* Chelsea Green Publishing.

Reid, M. (1934). *The economics of household production.* John Wiley & Sons; Chapman & Hall Limited.

Reinsdorf, M., and Schreyer, P. (2020). Measuring consumer inflation in a digital economy. In *Measuring economic growth and productivity* (pp. 339–362). Elsevier. https://doi.org/10.1016/B978-0-12-817596-5.00015-9

Reserve Bank of India. (2023, October 12). *Survey on computer software and information technology enabled services exports: 2022-23* [Press release]. https://www.rbi.org.in/scripts/BS_PressReleaseDisplay.aspx?prid=56542

Robinson, J. (1980). Time in economic theory. *Kyklos, 33,* 219–229.

Rochet, J.-C., and Tirole, J. (2003). Platform competition in two-sided markets. *Journal of the European Economic Association, 1*(4), 990–1029.

Rochet, J.-C., and Tirole, J. (2006). Two-sided markets: A progress report. *RAND Journal of Economics, 37*(3), 645–667.

Rodriguez, S. (2016, August 17). *Meet the Airbnb of 3-D printing.* Inc. https://www.inc.com/salvador-rodriguez/fictiv-is-the-airbnb-of-3d-printing.html

Rodrik, D. (2016). Premature deindustrialization. *Journal of Economic Growth, 21*(1), 1–33.

Romer, P. M. (1986). Increasing returns and long-run growth. *Journal of Political Economy, 94*(5), 1002–1037. https://www.jstor.org/stable/1833190

Rosen, S. (1981). The economics of superstars. *American Economic Review, 71*(5), 845–858. http://www.jstor.org/stable/1803469

Rosenthal, C. (2018). *Accounting for slavery: Masters and management.* Harvard University Press.

Rosling, H. (2010, December). The magic washing machine [Video]. TED Conferences. https://www.ted.com/talks/hans_rosling_the_magic_washing_machine?language=en

Roth, F. (2022). Intangible capital and labor productivity growth—revisiting the evidence: An update (Hamburg Discussion Papers in International Economics, No. 11). University of

Hamburg, Chair of International Economics, Hamburg. https://www.econstor.eu/bitstream /10419/253256/1/hdpie-no11.pdf

Sagonowski, E. (2018, September 21). *English court backs NHS in fight with Bayer, Novartis over off-label Avastin use.* Fierce Pharma. https://www.fiercepharma.com/pharma/english-court -rejects-arguments-by-bayer-novartis-over-off-label-avastin-use

Sainsbury, D. (2020). *Windows of opportunity: How nations create wealth.* Profile Books.

Samuelson, P. A. (1961). The evaluation of "social income": Capital formation and wealth. In D. C. Hague (Ed.), *The theory of capital* (pp. 32–57). Palgrave Macmillan.

Sandel, M. J. (2012). *What money can't buy: The moral limits of markets.* Macmillan.

Sandvine. (2023). *The global internet phenomena report, January 2023.* https://www.sandvine.com /hubfs/Sandvine_Redesign_2019/Downloads/2023/reports/Sandvine%20GIPR%20 2023.pdf

Satz, D. (2010). *Why some things should not be for sale: The moral limits of markets.* Oxford University Press.

Schelling, T. C. (1958). Design of the accounts. In *A critique of the United States income and product accounts* (NBER Conference on Research in Income and Wealth, pp. 325–333). Princeton University Press.

Schreyer, P. (2022). *Accounting for free digital services and household production—an application to Facebook.* International Association for Research in Income and Wealth. https://iariw.org /wp-content/uploads/2021/08/Schreyer_paper.pdf

Schreyer, P., and Pilat, D. (2001). Measuring productivity. *OECD Economic Studies, 33*(2), 127–170.

Schultz, T. W. (1961). Investment in human capital. *American Economic Review, 51*(1), 1–17. https://www.jstor.org/stable/1818907

Scott, J. C. (1998). *Seeing like a state: How certain schemes to improve the human condition have failed.* Yale University Press.

Sen, A. (1976). Real national income. *Review of Economic Studies, 43*(1), 19–39. https://doi.org /10.2307/2296597

Sen, A. (1999). *Development as freedom.* Oxford University Press.

Shackle, G. (1967). *Time in economics.* North Holland Publishing Company.

Shapiro, C., and Varian, H. R. (1999). *Information rules: A strategic guide to the network economy.* Harvard Business School Press.

Sheiner, L., and Reinsdorf, M. (Eds.). (2024). *The measure of economies: Measuring productivity in an age of technological change.* University of Chicago Press.

Shen, X. (2023, May 2). Chinese data exchange makes first sale involving personal data, paving the way for jobseekers to profit from their resumes. *South China Morning Post.* https://www .scmp.com/tech/tech-trends/article/3219135/chinese-data-exchange-makes-first-sale -involving-personal-data-paving-way-jobseekers-profit-their

Shi, J. (2023, January 5). Blossoming exchanges help data proliferate. *China Daily.* https://www .chinadaily.com.cn/a/202301/05/WS63b62411a31057c47eba7c14.html

Shiller, R. J. (2019). *Narrative economics: How stories go viral & drive major economic events.* Princeton University Press.

Shirouzu, N., and Stecklow, S. (2023, July 27). Tesla's secret team to suppress thousands of driving range complaints. Reuters. https://www.reuters.com/investigates/special-report/tesla -batteries-range/

Sichel, D., and von Hippel, E. (2021). Household innovation and R&D: Bigger than you think. *Review of Income and Wealth, 67*, 639–658. https://doi.org/10.1111/roiw.12477

Simon, H. (1971). Designing organizations for an information-rich world. In M. Greenberger (Ed.), *Computers, communications, and the public interest* (pp. 38–72). Johns Hopkins Press.

Smith, D. J. (2013). Power-by-the-hour: The role of technology in reshaping business strategy at Rolls-Royce. *Technology Analysis & Strategic Management, 25*(8), 987–1007. https://doi.org/10.1080/09537325.2013.823147

Sokolova, A., and Sorensen, T. (2021). Monopsony in labor markets: A meta-analysis. *ILR Review, 74*(1), 27–55. https://doi.org/10.1177/0019793920965562

Solow, R. M. (1957). Technical change and the aggregate production function. *Review of Economics and Statistics, 39*(3), 312–320.

Solow, R. M. (2000). Sustainability: An economist's perspective. In R. N. Stavins (Ed.), *Economics of the Environment* (4th ed., pp. 505–513). W.W. Norton. (Original work published in 1991.)

Stantcheva, S. (2023). How to run surveys: A guide to creating your own identifying variation and revealing the invisible. *Annual Review of Economics, 15*, 205–234.

Stapleford, T. A. (2009). *The cost of living in America: A political history of economic statistics, 1880-2000.* Cambridge University Press.

Steedman, I. (2001). *Consumption takes time: Implications for economic theory.* Routledge.

Stevenson, B., and Wolfers, J. (2013). Subjective well-being and income: Is there any evidence of satiation? *American Economic Review, 103*(3), 598–604.

Stigler, G. (1961). *The price statistics of the federal government.* NBER, Price Statistics Review Committee. Columbia University Press.

Stiglitz, J. E. (1974). The Cambridge-Cambridge controversy in the theory of capital; a view from New Haven: A review article. *Journal of Political Economy, 82*(4), 893–903.

Stiglitz, J., Sen, A., and Fitoussi, J. P. (2009). *The measurement of economic performance and social progress revisited. Reflections and overview.* Commission on the Measurement of Economic Performance and Social Progress.

Stojkoski, V., Koch, P., Coll, E., and Hidalgo, C. A. (2024). Estimating digital product trade through corporate revenue data. *Nature Communications, 15*, 5262. https://doi.org/10.1038/s41467-024-49141-z

Studenski, P. (1958). *The income of nations: Theory measurement and analysis: Past and present.* University Press.

Sundararajan, A. (2016). *The sharing economy: The end of employment and the rise of crowd-based capitalism.* The MIT Press.

Tahbaz-Salehi, A., and Carvalho, V. M. (2019). Production networks: A primer. *Annual Review of Economics, 11*, 635–663.

Tambe, P., Hitt, L., Rock, D., and Brynjolfsson, E. (2020). *Digital capital and superstar firms* (NBER Working Paper 28285). National Bureau of Economic Research. https://www.nber.org/papers/w28285

Taylor, C., Mubarak, S., Chant, K., Fisher, R., and Heys, R. (2024). From national accounts to inclusive wealth: A framework to bridge between market and accounting priced capitals. Economic Statistics Centre of Excellence Discussion Paper 2024-02. https://www.escoe.ac.uk/publications/from-national-accounts-to-inclusive-wealth-a-framework-to-bridge-between-market-and-accounting-priced-capitals/

Teece, D. J., Pisano, G., and Shuen, A. (1997). Dynamic capabilities and strategic management. *Strategic Management Journal, 18*, 509–533.

Thompson, E. (2022). *Escape from model land.* Basic Books.

Thompson, E. P. (1967, December). Time, work-discipline, and industrial capitalism. *Past & Present, 38*(1), 56–97.

Timmer, M. P., Dietzenbacher, E., Los, B., Stehrer, R., and de Vries, G. J. (2015). An illustrated user guide to the World Input–Output Database: The case of global automotive production. *Review of International Economics, 23*, 575–605.

Timmer, M. P., Erumban, A. A., Los, B., Stehrer, R., and de Vries, G. J. (2014). Slicing up global value chains. *Journal of Economic Perspectives, 28*(2), 99–118.

Timmer, M. P., Los, B., Stehrer, R., and de Vries, G. J. (2016). *An anatomy of the global trade slowdown based on the WIOD 2016 release* (GGDC Research Memorandum No. 162, University of Groningen).

Tooze, A. (2001). *Statistics and the German state, 1900–1945: The making of modern economic knowledge.* Cambridge University Press.

Topp, C. W., Østergaard, S. D., Søndergaard., S., and Bech, P. (2015). The WHO-5 Well-Being Index: A systematic review of the literature. *Psychotherapy and Psychosomatics, 84*, 167–176.

Trades Union Congress. (2021, November 5). *Gig economy workforce in England and Wales has almost tripled in the last five years—new TUC research.* TUC. https://www.tuc.org.uk/news /gig-economy-workforce-england-and-wales-has-almost-tripled-last-five-years-new-tuc -research

Trammell, P. (2023). *New products and long-term welfare* [Unpublished manuscript]. https:// philiptrammell.com/static/New_Products_and_Long_term_Welfare.pdf

Tuckett, D., Holmes, D. A., and Chaplin, G. (2020). *Monetary policy and the management of uncertainty: A narrative approach* (Bank of England Staff Working Paper 870).

United Nations. (n.d.). https://sdgs.un.org/goals

UN Economic Commission for Europe. (2015). *Guide to measuring global production.* UNECE. https://unece.org/DAM/stats/publications/2015/Guide_to_Measuring_Global _Production__2015_.pdf

UN Statistics Division. (2023). *DZ.8 measurement of cloud computing in national accounts.* United Nations. https://unstats.un.org/UNSD/nationalaccount/RAdocs/ENDORSED_DZ8 _Cloud_Computing.pdf

UN System of Environmental-Economic Accounting. (2012). https://seea.un.org/

UN Trade and Development. (2022, April 25). COVID-19 boost to e-commerce sustained into 2021, new UNCTAD figures show. UNCTAD. https://unctad.org/news/covid-19-boost-e -commerce-sustained-2021-new-unctad-figures-show#:~:text=In%202019%2C%20 these%20companies%20made,trillion%20(in%20current%20prices)

UN, European Commission, IMF, OECD, and World Bank. (2009). *System of national accounts 2008.* UN Statistical Commission. https://unstats.un.org/unsd/nationalaccount/docs /sna2008.pdf

Urzi Brancati, M. C., Pesole, A., and Fernandez Macias, E. (2020). *New evidence on platform workers in Europe* (EUR 29958 EN, JRC118570). Publications Office of the European Union, Luxembourg. https://doi.org/10.2760/459278

Välilä, T. (2020). Infrastructure and growth: A survey of macro-econometric research. *Structural Change and Economic Dynamics, 53*, 39–49.

Van Ark, B. (2010). Productivity, sources of growth, potential output in the Euro area and the United States. *Intereconomics, 45*(1), 17–20.

van Elp, M., Kuijpers, N., and Mushkudiani, N. (2023). *Free services in the Netherlands*. The Hague: Statistics Netherlands. https://www.cbs.nl/-/media/_pdf/2023/14/free-services-report -2023-v2.pdf

van Elp, M., and Mushkudiani, N. (2019). *Free services*. The Hague: Statistics Netherlands. https://one.oecd.org/document/COM/SDD/DAF(2019)15/En/pdf

Vanoli, A. (2005). *A history of national accounting*. IoS Press.

Van Reenen, J. (2018). *Increasing differences between firms: Market power and the macro-economy.* (CEP Discussion Papers, CEPDP1576). Centre for Economic Performance, London School of Economics and Political Science.

Varian, H. (2016). *A microeconomist looks at productivity* [Presentation slides]. Brookings Institution. https://www.brookings.edu/wp-content/uploads/2016/08/varian.pdf

von Hippel, E. (1976). The dominant role of users in the scientific instrument innovation process. *Research Policy, 5*(3), 212–239.

von Hippel, E. (2017). *Free innovation*. MIT Press.

von Hippel, E., de Jong, J. P. J., and Rademaker, D. (2017, July). Household sector innovation. Mohammed Bin Rashid Centre for Government Innovation, UAE.

Ward, M. (2004). *Quantifying the world: UN ideas and statistics*. Indiana University Press.

Wdowin, J. (2024). *A Senian approach to the relationship between the natural environment and the distribution of welfare: A new perspective on inequality measurement and choice* [Unpublished PhD dissertation]. University of Cambridge.

Weichenrieder, A. J., and Gürer, E. (2018). *Pro-rich inflation in Europe: Implications for the measurement of inequality* (SAFE Working Paper No. 209). http://dx.doi.org/10.2139/ssrn .3183723

Weitzman, M. L. (1976). On the welfare significance of national product in a dynamic economy. *Quarterly Journal of Economics, 90*(1), 156–162.

Weitzman, M. L. (1998). On the welfare significance of national product under interest-rate uncertainty. *European Economic Review, 42*(8), 1581–1594.

Whelan, K. (2002). A guide to the use of chain aggregated NIPA data. *Review of Income and Wealth, 48*, 217–233.

Williamson, O. E. (2008). Outsourcing: Transaction cost economics and supply chain management. *Journal of Supply Chain Management, 44*(2), 5–16. https://doi.org/10.1111/j.1745 -493X.2008.00051.x

World Bank. (2021). *The changing wealth of nations 2021: Managing assets for the future.* World Bank. https://hdl.handle.net/10986/36400

World Bank. (2022, February 22). *A digital stack for transforming service delivery: ID, payments, and data sharing*. https://documents1.worldbank.org/curated/en/099755004072288910 /pdf/P1715920edb5990d60b83e037f756213782.pdf

World Bank. (2023). *Digital progress and trends report*. https://documents1.worldbank.org /curated/en/099031924192524293/pdf/P180107173682d0431bf651fded74199f10.pdf

Wright, N., Nagle, F., and Greenstein, S. M. (2023). Open source software and global entrepreneurship. *Research Policy*, 52(9), 104846. https://doi.org/10.1016/j.respol.2023.104846

Young, A. A. (1928). Increasing returns and economic progress. *Economic Journal*, 38(152), 527–542. https://doi.org/10.2307/2224097

Zabelin, D., Yuyama, T., and Nakanishi, T. (2022, January 19). *The world is drowning in data. Why don't we trade it like on a stock exchange?* World Economic Forum. https://www.weforum.org/agenda/2022/01/data-trading-stock-exchange/

Zomer, T., Neely, A., Parlikad, A., and Martinez-Hernandez, V. (2020). Becoming digital: Enacting digital transformation in construction projects. University of Cambridge. https://doi.org/10.17863/CAM.47667

Zuora. (n.d.). (2024, August 24). Subscription economy. https://www.zuora.com/vision/subscription-economy/

Zysman, J., Murray, S., Feldman, J., Nielsen, N. C., and Kushida, K. E. (2013, March). Services with everything: The ICT-enabled digital transformation of services. In D. Breznitz and J. Zysman (Eds.), *The third globalization: Can wealthy nations stay rich in the twenty-first century?* (pp. 99–129). Oxford University Press.

ACKNOWLEDGEMENTS

I OWE MANY DEBTS OF GRATITUDE to people who have in different ways contributed to this book and the decade's worth of work underpinning it. First of all, my thanks to all my coauthors on the relevant papers: Mo Abdirahman, Matthew Agarwala, Ayantola Alayande, Anna Alexandrova, Eric Beinhocker, Tim Besley, Ioannis Bournakis, Sumedha Deshmukh, Stephanie Diepeveen, Stella Erker, Mark Fabian, Marco Felici, Luca Gamberi, Lucy Hampton, Richard Heys, Laurence Kay, Wendy Li, Kieran Lind, Annabel Manley, John McHale, Jen-Chung Mei, Rehema Msulwa, Leonard Nakamura, David Nguyen, Margaret Stevens, Will Stewart, Jeni Tennison, Manuel Tong, Andy Westwood, Julia Wdowin, Adrian Weller, and Dimitri Zenghelis. I received helpful comments on this draft as well as on earlier papers from a number of these, and also from Erik Brynjolfsson, Reda Cherif, Avi Collis, Hayane Dahmen, Shane Greenstein, Fuad Hasanov, Jostein Hauge, Bill Janeway, Julia Lane, Neil Lawrence, Margaret Levi, Gina Neff, Mary O'Mahony, Rebecca Riley, Debra Satz, Bart Van Ark, Tony Venables, and John Zysman. Stella Erker and Nick Testa were both wonderful research assistants who helped with the preparation of the book. Three anonymous referees gave valuable and constructive comments and advice on a first draft.

My work has been enabled and enriched by several intellectual communities, in particular the Economic Statistics Centre of Excellence and the Office for National Statistics (where I have been a Fellow for several years), the International Association for Research in Income and Wealth, the Productivity Institute, the Stanford Digital Economy Lab, the regular seminar on the Foundations of Values and Value run by Colin Mayer and Dennis Snower in Oxford, and a timely workshop run

Sophie from Romania. © Diane Coyle.

by Markus Gabriel and Anna Katsman in spring 2023 at The New Institute in Hamburg. I received helpful questions and comments from participants in seminars and talks over the years. Likewise, many colleagues from the Office for National Statistics have provided valuable insights, and I have particularly benefited from conversations with Sanjiv Mahajan, Josh Martin (now at the Bank of England), and Cliodhna Taylor. Much credit also goes to my academic home, the Bennett Institute for Public Policy at the University of Cambridge and our fantastic team; I'd particularly like to thank my colleague Michael Kenny, not only for his detailed comments on an early draft of this book but also for his constant support and friendship.

In relation to my research on economic measurement, I have been supported by several funders during the past decade: the Economic Statistics Centre of Excellence set up by the UK Office for National Statistics; the Economic and Social Science Research Council's (ES-RC's) Productivity Institute (grant number ES/V002740/1); an Arts and Humanities Research Council/ESRC grant on well-being (grant number ES/T005556/1); KPMG; Meta; the Gatsby Foundation; the Nuffield Foundation; and the Omidyar Foundation.

Huge thanks to all involved at Princeton University Press, especially Christie Henry for her leadership, the ever-patient and gracious Hannah Paul, and Josh Drake. My thanks also to the team involved in the production of this book.

Friends and family have borne the brunt of my book-related distraction, so a huge thank-you to them, especially the Salonistas (Bethan Marshall, Richard Marshall, Sian Kevill, Narinder Minhas, and Catherine Basset), Ruth Ben-Ghiat, Nita Juneja, Lindsay Shaw, and Adam, Franny, Clara, and Davy during the summer holiday in Tresaith, 2023. Nothing I do would be possible without the love and support of my husband, Rory Cellan-Jones, and—since she arrived overland from Romania, full of fear, on our doorstep in December 2022—Sophie.

INDEX

Note: Numbers in *italics* denote tables.

democratic institutions, living standards
and increasing, 221
diamond-water paradox, 126
digital disintermediation, 104–5; gig employment and, 116–20; time saving and, 121
digital intermediation, 101–2; household
capital and, 113–16
digitally disintermediated activities, 108–12
digitally enabled services, 22, 162–65, 164.
See also "free" digital services
digitally intermediated services, production
boundary and, 104–5
digital nomad visas, 163
digital platforms: enabling hybrid and
remote work, 120–21; subscription
economy and, 93–97
digital products, user-generated, 142–45
digital public infrastructure (DPI), 171–76,
248; components of, 172, 173
digital rights management (DRM), 95–96
digital stack, 171–76, 173
digital technology: changes in economic
activity, 18, 20; effect on time-use, 257–58;
time to produce and, 66–67
digital tools, highest productivity firms and,
52–53
digital trade, conceptual framework for, 175,
176
digitisation: alternative production structures and, 75–76; as driver of FGP and
servitisation, 85–88; shifting transactions
out of market into household, 99–102
digitised information, as intangible asset, 229
domestic capital, gig work and, 119–20
Donut Economics (Raworth), 220
Dyson, use of contract manufacturers, 77

Easterlin paradox, 236–37
e-commerce, 99–101, 112, 165–66, 166
econometric estimation, 189–90
economic activities, measuring economic
progress and classification of, 253–55
economic competencies, as intangible asset,
229, 231

Economic Consequences of the Peace, The
(Keynes), 155–56
economic discontent, extremist politics
and, 5–6
economic geography, 21–22, 255–56
economic growth: measuring, 11–15; productivity growth and, 37. See also economic progress
economic measurement: governments and
history of, 22–27; problems with, 15–22;
value laden character of, 261. See also
economic statistics
economic organisation, digital platforms
addressing, 117–18
economic progress: identifying, 8; productivity and, 34, 70–71; technological
progress and, 1–2, 34
economic progress, measuring, 240–41;
alternative indices for, 242–44; capabilities approach to, 243, 250–51; classification of economic activities and, 253–55;
comprehensive wealth and, 247–50;
dashboard approach to, 244–47, 246;
economic geography and, 255–56; focus
on well-being and, 241–42; principles for
measuring economic welfare, 258–62,
260; shadow prices and, 251–53; time-use
accounting framework for, 7–8, 143,
256–58
economic shocks, shifting public philosophy
caused by, 5–6
Economics of Biodiversity, The (Dasgupta), 253
Economics of Household Production, The
(Reid), 107
economic statistics, 6, 13; cautions about
weight placed on, 28–29; changes in
economy and need to reform, 262–63;
economic narratives and, 26–27; missing
activities and innovations, 15–17; social
construction of, 25–26; as social products,
220. See also economic measurement
economic value: dematerialisation of, 97–98;
human elements of, 42; identifying,
85–88; measuring, 263

A NOTE ON THE TYPE

This book has been composed in Arno, an Old-style serif typeface in the
classic Venetian tradition, designed by Robert Slimbach at Adobe.